# BROADCASTING IN THE
## 21ST CENTURY

*Also by Richard Rudin*

AN INTRODUCTION TO JOURNALISM (*with Trevor Ibbotson*)

# Broadcasting in the 21st Century

## Richard Rudin

*Senior Lecturer in Broadcasting and Journalism,*
*Liverpool John Moores University,*
*Liverpool, UK*

First published 2011 by
PALGRAVE MACMILLAN

Palgrave Macmillan in the UK is an imprint of Macmillan Publishers Limited,
registered in England, company number 785998, of Houndmills, Basingstoke,
Hampshire RG21 6XS.

Palgrave Macmillan in the US is a division of St Martin's Press LLC,
175 Fifth Avenue, New York, NY 10010.

Palgrave Macmillan is the global academic imprint of the above companies
and has companies and representatives throughout the world.

Palgrave® and Macmillan® are registered trademarks in the United States,
the United Kingdom, Europe and other countries

ISBN 978–0–230–01317–9 hardback
ISBN 978–0–230–01318–6 paperback

This book is printed on paper suitable for recycling and made from fully
managed and sustained forest sources. Logging, pulping and manufacturing
processes are expected to conform to the environmental regulations of the
country of origin.

A catalogue record for this book is available from the British Library.

A catalog record for this book is available from the Library of Congress.

10  9  8  7  6  5  4  3  2  1
20  19  18  17  16  15  14  13  12  11

Printed and bound in Great Britain by
CPI Antony Rowe, Chippenham and Eastbourne

# Contents

# List of Figures and Tables

## Figures

## Tables

# Preface and Acknowledgements

When colleagues and others who know of this book project ask me how long it took me to write it, I've been tempted to use the answer given by a comedian who was asked how long it had taken him to develop his routine. He replied: 'About 50 years, I should think,' This wasn't really a joke. He had shared and honed his material from a lifetime of observation, from listening to his parents and neighbours talk as he was sitting under the kitchen table as an infant, through childhood, adolescence, and all the bitter-sweet moments, the disappointments, the loves and rejections, the humiliations and triumphs of his life to date. All of that is true of me and my interest in broadcasting. Indeed, one of my mother's strongest memories of me as a small child was sitting cross-legged, listening intently to a transistor radio – then a new technology. I might well have been listening to the news reports of mankind's first walk in space. I clearly remember being fascinated by the exploits of the Soviet cosmonaut, Yuri Gagarin. About three years later, to be precise on the evening of 22 November, 1963, I was at the home of a friend, who was also aged six. We were excitedly discussing a fictional new 'space serial' – *Doctor Who* – which was being heavily trailed by the BBC, when the quiz programme (a British version of a US format *Take Your Pick*) on the commercial channel was interrupted by a newsflash that President Kennedy had been shot on a trip to Dallas, Texas. This news, and of course the subsequent announcement (followed by solemn music) of the President's death, clearly startled and concerned my friends' parents and provided the first example to me of the power and impact of dramatic news. Some 45 years later, I was exchanging texts with the same friend about speculation over which actor would play the 'regenerated' eponymous Doctor Who; news and special network sites were abuzz with rumours. This demonstrated to me how much of what were in the past private debates and gossip were now being influenced by a much wider network – a key theme in this book. In June 2009 it was a text from another friend who alerted me that a Hollywood gossip internet site was reporting the death of Michael Jackson. This was not confirmed for some minutes by the BBC TV news I was watching – the first major occasion at which I was aware of the broadcast media playing catch-up with the internet and it was fascinating to me to observe how those in my various social networks were negotiating with both new and old media.

Long before then my interest in which programmes people were watching and enjoying extended to an audience survey of my fellow school pupils at the age of 12, the results of which I sent to the BBC's weekly *Junior Points of View*

TV programme. It's a sobering thought that the broadcasting of my findings achieved what will almost certainly be the biggest audience – around eight million – that I will ever have for my research!

Along the way I have visited, listened, watched, and talked with a wide variety of personnel at a range of broadcasting services, including from (at the age of 16), small local commercial radio and television stations in Newfoundland, Canada, where my Aunt Barbara (Alexander) then lived – who then arranged for me to visit the Province's capital, St Johns, where the son of a friend was an announcer on the CBC; to radio and TV stations big and small, commercial, public service and community; national, international and local over several continents, with output as diverse as the popular Saturday night TV show, to *Wetten, Dass?*, to the BBC World Service, and out on the high seas, to Radio Caroline, defying the authorities and the law. I've been fascinated, beguiled and inspired by them all. As a child and adolescent I was also highly intrigued by foreign radio broadcasts such as Radio Moscow and its relentless Cold War rhetoric and from the other side of the ideological divide to the Voice of America and Radio Free Europe. Later on, I was to play my own tiny part in this, as my broadcasting in Germany on the British forces service was – I now know through Facebook contact – being avidly listen to and indeed recorded (at great risk) by those on the other side of the Berlin Wall. Later still, by the mid-1990s I was hugely excited by the ability to listen (via an often stuttering dial-up internet connection) to radio stations many thousands of miles away and indeed I wrote what I think may have been the first regular magazine column of reviews of such stations.

This book could not have been written without the help and support of many people and organisations. Of course, when creating a 'thank you list' one always runs a grave risk of offending through omission and there are many with whom I worked in broadcasting who deserve thanks but I think they all know who they are. As far as my academic and research career has been concerned I must pay acknowledgement to the team of the Centre of Mass Communications Research at Leicester University, with whom I did my MA by distance learning in the late 1990s and, a few years later, I was flattered to be asked to write a new unit for this course. There are many other academics in the UK I should thank but I will confine my list to just a few names. The first time I really appreciated how exciting it could be to be a part of an academic endeavour was when the Radio Studies Network was formed in 1998 which began as an email discussion list and led to a number of conferences in the UK and in other parts of Europe, as well as North America and Australasia, and has been an immensely important addition to the study and understanding of broadcasting. Part of the network from its early days was Sean Street of the University of Bournemouth who has been unstintingly supportive and helpful and Deborah Wilson from the University of Lincoln who persuaded me to submit a paper to the Broadcasting Education Association's festival in Las Vegas. This has now become an annual visit, incorporating the National Association of Broadcasters (NAB) and, (until 2011), the always absorbing Radio and Television Digital News Association (RTDNA) conventions. In 2007, with support and encouragement from Brian Pauling of the New Zealand Broadcasting School, I was elected Vice Chair of the International Division of the BEA, becoming Chair in 2009. It has been a joy and privilege, through this, to be able to engage with scholars and students from every continent.

In the USA, I must thank Christopher H. Sterling who edited the *Encyclopedia of Radio* to which I was honoured to contribute and who has been a source of inspiration and encouragement. Frank Chorba, Michael Brown, Sam Sauls, John Allen Hendricks and Michele Hilmes are amongst the many other US scholars who have been so helpful and friendly, and even shared some of my enthusiasms!

In the UK, I have been immensely fortunate to have such a supportive and understanding boss, in the form of my Head of Department, Professor Chris Frost and the members of the university's research committee which funded some of my research visits and conferences, as well some teaching remission. Other funding, including discounted rates at key conferences, has come from the British Academy, the Radio Academy and the organizers of the Media Guardian Edinburgh International Television Festival.

A great many people have given their time for interviews and other background research for this book. The BBC's written archives in Caversham and the library staff at the University of Bournemouth supplied some of the archive's television research figures. My thanks also to Alison Winter, Research Manager for BBC Audio and Music, and to the Institute of Practitioners in Advertising for permission to cite their respective research. Sheena Streather, Research and Learner Officer at Liverpool John Moores University, was unstinting in her efforts in responding to some rather imprecise requests for information! Thanks also to Hester Nevill of Radio 2 publicity who arranged my visit to the *Wake up to Wogan* programme and my interview with Sir Terry. I am grateful to Romie Singh for permission to use her work on community radio in Africa.

Those who are directly quoted as interviewees are, naturally, greatly thanked for their help and for giving me some of that precious and inelastic quality – their time. I particularly want to thank those both at the BBC's News Centre and at Sky News, who made me very welcome and were so ready to engage in debate both during and after my visits, which greatly helped clarify some of my thinking. There are many who presented and wrote conference papers who have also informed the work and who have spent, cumulatively, many hours with me in discussions at all sorts of levels. Some distinguished academics have been generous enough to compliment me on my own papers and presentations and I want to thank two Johns – Corner and Ellis – and a Jean – Seaton – for their encouraging words. There are other academics and writers, such as the University of Westminster's David Hendy, who have both inspired me, but also on occasion daunted me, with their scholarship and elegant style. I am well aware that my own academic career is slight compared with these and that I am standing on the shoulders of giants in this field and even a few words of encouragement from such major figures have been much appreciated.

A number of people, directly and indirectly, then looked through and discussed early drafts of the book, not least the three reviewers of the first complete draft and my office colleague, Glyn Môn Hughes, whose experience as a copy-editor and proof-reader, as well as his critical analysis, was put to much appreciated use. A friend from school days, Nigel Simons, brought the perspective of 'an intelligent outsider', as well as a love for robust debate, providing invaluable insights and testing my arguments and evidence, as well as helping me with the final checks and confirming 'permissions' from many dozens of sources, and in the vital task of indexing. A former academic colleague, Adrian Quinn, has been a sounding board for many years and has always been interested in and supportive of my work.

Also greatly appreciated is the unwavering support, patience and understanding of the small and dedicated team at Palgrave Macmillan, not least my original editor, Emily Salz, who moved to another company before the book's completion; Beverley Tarquini, Sheree Keep and Anna Reeve, and to Keith Povey (with the help of Linda McGrory), who performed the art of copy-editing – one of those unsung essentials of the publishing business.

Closest to home in every sense, I must thank my mother, brother and late father, who tolerated, encouraged and humoured me in my rather unusual interest in broadcasting.

Finally, but with the greatest possible gratitude, everlasting love, thanks and appreciation go to my wife, Alison, who has not only put up with my more than usually distracted air over a period of some four years but the seemingly unending piles and shelves of box files, books, and general clutter which threatened to infect the whole house – and to our son, David, who brings such happiness and is always ready with a gentle 'reality check' for me when I am too self-absorbed!

This book contains many facts and figures, and some contentious views; any inaccuracies or unwitting misinterpretations in the former are my responsibility and I welcome reaction to the latter. I am also conscious and excited by the fact that I have so much yet to learn and understand. My enthusiasm and fascination for broadcasting remains undimmed. Indeed, if someone had told me as a child that I could listen to my favourite radio stations in North America on a tiny device as I walked around at home, or listen to a former student 'live' on a station in the United Arab Emirates, watch the news services by countries as diverse as Iran, Russia, France, China, India and the USA on my satellite TV, or sit in bed and 'catch up' with a TV show I had missed, on a tiny but pin-sharp screen, I would probably have said 'take me there now!' So while what follows is, I hope, based on rigorous research and well-based argument, it is not the work of a cynic or 'lofty academic', but of a keen observer (as well as a participant for many years) and one who passionately believes in the potential and importance of broadcasting at many levels. My greatest wish is that this enthusiasm and fascination powers off the pages and that the reader will engage with the ideas and issues within them.

*June 2011*                                                                    RICHARD RUDIN

# Introduction

This book contains a great deal of discussion about the changes in the output and consumption of broadcasting as result of new technologies and convergence of media. Yet it is also striking how often the output of broadcasting and our relationship to it – 'live' coverage of world events, such as the Royal Wedding in Britain in April 2011, being seen at the same time by millions across the globe; the workplace conversation (and much of the tabloid newspapers) being dominated by a Saturday night TV show; rows between the broadcasters and the government and military about the effects and truthfulness of programmes – have remained unchanged. Broadcasters are still exposing injustices and wrongdoing and policy is still being changed as a result of these investigations.

On the other hand, during the period I was completing this book, there were several examples of significant events in society and culture in which broadcasting had played only a peripheral role. As will be discussed in the book, from the mid-1920s whenever there has been social upheaval, radio and/or television, whether licensed, clandestine or 'pirate', had played a crucial role; but when school students in England organised protests against planned rises in university tuition fees they did so through social networks such as Facebook; they didn't even need the official backing and organisation of the National Union of Students, let alone broadcasts on a 'pirate' radio station. Broadcasters were playing 'catch up' in covering the demonstrations, and much of the key material was shot by students themselves and initially posted up on YouTube. The 'kids' really were doing it for themselves. In the same period a string of 'secret' documents that were embarrassing to governments and the military were provided by the WikiLeaks' site. It seemed a key function of broadcasting 'to talk truth to power', to hold the powerful to account and to be the 'space' where scandal and wrongdoing was first revealed had, to some extent at least, been usurped by new media. Revolutions in Tunisia, Egypt, and UN-backed military action against the Gadaffi regime in Libya, in early 2011, as well as earthquakes in New Zealand and Japan – the latter also resulting in a devastating tsunami and damage to several nuclear reactors – were being 'covered' by ordinary citizens using mobile/cell phones, uploaded to social network sites. In turn, some of these contributions were being integrated into broadcasts by the mainstream media.

Although personal reflections are no substitute for proper empirical evidence and a clinical examination of case studies and examples, a good starting point for examining the uses of broadcasting and its effects on our lives is to consider our own experiences. The engagement and dominance of media has changed with each of the last three generations in my family; my grandparents were the first to have mass circulation, popular newspapers from their childhood; my parents were part of the first generation that had radio from infancy; mine was the first to have TV viewing as part of our earliest memories; my son's the first to have the internet from when they started school. Up until now new technologies have not replaced the former, although they have had to adapt. This does not mean, of course, that this evolution or adaptation will continue. Already the idea of waiting for someone to deliver you the news through the letter-box, presented in a fixed, permanent form in which you have no role or interaction, is as quaint as the thought of someone having to activate your street illumination by lighting the gas lamp outside your home seemed in the early 21st century. Many credible analysts are predicting the death of newspapers as a mass medium by 2020 – at the latest. The 2011 Royal Wedding in London gathered huge TV audiences, but it was estimated that some 400 million people around the world viewed the coverage on YouTube.

In my research for this book I asked almost all my interviewees and contacts one question: are we going through an evolution or a revolution? The unanimous response (at least from those in the editing and production side – one or two of the broadcasters were more circumspect) was the latter and, in particular, they believed that the relationship between the producer of broadcasting and the user was going through a fundamental change. However, the more I considered all these areas, the more I was struck by how much that history and the cultural 'baggage' of broadcasting imposed itself on the debates and developments in broadcasting today. An edition of the BBC's public discussion programme *Question Time* in November 2007 debated the issue of trust in broadcasting following the revelations of the malpractices outlined later in this book. Although his name was not mentioned in the question, and none of the panellists – nor, it seemed, any of the audience – were even born when John Reith left the BBC in 1938, his name cropped up four times in the discussion. There were similar discussions and invocations of the name Reith in 2008 over the so-called 'Sachs-gate' affair and in early 2009 over the life and death of Reality TV 'star' Jade Goody (both of these events are discussed at some length in the main chapters of this book). The Reithian legacy certainly casts a long – but not necessarily cold nor forbidding – shadow. The BBC's first Director-General set the parameters and the priorities of broadcasting in Britain: as a means of serving the public; to educate, inform and entertain, to make the good popular and the popular good, and which served neither as an arm of state propaganda nor a means of increasing shareholder profits.

How these principles are being adapted and adopted in the 21st century in the context of rapidly changing technology, and much else, became the focus for this book, which explores the significance of the past and the impact of the changes in broadcasting and how the public's relationship with the medium is evolving. In essence, there has been a tension between the ideas from the media effects tradition – what the media (in this case broadcasting) does to 'us'; and the theory of uses and gratifications – what 'we' do to/with the media. In short: who is in control? This book will address these questions through the use of case studies/examples, empirical evidence and the use of 'expert witnesses'.

Although there are many aspects concerning technology, regulation, owner-ship and control that impinge on these developments they are not in them-selves the main focus for the book. The concentration is always the impact on audiences, and the challenge I have set for the book is to gauge how and why broadcasting is changing in the 21st century compared to the 20th in terms of that relationship between the 'sender' (the broadcaster) and the 'receiver' (the viewer and listener). In doing so, this book will not contain a great amount of discussion of theoretical concepts. This is not because I believe them to be of no value: they can be excellent tools in enabling us to try and understand why broadcasting developed in particular ways in particular societies; they help us to 'join up the dots' and the reader is encouraged to explore these theories and test their usefulness in finding out why and how things are the way they are – the goal of all academic work. But whilst it is possible that the next decade or so will see the much strived-for single, unifying theory in quantum physics, I do not think the equivalent is possible to explain the range of political, cultural, sociological, technological and psychological factors and much else that are involved in broadcasting's development, and the motivations of its practitioners or its audiences.

Any book that lays claim to add, however modestly, to the sum of human knowledge must first define its terms and its parameters. By the end of the first decade of the 21st century (and those who believe the decade began in 2001 will be gratified to know that this book includes material up to the end of 2010) there were debates about just what broadcasting *is*. Of course, it is easy to get wrapped up in semantics and agonise too much over definitions and a substantial part of the book is concerned with how the traditional means of defining and explaining broadcasting are being eroded and lines are being blurred all the time, but perhaps this makes it even more important – or at least I feel I owe it to you, the patient reader – to explain what *I* mean by broadcasting.

Trevor Dann, who stepped down as director of the UK's Radio Academy in 2010, has complained in several speeches that the industry has (through the use of the same word – 'radio') unnecessarily associated the type of *content* with the type of *device* on which it is received and heard/viewed. Dann's central point is that it simply doesn't matter whether, in this case, audio content is listen to on an MP3 device or over a traditional radio receiver. But if the main focus of the book is on the changing relationship between listeners/viewers and broadcasting output then perhaps it *does* matter, because – to use a theoretical term – the 'uses and gratifications' of broadcasting may change in subtle or even fundamental ways, depending on the type of device on which the output is 'consumed'. But this is still dodging the question of what broadcasting *is* and how it differs from other types of audio and visual content production and distribution. Although, as will be discussed at some length in the book, technology has meant that limitations of time and space has been greatly eroded in the 21st century, I think we should hang on to the concept that *broad*casting output is intended for general public consumption (even if that public can be divided into increasingly small niches), rather than a specific group of people who can only receive the broadcasts if they are in a specific situation; this rules out all output over internal networks, such as supermarket radio stations, or any other closed network. The fact that you need special equipment, such as a satellite dish or cable connection, does not obviate the principle that anyone within a defined territory *could* receive the said broadcasts and even if they were not in the 'target market', were, in a broad sense, *intended* to be able to receive them.

The second important principle is the expectation that at least some of the audience will receive the content at the same time and in the linear order arranged by the broadcaster. Although a significant percentage – even a major- ity – of the audience may view and listen to content at a different time and may, indeed, reorder the content, the fact that the provider had arranged and publicized the programme output for particular times and in a particular sequence helps to define it as broadcasting.

Finally, my definition includes content that has been produced specifically for broadcast purposes. The mere relaying, for example, of movies on partic- ular, often subscription, TV channels, does not meet my definition of broad- casting, and here in a kind of reverse way, I'm agreeing with Trevor Dann. The fact that content appears on a TV channel button does not in itself make it broadcasting. It can, as in the case of non-stop TV movies, merely be using TV technology to relay output that was fully developed for a different medium or outlet, in this case the cinema.

Naturally, I would expect that you, the well-informed and alert reader, would think of many exceptions and potential conflicts with these definitions; certainly there are many 'grey areas.' That is to the good; all authors wish their readers to engage with the text, none more so than in the academic or schol- arly field.

## Outline and structure of chapters

Although it is impossible and possibly unwise or even counter-productive, to hermetically seal topics within particular chapters or even sections, the book organizes its main themes and discussions into three broad areas. These are preceded by the first chapter on broadcasting in the 20th century, because, as indicated above, we cannot hope to understand what is happening now, let alone see the likely trajectory, unless we have a handle on what came before. Clearly, even a substantial chapter such as this cannot hope to provide a comprehensive description or analysis of the whole of broadcasting in that century, so it concentrates on the themes and issues that are explored in the following chapters in the context of the early 21st century; mainly, but not exclusively, from the perspective of the UK.

Chapters 2 to 4 describe the characteristics and pattern of broadcasting in the 21st century, including how viewing and listening is measured and influenced and, in Chapter 3, asking if more broadcasting means 'worse' broadcasting, defining such a subjective term by comparing Public Service Broadcasting output in what I have identified as the peak year of 1977 for mass viewing to a small number of channels and before the mass take-up of video cassette recorders, to the situation in the multi-channel, multi-platform, interactive and time-shifted viewing and listening thirty years later. Chapter 4 is devoted to radio and argues that this is a distinct but constantly evolving medium which has confounded many critics and forecasters in remaining a vibrant and popular form of broadcasting and is therefore worthy of specific study and scholarship in its own right.

Chapters 5 to 7 can be considered the 'issues' section, starting with a discussion of the controversial genre of Reality TV and the wider question of how much broadcasting represents reality. Chapter 6 describes how the whole issue of trust in broadcasting and broadcasters has come under strain, and – very much twinned with this – Chapter 7 deals with the difficulty of maintaining fairness and impartiality and discusses the validity of accusations of bias.

The next section – Chapters 8 to 10 – discusses how the time and spatial dimensions of broadcasting have become blurred in the 21st century; starting with an examination of, literally, how time affects broadcasting and its output, the various pleasures and challenges this presents for both broadcasters and audiences, then the erosion of the distinctions between the global and local and, finally, the importance of television crossing borders, in both programmes and programme formats.

The final section, Chapters 11 and 12, considers the issues of convergence between broadcasting and the internet and how this has led to the phenomenon of user-generated content, including citizens' journalism. The last chapter tackles head on, using specific examples, the issue of the continuing power and impact of broadcasting in the 21st century and how new technologies and social media have affected that impact. Naturally, the conclusion draws together the evidence and arguments of the book and, in a slightly polemical style, makes the case for the survival of broadcasting as a public good, with distinct obligations and privileges.

As indicated above, there is a limited, direct use of theory in this book and where such terms are used it is hoped the broad thrust of the approach is clear from the context; however, the reader is urged to consult media and communications dictionaries and similar types of texts for fuller explanations, especially where these are of interest to their studies. Similarly, the use of industry jargon is kept to a minimum, and where it is used it is hoped the meaning is clear from the surrounding discussion. Where initials are used, the full name is given when first used in the chapter. Where possible, references are given for sources in the public domain, in the main free to access, with the full web addresses given in the 'Notes and References' at the end of each chapter. These were checked as close to the time of publication as possible and are from sites where there is a reasonable expectation that they will be kept online for some years from the date of publication. Direct quotations are referenced when taken from other sources; otherwise, and as will be made clear in the first quotation, they are from a personal interview conducted for this book. Following the main body of the work there is a list of suggested further reading, with indications as to which chapters these best support.

# Historical Background: Broadcasting in the 20th Century

This chapter considers the development of broadcasting in the 20th century. In particular it discusses:

- The early debates about what broadcasting should be and how it should be funded.
- Clashes between the state and broadcasters
- The role of radio in the Second World War.
- The popularity of television in both the factual and entertainment areas and the most-viewed programmes in the UK and the USA.
- The impact of technological innovations, including satellite transmissions and receiver and development of multi-channel, digital radio and television.
- How radio found a new role in the television age.

## The early days of broadcasting

The first scheduled transmissions in the world in a recognisable 'one to many' form of broadcasting were probably in the Netherlands, but historians have also credited the USA with setting up the first full-time radio station, KDKA in Pittsburgh, which went on air in time to broadcast the results of the 1920 Presidential election. Asa Briggs's authoritative account of the development of the BBC[1] describes the rapidity of the transition from the 'discovery' of the technological ability to transmit speech and music over long distances – which was described as 'radio telephony' – to fully fledged broadcast services in the UK. From the very earliest days, in addition to technical and economic issues, there were in fact questions about what broadcasting – initially of course, radio, or 'the wireless' – was *for*. Was it simply to broadcast events and material that had originated somewhere else – such as relaying an orchestra or a play, or reading aloud words that had already been produced from the print media – or should it have a particular and unique form? (Many of the early accounts of radio listening, including those very first ones of the BBC, use the term 'listening in': the audience is characterised as eavesdroppers.) What should be its 'grammar' and conventions? How should the audience be addressed: singly or collectively? Indeed, what involvement, if any, should the audience have in the making of the programmes or their consumption? The fascinating thing about this period in broadcasting history is, of course, there were no rules and no templates from which the pioneers could work. They were literally making it up as they went along.

One aspect though was immediately apparent and beyond argument. Unlike the print media, the means of distributing the output – the wavelengths – was limited. This was especially true at night-time, as AM transmissions travel further as the upper atmosphere cools. So unless there was some control over the number and power of transmitters, the airwaves would be a cacophony of inaudible noise, as each station battled to be heard over the others. So, from the start, there was a need to control and regulate the transmissions and from this, most countries concluded that as only a relative few would be able to broadcast, those that were committed were subject to regulation not only of transmission power but of content.

Nevertheless, as radio broadcasting developed in the 1920s and 1930s, different countries with a variety of different political systems and histories adopted different approaches to the new medium, especially its ownership and control. Even in the 21st century, broadcasting in different territories can still be categorised as falling into one or more of these broad definitions:

1.  Public service broadcasting (PSB), funded either by a licence fee as with the BBC, or directly through a government grant funded by general taxation, subscription by listeners/viewers and/or controlled and limited advertising. A strong element of independence and separateness from the state and its elites is essential, or the broadcasting would be better described as:
2.  Financed and run directly by the state (such as in France), though often (especially post-1990) partly or wholly funded by advertising broadcasting, often proclaimed to be in the national interest, but in reality has strong links with:
3.  An arm of state propaganda and control naturally favoured by, and common in, authoritarian states. Here there is little or no pretence that broadcasters have independence but that their broadcasting was under the 'dictatorship of the proletariat'.
4.  Run on a commercial basis and funded by advertising and sponsorship, generally 'free to air': although there may be some PSB requirements as in (1), perhaps especially in times of emergency, and requirements for accuracy, fairness balance and impartiality in news programmes and discussion of public affairs – such as in the 'Fairness Doctrine' in the USA. In

general, the aim is to maximise audiences by producing mostly popular entertainment shows and broadcasting popular sports and movies in order to produce the greatest profits for the private companies – in some countries these may be partly or wholly owned by the state.

5. Subscription services: the listener/viewer pays either a regular fee for access to certain channels – mostly by cable, or direct broadcasting by satellite (DBS), or on a pay-as-you view/listen basis. Income from this may also be supplemented by advertising.

Broadcasting in the pre- and immediately post-Second World War period tended to be mostly of the type defined in (1) above in the English-speaking countries of the British Empire and Commonwealth. For example, Australia had its ABC and Canada the CBC, both modelled very much on the BBC. Most Western European countries in the pre-and post-Fascist period tended to adopt a model described in (2), whereas of course the Fascist states in the pre-war European era and those in the Socialist/Communist post-Second World War era – up to approximately 1991 – tended to follow (3). The type described in (5) is dependent on technology – the broadcasters have to find a way of ensuring that only those who pay the required fees are able to access the material and this has tended to be via cable services or direct broadcasting by satellite. Until the beginning of the 21st century this was mainly confined to television.

The best-known development of (4) is, of course, in the USA and is often portrayed as being diametrically opposed to (1). However, many of the radio pioneers in the USA thought that the medium should remain essentially a public utility. Later, the public broadcasting system (PBS) and national public radio (NPR) used a combination of public funds and voluntary subscriptions to keep alive the idea of broadcasting as a public service.

## Early clashes between the state and broadcasters

In the UK, the 1920s and 1930s were especially eventful, with clashes between organised labour, capitalism and government and, in May 1926, the only General Strike in the country's history. Radio broadcasting was still then in the hands of an amalgamation of private operators under the single British Broadcasting Company. With nearly all newspapers affected by the dispute the government was, naturally, eager to use the new medium to communicate with the population and there was pressure inside the Cabinet for a government takeover. The BBC's then General Manager, John Reith, persuaded the Prime Minister, Stanley Baldwin, to resist this but in doing so assured him that nothing would be broadcast that would inflame the situation. Key figures supporting the strikers' cause were kept off the airwaves, but information which many trade unionists thought was helping to undermine the effectiveness of the strike *was* broadcast. This led to an enduring suspicion, even downright hostility, towards the BBC, with some activists urging the sabotage of the transmitters of 'the government wireless'.

Reith was keen to maintain government support and realised that if he upset ministers there would be pressure to either take over the company and run it as a state broadcasting service – as was already the case in many other countries – or, even worse in Reith's view, there would be commercial competition, and what Reith called (with pride) 'the brute force of monopoly', would be broken. He argued that competition would inevitably mean a race to the bottom in quality and content, in a bid to attract the most listeners. Reith believed that few people knew what they wanted and fewer still what was good for them, and was determined the BBC should be just ahead of the centre point of public taste, so that broadcasting would be challenging and elevating. He believed in a 'balanced' programme schedule – there would be light entertainment, but it would be almost impossible for a listener to select only the 'lollipops' from the output, because the times and days of these programmes were constantly shifted. Reith's BBC also thought that listening should not be passive – the public was expected to engage with the output. He later equated the introduction of a TV commercial network to an outbreak of smallpox. Reith's view prevailed and a monopoly company became a public monopoly corporation from the start of 1927, with Reith as its first Director-General.

Reith had realised from the start that there was bound to be trouble if the BBC operated its own news, as governments and other powerful interest groups would object to the perceived 'slant' of the bulletins. He therefore ceded control of the limited service it did provide to the national news agencies, who compiled summaries of news for the national radio service, but only in the evenings, and with no information which had not already been printed in that morning's newspapers. This also placated the powerful newspaper proprietors – who had greatly feared the impact of radio on newspaper sales. Crucially, the news was announced in strictly neutral tones and without commentary – indeed, the announcers did not even give their names until the Second World War, and then only because it was thought that, if the country was invaded and the studios taken over, the audience would be alerted to unfamiliar voices posing as BBC staff.

## The power and appeal of radio

The terrible human cost of the economic Depression in the decade or so before the outbreak of the Second World War in 1939, and the period of Appeasement towards Nazi Germany before this, as well as the Abdication Crisis of 1936, led to many such disputes about just how 'neutral' the BBC was in its treatment of highly controversial matters of public policy and debate. However, Reith, the BBC, nor the government could limit the reception of radio waves, which respected neither geographic nor political borders. Spotting a gap in the market and a market in the gap, entrepreneurs set up

English-language entertainment-driven, commercially funded stations broadcasting from the European Continent, such as Radio Luxembourg and Radio Normandy. These became hugely successful in Britain in the 1930s, especially on Sundays, which the BBC had determined should be dominated by religious programmes and 'serious' music and talk, which it thought befitting of the Lord's Day. For the working classes though, Sunday was often the only day of rest and surprisingly, these citizens sought more diversionary fare; 'the wireless' provided a cheap way of receiving entertainment, and the continental operators were happy to provide it. Such recordings as survive however indicate that even the commercial operators – who grew to be highly sophisticated, with top-notch recording studios in London, just around the corner from the BBC – were also presented by rather 'plummy' announcers and the tone was set to be 'respectable', so as to attract the middle classes, who would be in a position to buy the advertised products. Furthermore, the programme content was often integrated with its sponsorship – one of the things to which Reith was most opposed – most memorably with Radio Luxembourg's children's show *The League of Ovaltineys*.

The physical limitation on frequencies meant that even in the USA there was a large element of control and regulation, most particularly in the broadcasting of partial, biased coverage of news and current affairs. The partisanship and sensationalism of newspapers may be an important part of a free society but equally, it was widely thought, for radio, a measured and neutral approach was both necessary and desirable. Therefore, radio had the unique power of being both an entertaining and distracting medium, yet one that was thoroughly trusted. It was this power and authority of the medium that led to the extraordinary public reaction to the broadcasting of Orson Welles' Mercury Theatre production on CBS of H.G. Wells' *The War of the Worlds* on Hallowe'en night 1938. The production begins with a clear announcement that what is to follow is a drama, played by actors. However, two factors – at least one of which Orson Welles must have been very aware of – led to the confusion, and in some cases outright panic, of perhaps millions of Americans, who thought they were listening to coverage of a real invasion from space. First – and a factor which all radio producers have to bear in mind – is that audiences often tune in to a production after it has started, and in this case many did not hear the opening announcement. Second, the devices, conventions and 'grammar' of real radio reporting were used in a fictionalised context. Breathless announcers handed over to 'reporters' supposedly on the spot, interviewing 'eyewitnesses' and 'experts', just as they would for a real, dramatic news story. Whatever the intentions, the production caused a complete sensation during and immediately after its broadcast and in the coming days and weeks. At the very least, it may have been responsible for several premature deaths from heart attacks and even suicide.

The rise of a mass audience absorbing the same content at the same time in radio's so-called 'golden age' of the 1930s interested a number of academics, as well as other commentators who became concerned about the power of radio to mould opinion and attitudes. Those on the left of the political spectrum believed that a mass audience, listening to and absorbing the same material at the same time over large distances, could be manipulated into thinking and acting in ways conducive to the state and the economic and political elites behind it. Even when the influence was thought to be rather more benign and prosaic, such as the way that women, in particular, engaged with 'soap operas' (so called because they were often sponsored by the manufacturers of detergent powders) the effects were usually regarded as undesirable; radio being used as a distracter from the individual and group's 'real' economic and political situation. Prominent in this view were those from the Frankfurt School – many of them intellectuals who fled from Nazi Germany and set up or joined research establishments in the USA. They believed that, although the USA was not an authoritarian state, the mass media acted in a more or less uniform way that supported a single, homogenous ideology and there was clearly a danger that this ideology could be used against the interests of the working classes, and indeed the wider world. In addition, some complained that the BBC was far too keen to convey the opinions and interest of other nations and peoples. It certainly did connive with the government's then policy of appeasement in the late 1930s and kept a number of prominent voices from the airwaves, including those of Winston Churchill, then in his 'wilderness years' and warning of the dangers of Nazi Germany.

## Radio in wartime

In 1914 the British public learned they were at war, via the newspapers, some hours after the fateful declaration. In 1939 the whole country heard the news at the same time in a 'live' broadcast by the Prime Minister, Neville Chamberlain, from the Cabinet Room at Number 10 Downing Street. Radio now provided the ways in which political leaders and royalty could address their people simultaneously. Winston Churchill – British Prime Minister from May 1940 – adapted his style perfectly for the medium. Radio also boosted morale and helped production of armaments at home by giving airtime to comedians who could provide topical gags, mock Hitler and other leading Nazis, develop catch-phrases so beloved of the British, and in broadcasting music, both 'live' and recorded. And the broadcasts were not confined to the domestic audience: from its beginnings it was clear that radio could permeate geographical and political barriers far more effectively than any other medium. There were high hopes that radio could lead to greater understanding between peoples and reduce the likelihood of conflict – 'nation shall speak peace unto nation' as the (English translation of) BBC's motto puts it, and the Corporation began its Empire Service in 1932, connecting the citizens and leaders of the UK's far-flung territories. In the Second World War, carefully framed news and propaganda of various sorts were also broadcast overseas, to three main audiences. First, to British civilians, especially children, some of whom were evacuated to Canada – the Princesses Elizabeth and Margaret made a famous broadcast to them; second, to the potential fighting men in the British Commonwealth and Empire – notably Canada, Australia, New Zealand, South Africa and the Caribbean countries – many of whom travelled thousands of miles to fight for Britain and her Allies; and, finally, and perhaps most thrillingly, to the Resistance movements and those who had been shot down or escaped from prison camps in occupied Europe. British listeners became accustomed to hearing strange and clearly coded messages. Exiled leaders, such as France's De Gaulle, were able to address their people from the BBC's studios in London and encourage them to rise up against the occupying forces.

By the end of the War the status of radio could hardly have been higher. Wartime led to the rapid development of the BBC's own, independent (although subject to official censorship during the war), news service. Radio correspondents had been in the thick of the action – indeed often on the front line or, notably in the case of Richard Dimbleby, in a bomber over Germany. The integrity of the BBC was exemplified by Dimbleby when he accompanied Allied troops as they entered Belsen concentration camp. Dimbleby's account of what he had seen seemed so extraordinary and shocking to his masters back in London that they at first declined to broadcast his report, saying they needed confirmation from other sources. Dimbleby threatened to resign unless his report was broadcast; never had the claim that 'journalism is the first draft of history' been made more forcibly.

It was also quickly realised that radio could be used to spread hatred, mistrust and divisions, as well as sapping morale of the people and military in hostile countries. During the Second World War, William Joyce, a failed actor from Britain, though with strong Irish connections and dubbed 'Lord Haw Haw' because of his aristocratic accent and sneering approach, broadcast from Germany to the UK, telling the British that their leader was a drunk, that the war was going badly and that they were being lied to, not least about civilian casualties in the blitz. Opinion surveys showed people who heard the broadcasts *did* have a markedly less positive view of the progress of the war from Britain's perspective, compared with those who had not listened. In the Cold War period (1949–89) both sides used radio for propaganda purposes.

## Broadcasting as part of the rituals and routines of life

Sometimes governments with influence over public service broadcasters could 'encourage' the use of popular forms of radio, such as the daily serial or 'soap opera', in a benign way to spread important public service information. So it was that, a few years after the Second World War, BBC radio launched *The Archers*, (originally only in the English Midlands region, where it continues to be produced) to provide important agricultural information along with plot-lines about farmers and villagers in rural England for a country still subject to food rationing. The programme lost its educational purpose in 1972 but it continues to engage a significant and much-devoted audience, most of whom are not employed on the land or indeed live in rural villages. In an increasingly urbanized – or perhaps more accurately – *sub*urbanised population, the melo-dramas of the story-lines involving both familiar and newer characters, linked to a supposedly more 'natural' way of living through the rhythms and routines of agrarian society, hold continued appeal and the show celebrated 60 years of national broadcasting in January 2011.

The post-war broadcast schedules tended to follow a regular pattern and sought to both support and blend in with the routines and rhythms of the everyday lives of audiences, so that, for example, weekend schedules tended to feature more entertainment and diversionary programmes than those on week (working) days, although Sundays became established as the 'natural' day for TV costume dramas. But radio, then (also) television, also helped to unite the nation and solidified the rhythms of the year through the broadcasting of state and sporting annual events and rituals. In the UK, these ranged from the rather quintessentially British (perhaps specifically *English*) annual boat race on the Thames river in the spring between teams from Oxford and Cambridge universities, followed within a month or so by the climax of the football season with the Football Association (FA) Final, the Wimbledon lawn tennis championships in early summer and the Test and County cricket matches, through to the State Opening of Parliament and national Remembrance Day commemorations in the autumn. Christmas became one of broadcasting's most important periods in the calendar. Not only did the season often produce the biggest audiences of the year but families and nations could be united through the airwaves, by linking domestic and overseas transmitters, with music request programmes for kith and kin in far-flung corners of the earth, and the annual Christmas message from the monarch, the first being in 1932; the first on television – 'live' – in 1957. Although there was some initial resist-ance from the establishment, broadcasting quickly came to be regarded as a vital part of state rituals such as the weddings and funerals of royalty; in Britain, the 1953 Coronation of Queen Elizabeth II becoming the 'tipping point' in the public's adoption of television.

Moreover, broadcasting did not just relay existing national rituals and cultural and sporting events: it created its own fixtures in the nation's calendar, or, in the case of the Promenade classical concerts ('the Proms') – performed in London in the late summer – the BBC 'acquired' and so saved an important cultural season, which was facing collapse. The Corporation devised competi-tions for writers, musicians and budding scientists; it funded its own 'house' orchestras covering both classical and 'light music' repertoires, its own choral singers, its own radio repertory drama company – and a separate one for chil-dren's plays and serials. In other words, the BBC became a patron and creator – not just a disseminator – of the arts, culture, science and debate.

Of slightly more dubious cultural value was the annual *Eurovision Song Contest*, held every spring since 1956 – which was originally devised to 'show off' the network formed by members of the European Broadcasting Union, designed to enable easy exchange between European countries of a wide variety of television material. The contest – the butt of many jokes and much cynicism in the UK, partly due to the increasingly quixotic voting patterns – rather than bringing together the peoples and nations of the continent seemed, if anything, to magnify the cultural and political differences in Europe and produced surges of nationalistic fervour.

Children were thought to be needy and worthy of distinct programmes from early in the establishment of radio – the BBC had a *Children's Hour* (1922–61)[2] featuring stories and drama serials and younger listeners had their own entertainment programmes, as well as more 'worthy' and educational fare, from pre-school age through to adolescence. Television followed a similar development and (astonishing as it seems now) there was so much anxiety about the near-hypnotic attractiveness of the medium to younger viewers that both the BBC – from the resumption of television broadcasting after the Second World War in 1946 – and then also ITV – imposed a 'Toddlers' Truce'; an hour (6–7 p.m.) on weekdays when there were no programmes at all, in order that parents were able to prise their young children away from the sets and to bed. This was imposed until 1957, when it was abolished by both networks.

Television took hold of the public imagination and purse remarkably quickly after the Second World War. In the beginning it mostly adapted radio genres and formats – with the addition of being able to show movies although, in the UK's case, only some years after their theatrical release – but it soon developed its own conventions and 'grammar'. The control and financing of television generally followed the same pattern as had been established for radio.

The BBC's careful, deferential, unemotional and unimaginative approach to news, presented by telegenic announcers, was challenged though by the introduction of Independent Television News (ITN) in 1955. This service of national and international news bulletins for the new commercial network employed journalists as its news*casters* (not news*readers*), many of whom had come from the country's famously robust national newspapers. Their challenging, probing, persistent approach in interviews in particular, as well as their human-interest approach tone and style, combined with (unlike the partisan newspapers) impartiality and fairness, gave it both credibility and popularity.

Politicians found it hard to decide their attitude towards television: they courted it, resented it, and feared its impact on public support and voting behaviour. There was constant tension between the broadcasters and the politicians about the extent of legitimate enquiry and criticism, and for control of the 'news agenda'. Naturally, when politicians had important announcements to make to the nation, they did so on television.

In the UK, the political parties were given free airtime during and between elections, but in the USA politicians and parties had to pay for their slots, leading to a sort of arms' race, with campaigns costing hundreds of millions of dollars and resulting in candidates without access to big financial 'war chests' and who weren't backed by wealthy individuals and/or corporations being squeezed out of the political system. The first TV US Presidential campaign debates took place in 1960. Surveys showed that those that listened to the radio relay thought that the then Vice-President, Richard Nixon, 'won' the crucial first debate; the larger audience that watched it on television favoured the relatively youthful, tanned, and extremely wealthy John F. Kennedy. Given that the final result was so close it seems likely that television may have influenced the outcome of a hugely important political contest at a time of great world tension between the nuclear superpowers. Moreover, it 'proved' to politicians and their advisors that, in the television age, image was more important than substance.

Elections and broadcasting seemed made for each other. As it happened, the first radio broadcasts – at least in the USA – were made just at the time of the 1920 US Presidential election and two years later in the UK the then British Broadcasting Company came on air just in time for that year's general election. *The Times* recounts special 'listening-in parties' parties being held,[3] with guests gathering around the set for what must have been the extraordinary, novel experience of hearing election results across the country announced to the whole nation within minutes of their declaration. By the late 1950s the TV 'election night special' became established. Not only could the reactions of the victorious and defeated be shown at the time of reckoning, and their speeches relayed from the count, but studio guests could react to this fast-changing event and, using increasingly sophisticated polling sampling and computer software, predict the eventual outcome. Indeed, the use of exit polls – which in the 21st century were to be banned in the UK on the day of the election across all media until the close of polling – led to US networks 'calling' Presidential elections even before many citizens on the west coast, with a time zone three hours behind that in the east, had even cast their vote.

In Britain, the unusually swift transfer of power when the ruling party had been defeated (often less than 18 hours after the close of polls) provided further, live and dramatic evidence of the power of the voters, with television showing history as it was being made. As a guest on BBC television's programme for the 1970 election (when the Labour government was unexpectedly defeated by the Conservatives) noted however, at that time only perhaps 20 countries in the world were able to boast of such a peaceable, democratically induced transfer of power. Much of the world, notably the huge Communist countries, China and the Soviet Union, remained closed to the prying eye of the TV news reporter and camera, but when President John F. Kennedy was assassinated in Dallas in November 1963 the nation's citizens coast to coast learnt of his death minutes after it had been confirmed by the local hospital. Although transatlantic satellite time was expensive and had to be pre-booked – meaning that viewers in Europe initially had little more than newsreaders intoning information gleaned from the press wires – once satellite links were scrambled the continents were united in grief for the slain President.

However, the only pictures of the assassination came (some time later) from the home movie of a bystander; never again would a US President be in a public place – no matter how much the occasion lacked news value – without TV crews being present, 'just in case'.

Television took over from the weather as the main starting point – sometimes the *whole* point – of conversations. Public discourse was moulded and stimulated by the ideas and imagination of creative programme makers who used the medium to entertain, enlighten, educate and sometimes to provoke. The British also seemed to be especially fond of catch-phrases, used in comedy and entertainment shows and some dramas, as well of course as a deliberate ploy in advertising slogans (although these would often be 'reproduced' in an ironic or facetious manner in social discourse). A society still riven by class divisions – often nuanced to an extraordinary degree – industrial disputes, and tensions caused by differences in manners, dress and accents, found a common ground in using such phrases in all manner of conversations.

There were tensions in some countries, including the UK, about the balance between national and local/regional broadcasting. John Reith forcibly merged the many local stations that his new company inherited in the early 1920s, and developed a National Programme, imposing the accents, views and attitudes of the English upper middle-classes across the nation or nations. Some variety was allowed in the 'Regional Programme', which led to some ground-breaking features and documentaries, but many parts of the UK, such as in northern England and most especially in what the BBC referred to as 'the national regions' of Scotland, Wales and Northern Ireland, continued to feel throughout the 20th century that their cultures and languages/dialects were being suppressed, or at least not being given sufficient airtime. This was partly dealt with by regional 'opt-outs' on TV and radio, the establishment of a commercial TV network based on regional franchises, a Welsh-language channel formed from a unique partnership between commercial operators and the BBC, the development of local radio on the BBC from the late 1960s and commercial (or 'independent') local radio from the early 1970s – which was generally more successful the further the location from London, and especially so in the central belt of Scotland, south Wales and in Northern Ireland. Nevertheless, the tensions remained between the national and the local/regional – as they did over the larger constitutional question of the proper relationship between the constituent parts of the United Kingdom.

## Continued conflicts between broadcasters and the state

National and international radio broadcasts from the BBC infuriated the British government during the Suez Crisis of 1956. In an uncanny parallel to the invasion of Iraq in 2003, the British – this time with the French, and without the support, or even knowledge, of the Americans – used a pretext to invade the Suez Canal, a hugely important conduit of oil from the Middle East to Europe, which had been nationalised by the Egyptian President, Colonel Nasser. Like Iraq nearly 50 years later, the action divided the nation. The BBC sought to reflect opposition to the invasion but the Prime Minister, Anthony Eden, thought the Corporation should uncritically support government policy, especially after 'our boys' were sent into action, and threatened to cut the Foreign Office grant that funded the Corporation's external services. The military action quickly ended when a furious US President threatened to bring down the UK economy – the country was still hugely in debt to the Americans due to loans given during and after the Second World War. Eden resigned soon afterwards, supposedly due to ill health, and, as in the aftermath of the Iraq war, public opinion surveys indicated that it was the government's reputation that was tarnished and the broadcasters' enhanced.

Politicians, the military and (often self-appointed) 'moral guardians' constantly fretted about the impact of television, which was blamed, amongst many other things, for eroding the American public's support for the Vietnam War (1963–75). When, in February 1968, CBS TV news' main 'anchor', Walter Cronkite – whom polls had shown was the most trusted person in America – returned from visiting the front line in Vietnam and told his viewers that, in his opinion, the country was involved in a conflict which it was not winning and could not win, the then US President declared that he knew he had 'lost America' and, within a month, announced he had decided not to contest another term in office. This was a lesson not lost on the British military who, some 15 years later, in the relatively small war over the Falklands (Malvinas) Islands – British territory in the South Atlantic which was invaded by Argentina in 1982 – told broadcast journalists that they would not enable them to 'do a Vietnam', and greatly restricted access to, and broadcasting from, the front line, or from ships that had been bombed. The military successfully blocked the transmission of moving pictures until the British forces had successfully recaptured the islands. In the age of television 'live' satellite feeds, the Falklands conflict was a 'radio war'.

The British government was also concerned regarding broadcasters giving legitimacy to 'terrorists' involved in the 30-year period (1969–98) of 'The Troubles' between Britain and (Northern) Ireland. Most countries had debates about the medium's 'responsibility' for increasing licentious behaviour and use of 'bad language' – especially by the young. And there was concern for the erosion of communities and deference towards authority and institutions – secular and religious – and all manner of psychosocial phenomena.

## Continued debate over the purpose and potential of television

Throughout the 1950 to the 1970s there were continued tensions over the purpose of television: was it simply a 'goggle box', there to provide light relief and entertainment, or did it have a higher purpose; to educate, inform, stimulate debate and hold the powerful to account? Perhaps both – but who decided how much of the former compared with the latter? Overall, three main types of output attracted mass audiences and, even in many authoritarian states, tended to dominate the airwaves, certainly at peak times. These were: dramas or 'soaps', quiz shows and sport. Most television in most of the world consisted either of government-sponsored propaganda, both covert and overt, or of mass entertainment programmes. In South America *Telenovellas* or soap operas produced the highest audiences. In Asia the Japanese-made drama *Oshin* was broadcast by 26 countries, including China and India. The Hindu story *Ramayana* was so popular that riots occurred when a power cut occurred during one of the transmissions, and the opposition BJP persuaded one of its stars to stand for election. In the USA, the drama *Roots* (1977) promoted better understanding about its racist history and thus creating greater empathy by its white citizens of European origin towards African–Americans, and the sitcom *M*A*S*H* (1972–83), although ostensibly about the Korean War of the 1950s, was 'really' about the Vietnam War, which was still in progress during the first couple of seasons of the show and, through dialogue and situations which provoked laughter and tears, helped heal a very divided nation.

In the UK, the commercial broadcasters, as well as the BBC, were required to be public service broadcasters in ethos and practice – and this was specified to a large extent through particular requirements for quality and quantity of, for example, news and current affairs, and in catering for a wide variety of taste and interests. Advertising on the commercial network was limited to 'natural breaks' between and within programmes and advertisers could not sponsor the output or directly influence programme-making decisions and both the BBC and commercial channels demonstrated that they could be both educational and entertaining. Even the 'soap operas' reflected many of the changes and debates in society. Many also contained profundity and wit, not least *Coronation Street*, which began in 1960, networked from the following year and which has rarely been out of the top 10 most viewed programmes ever since. The 50th anniversary celebrations in 2010 (by then the longest-running programme of its type in the world and shown in some 35 countries) not only included many tributes from politicians, artists and other commentators, but a dramatisation – on the BBC – of its beginnings.[4] This highlighted the conflict between its writer and creator and some of the executives and shareholders at the network that produced it, Granada Television, based in Manchester, as to whether a show about 'ordinary' people, who had strong north of England accents (which had until then had mostly been heard in the national media only in a comedic context) would have resonance over the whole nation – or even be understood. It may have been designed to appeal – and certainly did appeal – to 'ordinary' working-class viewers, but it was admired by many from the cultural elites who compared its writing and performances to the best that has ever been achieved in any medium and, most impressively, the standard was achieved not just a few times in the life of the artistes and producers, but week after week.

Its theme tune, as with those of other popular shows, became like trumpet calls to the nation's citizens, who gathered around the television set, which mostly had pride of place in the main living room. The TV became the electronic fireplace of the 20th century; the equivalent of the gathering of family and tribe around the fire in pre-industrial times; a place in which stories would be heard, songs would be performed and where discussions on matters of the moment would be generated and conflicts resolved. In TV's case, however, the *same* entertainments, the *same* debates and the *same* instruction and transfer of knowledge took place simultaneously in homes across the country at the *same* time. The impact of entertainment programming being seen across a nation was exemplified by the appearances of The Beatles on *The Ed Sullivan Show* on the US network CBS in February 1964. So large was the audience (for the first of the three consecutive Sunday night appearances this was estimated to be 73 million, then the highest on record) and so intense the interest in the 'Fab Four' young men from England that in many American cities recorded crime fell to almost zero!

Although it is usual to discuss the medium's reception in group form, there is no doubt it was also a tremendous alleviator of loneliness, boredom and isolation – geographic and/or socially by those living on their own, out of choice or necessity and whether forcibly confined to the home through disability or other factors. The 'baby boom' generation who entered their teens and twenties from the late 1950s to the early 1970s, benefited from post-war affluence. However, many did not live in or near the big cities, so programmes featuring the latest music, fashion and dance steps could be followed through programmes such as *Ready, Steady, Go!,* broadcast early on Friday evenings from 1963–66 on the UK's commercial TV channel, which kept the youth of the country connected to the fast-changing cultural scene, wherever they might live. The BBC's *Top of the Pops* (1964–2006) did the same job for a much longer period – although arguably with less flair and zest.

Debates and controversies, as well as the 'pleasures' of entertainment programmes and dramas, could be followed in the ensuing press coverage. Some of these had a strong 'message' about aspects of society; one BBC play, *Cathy Come Home* (1966), led directly to the start of a national charity for the homeless. By the end of the 1960s, television was the main conduit through which intellectuals, artists, writers, historians and scientists, as well as entertainers, were able to obtain a mass public impossible in the pre-broadcasting age.

Television was especially effective in bringing the natural world into living rooms and, in many countries, education in the broadest sense was augmented in television (as it had been from the early days of radio) by formal education programmes, both to support school curricula, then for adult education, and in Britain, from 1971, by the Open University. This new form of distance learning, supported by written materials and some traditional lectures at weekend and summer schools, allowed many people who, for a variety of reasons, were unable to attend traditional universities to acquire a degree –

and one which was internationally respected. Moreover, the TV and radio programmes provided a first-class higher education teaching to those who were not enrolled on the course but nevertheless were able to learn about diverse subjects, from astronomy to sociology. This was broadcasting that met the highest purposes that Reith and other originators of broadcasting systems would surely have approved. Indeed, the original meaning of 'broadcasting' was to spread seeds – so broadcasting can be seen to be spreading seeds of knowledge and promoting debate, based on rational discussion, something that was also true to the spirit of the European Enlightenment.

## The demands and rewards of 'the golden age of television'

Television, like radio, gobbled up material and comedians, in particular, realized that, in contrast to a career in theatrical and club performances where they could build a whole career on perhaps a thirty minutes' routine, in radio and then television they needed fresh material each week, so writers and producers became hugely important in the entertainment industry. The performers also needed to realise that, just as radio required a very different speaking style (intimate and conversational, rather than the declamatory and hectoring approach often used for public meetings), so the use of exaggerated gestures and strong vocal performances, essential to reach the back rows of a theatre audience, were completely unsuitable for television. Some, some such as Britain's Eric Morecambe and Ernie Wise, took a while to realise this. Their early TV forays were a disaster. One critic wrote that a TV set could be defined as 'the box in which they buried Morecambe and Wise' – and they nearly gave up the business. But when a strike denied them their usual big stage sets and cast they were forced to work close to camera and to rely on their charm and personal relationships to engage the audience, who were watching them on a flickering black and white screen at home. They then became so successful that their Christmas TV Shows on the BBC (1969–77), by then in colour, were watched by the end of this run by half the population, including the Royal Family who, in the days before video cassette recorders, would, like millions of their subjects, organise their Christmas Day activities around the show. Eddie Braben, Morecambe and Wise's scriptwriter in this period, later talked about the pressure he felt for being responsible for the success and happiness of so many people's Christmases.

Situation comedies (sitcoms) often had the most impact both in audience ratings – and often come top in polls of the most fondly remembered television and because, in most cases, the comedy derived from the characters and situations, rather than 'gags' or visual set-ups, they had a vitality and relevance to the politics and culture of a nation. One of the most significant of these in the UK was the BBC sitcom *Till Death Do Us Part*, which ran from 1965 to 1968 and then in various forms, including a spin-off, in the 1970s and 1980s. Recorded as close as possible to transmission in order to ensure topicality, it centred on clashes between the generations (forced by economic circumstances to live under the same roof), and discussed politics, attitudes towards race issues, immigration and other highly controversial issues at a time when society was in flux. Its use of 'strong' language and its rawness in the attitudes of its characters led to opposition by 'moral' campaigners, as well as questions in Parliament. And this was not a purely British phenomenon; there were versions in many other countries, including Germany, Brazil and Hong Kong and the USA (*All In The Family*), which was also shown in the UK.

Traditional variety shows continued to flourish for the first three decades or so of television as a mass medium. In the UK, jugglers, magicians, acrobats and ventriloquists found employment on both BBC and commercial networks, especially at the weekends, with the BBC featuring a Saturday night show, 'live' from its own television theatre – a converted former music hall (vaudeville theatre) in west London – often hosted by a 'pop' star; the old and new popular cultures often sitting uneasily with each other. The BBC gave its support and airtime to the surreal and cerebral comedy of *Monty Python's Flying Circus* (1969–74) and the more eclectic end of the rock/folk/blues genres in *The Old Grey Whistle Test* (1971–88), but it also featured the easy-listening music and whimsical comedy of *The Val Doonican Show* (1965–86) and the singing and dancing of white singers 'blacked up' in *The Black and White Minstrel Show* (1958–78), featuring – although not limited to – the Dixieland routines (complete with period costumes) of an earlier period in the deep south of the USA. The artistes and producers said they were both baffled and hurt by suggestions that the performers used racist gestures and mannerisms, but in the end the Corporation accepted that, despite the programme's enduring popularity – it reached audiences of 18 million – in an increasingly multi-ethnic country, which was becoming more sensitive to the portrayal of racial and other minorities, it had to go.

## Television transformed by technology and politics

The broadcasters' use of satellite communications and the use of increasingly lightweight cameras, video replacing film – meaning material no longer had to be developed and processed – and synchronised sound meant that reports had an increasingly 'real' feel to them and could either be sent 'live' or completed shortly before transmission. Now, the tragedies of mankind were laid bare on the evening news. Consciences were stirred, protests organised and, sometimes, politicians and military leaders were shamed into relieving suffering, and gathered round the peace table. Television provided a truly global, communal experience – an extraordinary development in human history – for everything from the viewing of the Moon landings (1969–72), to the Olympics and other international sporting events and the Live Aid pop/rock events in 1985. The impact of 'live' worldwide transmission of events did not go unnoticed by those with malign intent, and just as revolutionaries, counter-revolutionaries and invaders quickly learned that the occupation of broadcast stations provided both legitimacy and confirmation of their success, so terrorists realised that the taking of hostages, the blowing up of aircraft and the planting of bombs would have far more impact if they could be sure it would be broadcast on 'live' TV. The abduction and murder of Israeli athletes at the 1972 Munich Olympics provided the grisly and tragic proof that television did indeed have the power to show the greatest and worst aspects of humanity.

For the viewer, the most important single change was the arrival of colour television. There was rapid take-up of new sets in the late 1960s through to mid-1970s and although the move to colour did create considerable extra cost for the TV companies, public service broadcasters such as the BBC benefited from a huge increase in income through a higher colour licence imposed on all households with such a set, and commercial broadcasters were able to raise their rates as advertisers found the medium was now even more effective in selling their wares. International sales of programmes increased, especially from the USA, but some from the UK went in the reverse direction; certainly the UK television industry fared better than its movie equivalent in persuading the Americans of the value of British cultural production.

The 1970s saw the high point of television as a medium in which the population watched the same programmes at the same time. Only by the end of the decade did the domestic video cassette recorder (VCR) offer the prospect for 'time-shifted' viewing. The launch of music television (MTV) in 1981, featuring the fast-moving pop promo videos, linked by video jockeys (VJs) led to a host of imitators and challenged radio's dominance as the chief way that young people would have access to music any time of the day or night.

The UK then initiated another form of PSB. Channel 4, which began broadcasting in 1982, was designed to complement the main ITV commercial channel by providing different perspectives, forms and attitudes. This included the UK's first daily hour-long news programme. Supervised by a non-executive Board of 'the great and the good' and funded by advertising, with airtime initially sold by the regional ITV companies, who also subsidised it in its early years, it revolutionised the UK television industry because nearly all its output was commissioned from independent producers. No longer did you have to be directly employed by an ITV company or the BBC to work in television. Ironically, given that it was created by the first of the governments under Prime Minister Margaret Thatcher – the most right-wing since the Second World War – the station quickly became known as the most subversive anti-Thatcherite channel. Even the news, although maintaining due impartiality in strict terms, in tone and attitude had a clear leftish approach.

By the end of the decade, the BBC and ITV companies were also compelled to offer a significant portion of airtime to independent producers. ITV companies were then auctioned to the highest bidder – subject to a 'quality' test – and commercial radio was freed of its PSB obligations, with new, national stations also auctioned to the highest bidder, but all British broadcast news, on whichever channel/medium, had continued obligations to be fair, accurate and impartial. The 1990s saw market forces, de-regulation and other political, economic and technical factors having a major impact on most broadcasting systems. By the end of the century, direct broadcasting by satellite (DBS) in the UK and a multiplicity of channels afforded by cable in the USA, including a 'rolling news' channel, CNN, meant that the dominance of the free over-the-air broadcast networks would be greatly eroded.

## The most-watched TV programmes of the 20th century

Identifying the most watched TV programmes of the 20th century can provide a useful indication of the attractiveness of different types of output – of *genres* and the sort of programmes that have brought the public to the TV sets *en masse* at the same time. Such tables do not necessarily reflect the most-watched programmes week in and week out – generally in the UK, aside from the occasional sports' event, these tend to be the 'soaps' and other popular dramas – but rather tend to reflect the extraordinary pull of 'special events' (see Tables 1.1 and 1.2).[5]

Although there is a preponderance in the USA of 'live' coverage of the Super Bowl finals, supplemented by coverage of two days of a Winter Olympics, with only the final episodes of two enormously successful sitcoms and the most talk-about episode of the most successful 'soap opera' otherwise making it to the list, it is the UK that has a sporting event at the very top; a figure that is unlikely ever to be surpassed (and not just because, at the time of writing, it seems unlikely, in my opinion, that England's soccer team will ever again reach

**Table 1.1** All-time most watched TV programmes in UK to 2000

|  | Programme | Year | Audience (millions) |
|---|---|---|---|
| 1* | World Cup Final 1966 | 1966 | 32.30 |
| 2* | Funeral of Princess Diana | 1997 | 32.10 |
| 3* | The Royal Family | 1969 | 30.69 |
| 4 | EastEnders | 1986 | 30.15 |
| 5* | Apollo 13 splashdown | 1970 | 28.60 |
| 6* | Royal Wedding – Prince Charles and Princess Diana | 1981 | 28.40 |
| 7* | Royal Wedding – Princess Anne and Capt. Mark Phillips | 1973 | 27.60 |
| 8 | Coronation Street | 1989 | 26.93 |
| 9 | Only Fools and Horses | 1996 | 24.35 |
| 10 | EastEnders | 1992 | 24.30 |
| 11 | Royal Variety Performance | 1965 | 24.20 |
| 12* | News – assassination of President Kennedy | 1963 | 24.15 |

* Aggregate of audiences from BBC1 and ITV. Nos. 4, 9 and 10 were shown on BBC1; 8 and 11 on ITV.
*Source*: 'BFI most watched' 1950s–1990s.

**Table 1.2** All-time most watched TV programmes in USA to 2000

| | Programme | Year | Audience (household/millions) |
|---|---|---|---|
| 1 | M*A*S*H (last episode) | 1983 | 50.15 |
| 2 | XV11 Winter Olympics 2nd Wed. | 1994 | 45.69 |
| 3 | Super Bowl XXX | 1996 | 44.15 |
| 4 | Super Bowl XXV111 | 1994 | 42.86 |
| 5 | Cheers (last episode) | 1993 | 42.36 |
| 6 | Super Bowl XXX1 | 1997 | 42.00 |
| 7 | Super Bowl XXV11 | 1993 | 41.99 |
| 8 | XV11 Winter Olympics – 2nd Fri. | 1994 | 41.54 |
| 9 | Super Bowl XX | 1986 | 41.49 |
| 10 | Dallas (Who Shot JR?) | 1980 | 41.47 |
| 11 | Super Bowl XV11 | 1983 | 40.48 |
| 12 | Super Bowl XV1 | 1982 | 40.02 |

*Source*: Nielsen Media Research, 1961–1999.

the final of a world tournament). Aside from that World Cup Final, four from the UK chart are aggregate figures from 'live' coverage of events – a brace of royal weddings, the funeral of Princess Diana, the dramatic Apollo 13 splashdown, when the American astronauts were in mortal peril, plus the (never repeated) documentary on the Royal Family, one sitcom and three 'soap' episodes. Perhaps surprisingly, according to these figures, only one Christmas Day show makes the list – the 1986 episode of *EastEnders*. The latest date for a top-12 rated programme was 1996 (USA) and 1997 for the UK, but in the latter case this was for the extraordinary circumstances of the funeral of Princess Diana and, despite the ever growing coverage of TV and the ownership of sets, half of the most-watched programmes date from 1973 or earlier. Further audience figures, comparing those at the peak of television's 'golden age' with figures from thirty years later, are discussed in Chapter 3.

## Radio finds a new role

In the meantime, the senior broadcast medium needed to find a new role, purpose and attraction in the latter part of the 20th century. Fortunately, two developments provided salvation. First, the invention of the transistor radio meant that the medium could now be truly heard 'anytime, anywhere'. Second, was the development of a new form of popular music – rock 'n' roll – and the post-war affluence in the west, which created new identities and patterns of consumption. The radio companies developed formats that could accompany daytime activities and provide companionship, whilst at nighttime many geared themselves towards teenagers and young people. In the USA, network programming with a full and varied schedule of programmes, gave way to locally based (although the 50,000 watt clear-channel stations could be heard over much of the continent after dark) mostly music-based services, hosted by high-energy disc jockeys; so program*mes* were largely replaced by program*ming* of a single genre. Unlicensed radio from international waters broadcast to many European countries from 1958, such stations peaking in the British case in the period of 1964–70 but not finally extinguished until 1990, and to New Zealand from 1966 to 1970. Both north and south of the equator the 'pop pirates' led to the breaking of monopolies and to licensed commercial radio. Nevertheless, public service broadcasters, such as the BBC, maintained high-quality, well-produced radio news and current affairs, documentaries, music concerts, comedy, quizzes and drama – with the 'mixed speech' network, Radio 4, continuing to achieve a mass audience, indeed becoming the most listened-to station in London – the most competitive radio market in Europe. Radio was still the entry point for many people to types of music, drama, science and philosophy, which might otherwise have remained closed to them. BBC radio continued to nurture writers, producers and performers, with many (especially in the comedy sketch-shows and sitcoms' genres) transferring shows first established on radio to television – where the financial rewards were greater.

The lack of representation of 'ordinary people' though exercised many, including BBC radio producer Charles Parker, who, from the late 1950s, produced a series of ground-breaking documentaries on various aspects of the lives of working people and those – such as 'travelling people' – whose experiences and perspectives are hardly ever reflected on mainstream media. The work of Charles Parker and his associates continues to inspire radio producers and educationalists – there is an annual prize for radio-feature making in his name, and his archive, contained in Birmingham Central Library, receives many appreciative visitors. The talk-back or radio phone-in type of programme took off in the 1970s, becoming a staple of most local radio stations and seemingly provided radio with a democratic flavour, often lacking in television.

Mirroring the much later development of digital audio broadcasting (DAB), broadcasts on FM from the mid-1950s and then the advent of stereo, greatly improved the listening experience, as well as enabling many new stations to take to the air. The early development of FM in many countries – including the USA – meant that a greater variety of 'voices', music and opinions, especially those of African–Americans, were given airtime, but gradually, as FM listening matched then overtook AM, most of the stations became incorporated into the mainstream. In the UK, the 'rationing' of recorded music on licensed stations forced the broadcasters to seek new, unsigned talent, or bring in established artists to record new material in specially recorded sessions. This enabled DJs such as John Peel on BBC Radio 1 to provide a much wider range of material for his listeners than was usual on commercial stations, which tended to rely on records from artists who were already successful. As will be argued in Chapter 4, the death of radio, so often predicted from the beginnings of television, was to be disproven not only in the latter part of the 20th century, but well into the 21st.

## Notes and references

1.  Briggs, A. (1961) *The History of Broadcasting in the United Kingdom, Volume 1 – The Birth of Broadcasting*, London: Oxford University Press.
2.  It continued until 1964 under the title *For The Young*.
3.  The Times (16 November, 1922) *Broadcasting Results – Listening-In Parties*, p.12.
4.  (BBC, 2010) *The Road to Coronation Street*, first transmitted BBC4 and BBC HD, 16 September.
5.  There is a problem of inconsistency with the different methods of ratings: the USA continues to quote the numbers of *households* from their sample viewing particular programmes, and ranked in order of percentage of TV-owning households tuned in to the programme, whilst Britain quotes the *total* audience. Not only that, but Britain's ratings aggregate the total viewing audiences when either the same programme is being simulcast, the same event is being covered, or – as in the case of no.12 – when they are news broadcasts on the same approximate time period following the same event (the assassination of President Kennedy). The figures from the USA do not take into account any of these factors, but as there is not the 'tradition' of simulcasting the same programme and there is more likely to be exclusivity in the coverage of sporting events, there could well be higher figures and a change in the rankings if, for example, news programmes across the networks had been amalgamated. This might also have skewed the eras represented in the ratings; the UK's includes programmes from 1963–97; whilst in the USA the earliest show represented is in 1982.

# Broadcasting Output and Consumption

*2*

This chapter considers the quantity and nature of broadcasting; how it is measured and how it is consumed. In particular it discusses:

- The overall number of radio and television stations and international comparisons of levels of listening and viewing.
- How listening and viewing figures are compiled.
- The impact of a multi-channel, multi-platform world on both audiences and advertisers.
- Claims that subscription cable services have led to 'better' output, especially in drama.
- What detailed studies of audience behaviour tell us about how people 'really' use broadcasting.

## How much broadcasting is there?

This is in fact a far trickier question to answer than might be supposed: even the UN's official agency for broadcasting and telecommunications was unable to provide a definitive answer and the most comprehensive information was compiled by the University of Berkeley in the USA, which collated information from the CIA's world fact-books. This indicates that there are (or were – the information was first published in 2000) around 44,000 radio stations worldwide, broadcasting over 65 million hours of original programming, and some 33,000 TV stations globally, broadcasting 48 million hours of original programmes. So, who is listening to and viewing these programmes? Before investigating the ratings' figures for the UK and USA in more detail, here is a wider international comparison, comprising six of the world's leading industrial economies, plus China (see Figure 2.1).

This international comparison indicates that two of the biggest economies

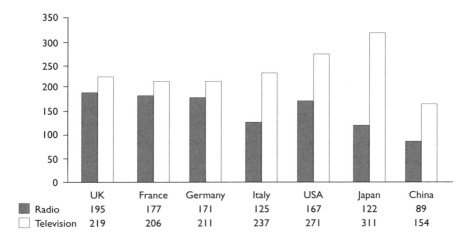

| | UK | France | Germany | Italy | USA | Japan | China |
|---|---|---|---|---|---|---|---|
| ▮ Radio | 195 | 177 | 171 | 125 | 167 | 122 | 89 |
| ☐ Television | 219 | 206 | 211 | 237 | 271 | 311 | 154 |

**Figure 2.1**    International comparisons of daily consumption of broadcasting services (minutes per day)

*Source*: Ofcom (2007) *International Communications Market (December)* available online at: http://www.ofcom.org.uk/research/cm/icmr07/.

in the world – the USA and Japan – are also first and second, respectively, in their average overall daily consumption of radio and television. The UK population, however, has the highest amount of daily radio listening. We might expect there to be significant differences between Japan and China – the latter took over from Japan in 2008 as the second biggest world economy.[1] However, in per capita (personal) income, the USA had – according to estimates in 2009 – eight times greater wealth per person than those in China and an astonishing 16 times that of the average person in India.[2] An indicator of the remarkable rise in China's global position is that between 2002 and 2007 the number of television households grew by 50 million, compared with a growth of just 600,000 in the UK.[3] The Italians are the most enthusiastic TV viewers but least prone to radio listening, giving some weight to the argument that use of media is a 'zero sum' calculation, with more consumption of one invariably leading to a fall in others; however the differential between daily radio and TV consumption is less than 30 minutes in both France and the UK, indicating a strong historical culture of radio listening and continued attractiveness of the medium's output. Public service broadcasting (PSB) has a strong tradition in western European countries and of course this began in radio.

Further research released by Ofcom in 2009[4] comparing 2008 with 2007, showed an increase in daily viewing time in the UK of 3.2 per cent – the biggest year-on-year increase of eleven countries surveyed (UK, France, Germany, Italy, USA, Canada, Poland, Spain, Netherlands, Sweden and Ireland). The 3 hours 45 minutes a day were exceeded by Italy (3 hours 54 minutes) and, as might be expected, dwarfed by the USA (4 hours 37 minutes).

**Table 2.1**    Terminology used in discussion of ratings

| | |
|---|---|
| **Reach** | The percentage of the entire population in the transmission areas who listen/view to the programme service/channel or programme, expressed either as the actual numbers or as a percentage. |
| **Cume (cumulative)** | Expresses the cumulative audience (either as a percentage or in actual listeners/viewers) for a specific period, which could be a part of a day or hour, day, week, month. |
| **(Household) rating** | Particularly used in the USA, this expresses the numbers of households who have tuned into a television programme (television is still regarded as a 'group activity', in comparison with the overwhelmingly individual consumption of radio). There are just over 100 million households in the USA, so a ratings point equates to just over a million. |
| **Average hours** | Can be either the average hours of overall listening/viewing to the medium as a whole, or to particular programmes or part of programmes (e.g. of a half-hour of a daily radio programme); can be expressed in total numbers, or as a percentage of the audience, or of the available population as a whole. |
| **Share** | Usually regarded as the 'fairest' calculation of the relative consumption of programme channels or individual programmes, as it includes both the numbers tuning in ('reach' and/or 'cume') and for how long they tuned in (average hours) and can be expressed as a percentage of the overall listening/viewing 'cake'.<br><br>Unless otherwise stated though, when discussing 'share' as a percentage, this is referring to the share of overall listening or viewing, i.e. 'ignoring' those who do not listen to the radio or watch TV at all. |

The same report showed that, in 2008, despite the digital switchover not due to be completed in the country until 2012, that the UK had the largest percentage by far (88 per cent) of homes with at least one digital set.

There is some rather confusing terminology used in ratings, so before more detailed consideration is given, Table 2.1 shows a summary of the terms used in this discussion.

## How audiences are measured

The question that needs to be answered at this stage is how do 'they' know how many people are watching or viewing? Table 2.2 shows the main methodologies of making audience calculations used in the UK (with similar methods used in the USA and many other developed markets) and how the figures are made known.

**Table 2.2**   Methodologies used to compile UK audience ratings

| Television (BARB) | Radio (RAJAR) |
| --- | --- |
| Figures compiled from a panel of 5,100 homes, returning data from around 11,500 viewers (including visitors to the home) 'representative of the whole of the UK',[1] including children, mostly by using electronic meters, backed up by home visits. | Surveys around 130,000 adults over a year (each surveyed for one week), who are asked to complete a listening diary, by putting a cross in a daily grid, divided into quarter-hour segments along one axis, and stations on another. Only one person in the home is surveyed. Trials of personal people meters (PPMs) which record the radio output in 'real time' and then matched against a database were experimentally used alongside the diary methods (see below for a discussion about the more advanced use of these devices in the USA). |
| Electronic device attached to TVs: 'All viewing environments in the home are represented'[2] and measures both analogue and digital delivery via cable, satellite and terrestrial distribution. | Diaries ask for location of receiver and which platform used – e.g. analogue radio, digital radio, TV audio channel. |
| PVR and VCR playback is incorporated within seven days of transmission. | 'Listen Again' and podcasts not included in main survey but separate survey indicates general usage of these listening methods. |
| Weekly figures published, but available overnight to subscribers and some published online by Broadcast magazine (www.broadcastnow.co.uk). | Produces 'top line' figures every three months, placed on its website, but (to ensure a sufficiently large sample) detailed data from individual stations available every three, six or twelve months, depending on size of station. Subscribers receive quarter-hour break-downs and sub-divided according to age and other socio-economic factors. |

[1]  Quoted from front page of BARB website, available at: www.barb.co.uk
[2]  *Ibid.*

The revelation that audience figures are based on the actual (in terms of TV) or recalled (in terms of radio) viewing/listening of only a small sample of the population is often received by many outside the industries with incredulity, quickly followed by scorn. How can 'they' be sure about these figures based on such a small sample? This reaction is almost invariably followed by an indignant: 'Well, they've never surveyed me' (and perhaps '... or anyone that I know!'). This incredulity/scorn is undoubtedly made worse in many cases because the 'ordinary' person feels fooled and misled; often otherwise well-informed people believe that somehow all listening/viewing is 'picked up' by some sort of device.

## What type of output is being most viewed and listened to, when and how?

Although there are some distinct variations according to socio-demographic factors, discussed further below, UK television audiences broadly favour entertainment (including drama, comedy and game shows) types of output over what can be broadly described as factual (including news/current affairs/documentary). Television programmes that are high in human interest and featuring characters/personalities with whom the mass audience can relate – be that popular dramas and 'soaps', or Reality TV shows (discussed in Chapter 5) – are overwhelmingly the most popular; with sport and 'special events' on specific occasions. Viewing for the fixed television news programmes and some other types of factual programming though remains relatively high in the UK, compared with many other developed countries. Television peak viewing times are 7.00–10.30 p.m., with 23.3 million Britons viewing TV at 9.15 p.m. on weekdays, with the weekend peak slightly higher. Afternoon audiences are around 50 per cent higher at weekends than weekdays, in line with the availability of the audience. BBC1, with its mixed schedule across virtually all programme genres (with the notable exceptions of 'shopping, 'gaming' and 'adult'), is the most-watched UK service. Cultural and social/work patterns provide some interesting variations in peak viewing.[5] Whereas Germany, the UK and USA have their peak viewing period within the same 45-minute period (9.00–9.45 p.m.), there are two distinct viewing peaks in France and Italy, with a lunchtime peak higher than that in the evening, but in Japan there are three peaks: those at 07.45 a.m. and 12.45 p.m. being only 26 per cent short of the evening peak.

These figures tell us something interesting about social, work and life patterns but, of course, for commercial broadcasting they are of vital importance as they determine the advertising rates that can be charged. The usual way of determining advertising rates is on a cost per thousand (CPT) basis. So shifts of a few thousands, let alone tens of thousands, in the ratings can make a big difference to the broadcasters' revenues. Of increasing importance, though, in a fragmented, multi-channel media landscape is the sociodemographic make-up of the audience. Age and social class are the key factors – advertisers generally preferring the young (aged 15–34) above all else, as they are thought to be the most receptive to influences on their spending behaviour. Breakfast-time commercial TV broadcasting attempts to reach 'housewives with children'. Whilst it is true that most of the richer, developed countries are experiencing an age shift in their populations towards the higher end, with consumer and political 'grey power' certainly being a phenomenon in many countries, the fact remains that, in general, as people get older they tend to be more conservative in their tastes and less willing to experiment with new products or services and so are, on the whole, less attractive to advertisers. Social class is important as, generally, those with higher incomes are thought to have more discretionary income and therefore more money to spend on advertisers' products and services. There is often a premium for advertising breaks in news programmes, as these attract disproportionate numbers of higher income groups, even if this is mitigated by the ageing profile of audiences to such output. One factor, however, which has become less important in the 21st century is gender. Cultural and economic factors meant that, in the 20th century, many advertisers targeted women viewers and listeners, as it was thought they were most likely to make spending decisions, but changing gender roles and work patterns means there is less concentration on the 'housewife' audience.[6]

Great scepticism, though, should certainly be applied when claims are made about global viewing figures for specific events. It has become common since the 1960s for broadcasters to breathlessly declare that so many hundreds of millions, or even billions, have watched a particular event and it seems as if many people believe there is some sort of United Nations-type of body which compiles and supervises the figures behind such claims. In fact, when dealing with aggregates over many countries (some of whose sampling may, to say the least, be less rigorous and credible than those described above), such figures should be regarded as intelligent guesswork at best. Nowhere is this truer than disputes about coverage of worldwide sporting events. Following the 2006 tournament, the governing body for the FIFA World Cup admitted that claims that more than a billion people viewed the games were exaggerated.[7] However, the 2010 World Cup final between Spain and the Netherlands did not just excite interest amongst the participating nations but much further afield. According to the Canadian Press[8] an average of 5.816 million (about a sixth of the country's entire population) tuned into CBC and its French sister station Radio-Canada, and the online broadcast attracted a total of more than 230,000 'live' streams.

In British radio, the RAJAR figures are invariably controversial. This is because of the recall/diary method, which relies on the members of the sample accurately remembering which station they listened to and when. Not surprisingly, those stations that do not do as well as they believe they should question the methodologies far more vociferously than those who do relatively well. Speech-based stations, in particular, believe that they are under-represented because the more aggressive and compelling promotions and advertising of music-based stations are likely to lodge in the mind. Many listeners complain about the constant repetition of station names/call letters/slogans, often on the basis that they know what they are listening to (thank you very much!) and don't need to be constantly reminded. The fact is though that the use of catchy jingles, big prize contests, as well as the 'station name in every (presenter) link' – sometimes 'station name twice every link' – policy are all aimed at the few hundred people who at that time have those diaries. Stations use a form of 'brain-washing' (albeit of a relatively benign type) in the hope that, once a member of the sample settles down to complete a listening diary, their station name will be at the forefront of his/her mind.

Because of this, in the UK speech stations such as talkSPORT have been the most enthusiastic proponents of the various 'personal people meter' devices, which use an audio code – inaudible to the human ear – broadcast along with the programme signal, which is detected by the meter. Information can be downloaded to a central computer base at the end of the day. Comparisons between the RAJAR and PPM results have indicated some very significant differences. As this then tends to reduce advertisers' confidence in the reliability of the audience data, other stations have countered with claims about the inconsistencies of the PPM service. In the USA, PPMs were used in most of the major markets and replaced the diary method in all of the so-called 'metro' (major urban) areas by 2010. The meters provide much more detailed information to the programmers as they show minute-by-minute changes between stations; so, for example, a programmer can see whether a particular new music track, news bulletin, or other programming element was a 'tune in' or 'tune out' factor and which stations were tuned to/from (or, indeed, whether the set was switched off). In the USA, the results of the PPM have directly led to changes in programming: rock stations gained a higher patronage when radio is measured though this method, so this format has seen an increase.

For a variety of political, economic and cultural factors, Britain has a strong tradition of national radio listening compared with the USA. The UK has a population only about fifth of that in the USA and it is of course a much smaller country physically, and with a single time zone, which means the whole country is (broadly speaking) getting up at the same time; unlike in the USA, where, for example, the residents of Los Angeles are mostly still fast asleep by the time New Yorkers are well into their working day. The importance of time in broadcasting will be explored further in Chapter 8.

Most of radio output is designed to accompany – rather than dominate – social, domestic and work routines. The 2010 Ofcom report on the communications market in the UK highlighted the fact that, more than two-fifths of radio listening took place outside the home, much more than any other medium.[9]

## Fragmentation and convergence

Convergence technologies – discussed further in Chapter 11 – have opened up many more revenue streams to broadcasters and much better ways of advertisers to target particular types of consumers. These were discussed in some detail in a blog by Olivier Wellmann,[10] Senior Director of Project Management at Open TV, who argued that ways of reaching the consumer through television were changing rapidly. He identified four main strands:

1. The ability for advertisers to target individual viewers by studying their set-top box profile ('addressable advertising').
2. The ability of viewers to interact with the advertiser's brand ('interactive advertising').
3. The ability of advertisers to reach consumers on a variety of screens, e.g. mobile phones, games consoles and PCs ('multi-screen approach').
4. Perhaps most importantly, in addressing the 'half of advertising is wasted' issue, to measure audience response to individual messages ('measurement and accountability'). This may be good news for broadcasters' revenues as, he argues, with less wastage, the CPT rates could be increased.

Direct revenue to the broadcasters themselves, in alliance with the producers of goods and services, is also increasingly important. These are most obviously connected with shopping channels, gaming and 'adult' entertainment. At the end of 2009 these channels occupied some 15 per cent of the UK's most popular digital television platform, Freeview (although some of these, especially the 'adult' channels, are evenings/overnights only and share time with other channels) and five out of the twelve data services were devoted to text gaming, dating and 'adult chat'.

Another important of audience measurement that needs to be discussed – and one which will certainly become increasingly important and indeed problematic for broadcasters and advertisers – is how to measure time-shifted viewing and listening. In the UK, the success of the Sky Plus personal video recorder (PVR), much praised for its simplicity of use, has resulted in considerable additional audiences to programmes after their original transmissions. But, as Gareth Maclean notes, every technological change – from VCRs to the iPlayer – has seen ratings shrink.[11] The UK's TV audience measurement company BARB started reporting time-shifting viewing in the early 1990s and from 2006 produced two types of figures: overnights, which include time shifted programmes – known as 'viewing on same day as live (VOSDAL) – and consolidated figures, which take in viewings within a week of the programmes' first broadcast. Sky Television has a further panel of 33,000 homes of its subscribers because it believes that overnight audience figures tell only part of the ratings' story. An example given by Sky[12] was its drama *Bones*. For the first episode of the fourth series on Sky One, 537,000 people watched it 'live', but this audience more than doubled if taking into account those who watched it via Sky Plus, the Sky HD channel, multi-start, Sky Anytime and repeats on Sky 1 and Sky 2. This is interesting for the broadcaster when determining the true cost/revenue for each series but is a major problem for advertisers – and that in turn of course also means for the broadcasters – because all the time-shifted viewing does not help in assessing the impact of the commercials and sponsorship messages which surrounded, and were included, in the original broadcast. How is it possible to determine how many viewers sped through the commercials – or if so, which ones? The impact of all of this will be that advertising on television will become increasingly subtle; advertisers will seek ways of integrating their messages *within* the programmes, including 'product placement'. Long since a feature of US TV, such practices were completely barred in Britain until the second decade of the 21st century[13] – indeed for the first few decades of television, 'real' products were not even allowed to be shown in dramas and the like; a corner shop in a 'soap', for example, would have to be stocked by completely fictitious products and packaging; TV presenters would have to be careful not use a brand name which had become synonymous with the article, so it had to be 'sticky tape' rather than Sellotape, and 'ball-point pen' for Biro.

'Pre-roll' advertising, which cannot be fast forwarded, and so-called 'viral campaigns' using the web and other convergent technologies, seem certain to become increasingly important. It seems likely that by 2020 the standard thirty-second commercial spot, the mainstay of television advertising for some 60 years, will seem old-fashioned and quite possibly redundant.

## Implications in changes of financial models and audience behaviour for the funding of programmes

In the 21st century, however, the increasing importance of subscriptions as a form of income has skewed television output further in the direction of the premium sports events and movies and to high-quality drama. For example, critically acclaimed shows such as *The West Wing* and perhaps especially, *The Wire* – cited by some critics, notably in the USA, UK and Australia, as the greatest television show ever[14] – were produced for the American cable channel Home Box Office (HBO).

The show's creator David Simon told the 2009 Media Guardian Edinburgh International Television Festival[15], that the economics of cable had 'freed' programme-makers from the tyranny of the ratings:

> Their [HBO's] economic model is that if certain shows bring people into our tent to pay $17.95 a month, OK then we can fund that show. And *The Wire* bought some people into HBO and some people who were subscribers didn't dig it and they watched *The Sopranos* and other people watched boxing and other people watched *Sex and The City*, but as long as they stayed in the tent … so in effect the ratings no longer mattered as much. The Nielsen's [TV ratings] were emasculated as a force … eventually the DVD concept – which didn't exist when we were planning *The Wire* – caught up to the show. And so our ratings became more and more meaningless with every season. I think by the end we had our worst ratings – the fifth season – and more people were watching the show. (Transcribed by author from video of interview.)

Programmes which gather the most views on the BBC's web catch-up service iPlayer demonstrate that such technologies and ways of consuming broadcast media are particularly popular with young – and often young male – viewers. Of the top ten individual episodes viewed on the iPlayer in 2009[16], eight were for the motoring show *Top Gear*, one was for a stand-up comedy presentation, and one was an episode of the sitcom *Gavin and Stacey*. BBC research also showed that the most popular time for watching programmes on the iPlayer was 10.30 p.m. – about an hour after the peak-time audience for broadcast TV – and it seems likely that viewers were taking their laptop computers to bed and watching the shows there.

Listening to radio services over the Corporation's web service was very different: here the main benefit for the audience seems to be the ability to listen to 'streamed' programmes at work over the internet. The most listened to radio show via the iPlayer in 2009 was BBC Radio 5 Live's *Test Match Special* on the second day of the fifth (cricket) test in August that year, which resulted in 183,300 streams. Other popular shows included the comedy panel game *I'm Sorry I Haven't a Clue* (discussed further in Chapter 4), a premier league soccer match, and a special programme featuring the boy-band (by then well into their middle age) Take That. Intriguingly, the BBC was also able to reveal the different hardware used to view the iPlayer:[17] comedy was most popular on Mac computers and PS3 (gaming) devices, while drama was more popular on PCs. At the risk of ditching rigorous research in favour of pure speculation, this may well be that gaming devices, in particular, are more of a male preserve and males favour comedy compared with females, whereas females disproportionately favour drama.

In any event, there are technical limitations in further moves to online delivery of previously over-the-air delivery of content. Part of the unique quality of traditional means of delivering broadcasting is that you don't need to 'log on' to some kind of server, you will not have frequent nagging messages demanding that you download more pieces of software or renew a subscription, or do anything. Simply press the button. There is certainly a strong feeling in much of the population in the advanced industrialised – or post-industrialised countries – that life is getting too complicated and this is causing stress and anxiety. However, one major technical factor alone that is so obvious that it is often overlooked, means that broadcasting is likely to have the edge over other forms of mass communications for the foreseeable future. In fact, it is as much an economic factor as it is a technical one: the cost of providing radio and television programmes over the air, whether through terrestrial transmitters or via direct broadcasting by satellite, does not increase however many extra people start using the service. There is no requirement or demand to add extra bandwidth; no drain on a finite resource. The transmitters or transponders do not require extra power output no matter how many people 'tune in' in their transmission area. It is hard to think of any other product or service to which this applies, certainly not in the communications area. Every extra newspaper or magazine printed to meet extra demands leads to an extra cost to the publisher; every additional subscriber to a broadband/internet service has an impact on the availability of the services other users, or requires extra bandwidth; every user of a wireless connection (and radio was the original 'wireless') is consuming part of a finite transmission spectrum.

## Quantity versus quality

For all this discussion of how many people are watching and listening, what, how, when and to some extent why, there is little that tells us how much they are *enjoying* or valuing their broadcasting consumption. As discussed above, commercial broadcasters are, of course, primarily concerned with the size and make-up of their audiences that they can sell to advertisers and sponsors, or through subscription. Public service broadcasters, however, are likely to be at least as interested in how well they are serving their audiences in other ways: how much their audiences enjoyed or appreciated the output and what they would like to see or hear more or less of. For example, a programme on steam trains or church organs may attract few listeners or viewers, but those that do watch/listen – who are likely to be very interested in those subjects and been alerted to them via internet sites, appreciation societies and so on – are probably going to enjoy them very much indeed. To such a broadcaster, should the great enjoyment by a relatively few number of people be regarded at least as important as gaining very large audiences and satisfaction at beating their commercial rivals in the ratings' game? This is, as will be discussed in Chapter 4, especially true in community radio. Broadcasters such as the BBC say they need to do both – to have the mass *and* minority appeal – and, of course, it's perfectly possible for ratings' hits to also be greatly appreciated. The shorthand for this approach is 'to make the good popular and the popular good.'

A good example of this was over Christmas 2009. On Christmas Day, David Tennant starred in his final *Doctor Who* story – a two parter, with the second episode being shown on New Year's Day 2010. The Christmas Day episode was a big ratings' hit, with 10 million viewers[18] and the following day Tennant was seen in the lead role in the televising of the Royal Shakespeare Company's acclaimed production of *Hamlet*. The three-hour transmission garnered 900,000 viewers.[19] Although *Doctor Who* certainly achieves a huge amount of interest and obvious enjoyment, it seems plausible that the televising of *Hamlet* was appreciated more. Whilst there were no doubt some who have little knowledge or interest in Shakespeare's work and may have tuned in out of curiosity to see Tennant, the bulk of the audience that gave up three hours on Boxing Day are likely to be knowledgeable about the play and, if they hadn't seen the stage production, will have seen the reviews and be receptive to the production and greatly enjoy it. One thing is for sure; the televising of the production brought around 15 times the whole of the audience who saw the RSC's production at Stratford upon Avon. Furthermore, many of those viewers may have been unable, for economic reasons (tickets were selling online for £500) or because of their location, or mobility, to see the stage production.[20] The BBC's first Director-General, John Reith, would surely be pleased that his greatest ambition – to bring the 'fine' arts to everyone, what-ever their location or position in life – was still being achieved more than 80 years since the founding of the Corporation.

Unfortunately, however, we do not know how much the audience enjoyed this screening, because the only survey to routinely test such things is the BBC's audience appreciation index (AI), which asks an online sample of 15,000 view-ers and listeners how much they enjoyed specific programmes, and how much an effort they made to view it ('made a special effort', 'made some effort', or 'because it was on'),[21] then giving programmes a percentage, is not put in the public domain. The Corporation guards these figures jealously, to the great frustration of many – not least the programme makers themselves: only occa-sionally do these figures – or rumours of the figures – appear even in the press. According to media journalist Gareth McLean,[22] by this measure *Criminal Justice* gained an AI of 90, *Spooks* was on 92 and *Cranford* registered 93, against an average drama AI of 84. In a comment piece in the trade magazine *Broadcast*,[23] producer William G. Stewart recounted that, in the early 1960s, the BBC regarded 70–75 as fine for sitcoms, anything under would result in 'long faces'; 80 and above 'would be dropped into conversation in the BBC club at lunchtime.' But neither the advertisers nor the press saw the figures and nor did the public – who were, after all, paying for this research.

In the 21st century a marketing concept of what is termed 'emotional connection' to consumer brands was applied to individual television shows, the assumption being that if viewers feel such an engagement they are more likely not only to keep viewing the programme but there will be a correspond-ingly positive attitude towards the show's advertisers and sponsors. The Q Scores Company puts regular updates in the public domain on the rankings of television shows according to such feelings of attachment. In the fall (autumn) of 2008, for example, its emotional bonding index (EBI) demonstrated the commitment viewers had to have to continue watching a show for the reast of the season.[24] This showed that what the company termed 'compelling dramatic formats' topped the list, with CBS's *Survivor* programme scoring the highest EBI at 177 (the average is 100), although in its IQ Index – which the company says 'indicates the programme's capacity to satisfy key viewers' – this was beaten by four other shows: *House, CSI: Crime Scene Investigation, Heroes* and *Grey's Anatomy.*

## How people 'really' use broadcasting

Having considered so many different aspects of the broadcast audience, this chapter concludes with a short summary of what we know about how people really use the broadcast services and how this consumption relates to other aspects of their lives. In many respects the ultimate lifestyle/broadcasting research providing rich, qualitative data has been carried out by researchers from Ball State University's (BSU) Center for Media Design in Indianapolis,

USA, in Middletown Media Studies 2 (MMS2), and this will be compared with a survey by the UK regulator Ofcom in 2010 which, for the first time, considered people's *simultaneous* usage of different media and technological communications, and a further piece of research on Britain's TV viewing habits, conducted by ICM for the *Radio Times* and online TV service Seesaw.com in July 2010.

MMS2 was an extraordinary piece of work of immense value at many levels for anyone interested in how people use the media, in which the researchers followed a representative sample of 400 people in what are regarded as 'typical' towns in the USA, Muncie and Indianapolis, as they went about their day-to-day activities. This research built on Middletown Media Studies 1, conducted in 2004, which itself picked up on research in Muncie in the 1920s and 1930s by sociologists Robert and Helen Lynd. The good people of Muncie are almost certainly the most 'observed' people in America over many generations.

As explained by two of the key researchers – Bob Papper, BSU telecommunications professor and Michael Holmes, communication studies professor – at the 2006 Radio and Television Directors Association (RTNDA) Convention in Las Vegas, the researchers entered the homes as early in the day as they were allowed, and stayed until finally kicked out at bed-time. When the people being sampled went shopping, to work or anywhere else outside the home, the researchers went with them, recording all the media they consumed – and which media were used simultaneously with others. The researchers recorded on electronic keypads the sample's use of 15 types of media and communications in 15 second periods – 1.2 million separate observations in 5,000 hours of study. If nothing else (and there is a *lot* else) the research surely lays to rest any idea that the study of media – especially broadcast media – is of peripheral interest, compared to that of other human activities: it demonstrated that people spend more time with media than doing *anything* else – including sleeping. Papper declared that:

> Television is still the 800-pound gorilla because of how much the average person is exposed to it. However, that is quickly evolving. When we combine time spent on the Web using e-mail, instant messaging and software such as word processing, the computer eclipses all other media, with the single exception of television.[25]

The key findings of the research are:[26]

- About 30 per cent of the observed waking day was spent with media as the sole activity, versus 20.8 per cent for work activity, while an additional 39 per cent of the day was spent with media while involved in some other activity.
- In any given hour no less than 30 per cent of those studied were engaged in some way with television, and in some hours of the day that figure rose to 70 per cent.

- While television is still by far the dominant medium in terms of the time average Americans spend daily with media, at 240.9 minutes, the computer has emerged as the second most significant media device at about 120 minutes.
- About 30 per cent of all media time is spent exposed to more than one medium at a time.
- (Counter-intuitively) that people aged 18 to 24 spend *less* time online than any other age group except those older than 65 (as this was 2006, this was before Facebook and other social media really took off we could expect this figure to have changed quite dramatically since then).
- Levels of concurrent media exposure were higher among those aged 40 to 65 than people 18 to 39.
- Women spend more time multi-tasking with two or more types of media than men.
- Use of the web, email and phones is substantially higher on Fridays than any other day of the week'

Another highly revealing aspect of the research demonstrated was the lack of reliability of recall by the sample (with significant implications for both the Ofcom survey and the RAJAR diary method for radio measurement, discussed above). When some members of the sample were called the day following the sample period – when, as the researchers pointed out, you would have thought they would be especially sensitised to the whole business, having had researchers following them around for nearly all of their waking hours – and asked them to recall their media use, they *under-estimated their use of television by 50 per cent*. This factor emphasises the view that people are inclined to give answers which they think are socially acceptable, rather than the truth – or at least the full truth. Even more starkly, in the initial questioning of the sample, over 90 per cent claimed they had voted in the previous Presidential election – unlikely to be true when national turnout was barely 50 per cent. Scarcely more credible was the response to the question about use of 'adult entertainment' (pornographic) channels or websites: none (not even the young men) admitted to this! Pornography was likely to have been consumed when the researchers were 'kicked out' for the day, or possibly those who regularly use pornography on the numerous cable TV channels devoted to it, or via computer, did not do so during the time they were being researched – 'just in case'!

In the UK, the 2010 Ofcom Communications Market Report's study of simultaneous use was derived from a nationally representative sample of 1,138 adults aged 16 plus, who participated in the survey in April and May that year.[27] This was a mixed-mode online and telephone survey. Respondents recorded all their media behaviour in a diary for seven days, and this data was captured on a daily basis, online or by telephone. People recorded when they were watching or listening to video or audio or playing games on any device, reading a newspaper, magazine or book, making phone calls (on any device) or using a computer or mobile phone for any reason. The survey included personal and business use, in-home and out-of-home use.

The survey found (again, amongst many other things) that, of the average waking day of 15 hours 45 minutes, 7 hours and 5 minutes is spent in media and communications activities, but 3 hours and 6 minutes was used with two or more media/communications. If this is taken account, then on average 8 hours 48 minutes is spent on media/communications – as in MMS2, more than any other human activity, including sleeping. As would be expected, the amount of concurrent time was highest amongst 16–24-year olds, but this group spent the least amount of *actual* time – the highest of which was in the 45–54-year-old group. Again, as was found in MMS2, television dominated activities in the evenings and over half of all media/communication activity involves a TV or radio set, and TV in the evenings was most likely to be a solo activity.

Both studies suggest that, despite the wealth of alternative methods of consuming media, including time-shifting and multimedia devices, the 'traditional' sitting down in front of a TV set and watching programmes as they are broadcast (linear viewing) still dominates leisure activities. As many commentators noted in the days after the report, 'the death of television has been greatly exaggerated'.

Radio listening was very healthy in the UK study – the report came out shortly after the RAJAR figures had registered the highest ever radio listening since that methodology began in 1999. An intriguing question asked in the questionnaire section of the Ofcom survey was which media would be most missed, and here there is some cause for concern for the radio industry. Amongst 16–24-year olds the mobile phone remained the second most-missed medium, with one-third citing it compared to one in ten adults overall. In contrast, listening to the radio is the second most-missed activity among older users (16 per cent of 55–64-year-olds), far higher than younger adults and the adult population overall.

At the start of the 21st century, digital audio broadcasting (DAB) – originally developed in Germany, adopted by the BBC and backed by the European Commission in order to provide a new microelectronics industry for member states – was being touted as the logical and impressive successor to analogue radio transmissions. The then fledgling in-band on-channel (IBOC) standard, being developed in the USA, was dismissed by the BBC and other European broadcasters as an untried and probably never-viable technology. Ten years later, the 'bribe' to UK commercial stations to have their licences 'rolled over' without facing competition if they agreed to join the DAB platform, was being seen by many operators – faced with having to cut programming budgets to pay for expensive additional transmission costs, which yielded almost no extra listeners – as the most foolish commitment they had ever made. The costs of going onto the DAB platform had resulted in them having to abandon a reasonable level of local news and other content. The much-vaunted improved technical quality provided by DAB over FM has been compromised due to the relatively low bit-rates allocated to most services, in order that a large number of services can be squeezed onto each multiplex transmitter. In any event, the willingness of most of the public to trade the much higher quality of CD audio for the portability of the compressed MP3 files format demonstrates that, in this area, for all but the relatively few audiophiles, technical quality is of very much secondary importance. In the meantime, in the USA, the now re-branded HD Radio, which 'piggy-backs' on existing FM and AM transmissions, was providing both markedly better sound quality than on analogue and sufficient numbers of extra stations to enhance the US broadcasters' portfolios. The 'bouquet' of different digital radio standards – at least two others were being adopted in different parts of the world – means that, within another decade, the international traveller will no longer be able to assume that a radio bought in one country will work in another.

Commenting on further research for the weekly TV and radio listings' and features' magazine *Radio Times*,[28] the TV critic Mark Lawson identified some important differences in the consumption of broadcasting by different age groups.[29] Whilst those in the older (65 plus) age brackets 'expect to continue using the medium as their parents taught them to', those in the 18–24 category were much more likely to time-shift their viewing. The increase in daytime TV, Lawson notes, has been linked to the growth of further education, with more students available during the day: 'bringing an unexpected boost to the audiences of shows never intended for them, such as (the shows aimed at the pre-school ages) *Countdown* and *Teletubbies*'. In the evenings, however, students and other young people, being far more comfortable with using new technology, were more likely to use 'catch-up' services. However, 93 per cent of viewing to TV occurred 'live' or in linear form; being viewed at the time scheduled by the broadcasters, and, as Lawson notes that: 'some tribal instinct still seems to compel us to gather around a box for disasters, football games and talent-show finals' (*ibid*).

Working with that desire for communal experience is interactive, social media, instant messaging and texting, but that this may not even be with people in the same country: in one sense broadcasting is leading to a global conversation. Changes in British society, most notably (in common with most of the rest of the industrialised/'western' world) the increase in one-person households – due to increasing rates of divorce, decline in marriage and an ageing population – has meant that much more TV viewing was taking place by individuals alone, compared with the social, family experience that predominated in the 20th century – making TV much more akin to the common use of radio services.

I would add one further piece of speculation and prediction: with the economic crisis in Britain and many other countries and the increasing cost of housing, plus student debts, leading to many not-so-young people returning, or never leaving, their family home, the importance of connecting to others in their own age and peer-groups, through discussion of broadcast events and personalities, will be even more potent. In the 20th century broadcasting was often said to be the 'glue' that held society together; in the 21st it may well be social media *linked* to broadcasting that eases geographical and social isolation.

## Notes and references

1.   Sunday Telegraph (2009) 'A Stark Warning from the Four Corners of the Globe', *Business Comment Special*, 27 December, B5.
2.   *Ibid.*
3.   Ofcom (2008) *International Communications Market (December)*, available online at: http://www.ofcom.org.uk/research/cm/icmr08/emerging.pdf.
4.   Ofcom (2009) *International Communications Market (December)*, available online at: http://www.ofcom.org.uk/research/cm/icmr09/stats.pdf.
5.   Ofcom (2006) *The International Communications Market (November)*, available online at: http://www.ofcom.org.uk/research/cm/icmr06/tv.pdf.
6.   Even in the early to mid-1990s, when I was working in UK commercial radio, the mid–late morning period was still referred to in the advertising rate card as 'AAA housewives', as it was thought this was the time period in which women were likely to be making out their shopping lists and generally making their purchasing decisions. The term 'housewife' had by then fallen into disuse in most of the rest of society, as it was regarded as both sexist and patronising.
7.   Harris, N. (1 March, 2007) 'Why Fifa's claim of one billion TV viewers was a quarter right', *Independent.co.uk*, available online at: http://www.independent.co.uk/sport/football/news-and-comment/why-fifas-claim-of-one-billion-tv-viewers-was-a-quarter-right-438302.html.
8.   *The Star* (13 July, 2010) 'World Cup final draws record TV ratings', available online at: http://www.thestar.com/sports/soccer/worldcup/article/835107—world-cup-final-draws-record-tv-ratings.
9.   Ofcom (19 August, 2010) *Communications Market Report*, available online at: http://stakeholders.ofcom.org.uk/binaries/research/cmr/753567/CMR_2010_FINAL.pdf.
10.   Nagravision – Online (July 2009) *The Opinion: A Vision for Television Advertising – Consumer Addressability*, available online at: http://www.nagravision.com/online/online03/article_5.html.
11.   McLean, G. (1 June, 2009) 'How do I rate thee? Let me count the ways', *Guardian.co.uk*, available online at: http://www.guardian.co.uk/media/2009/jun/01/television-ratings/print.
12.   *Ibid.*
13.   Neate, R. (9 February, 2010) 'TV product placement ban lifted in UK', *Telegraph.co.uk*, available online at: http://www.telegraph.co.uk/finance/newsbysector/mediatechnologyandtelecoms/media/7197867/TV-product-placement-ban-lifted-in-UK.html.
14.   Hassall, G. (1 September, 2009) 'ABC2 screens 'best TV show ever', *Sydney Morning Herald-Entertainment*, available online at: http://www.smh.com.au/news/entertainment/tv—radio/best-ever-tv-show-starts-tonight/2009/09/01/1251570694644.html.
15.   *Guardian.co.uk* (29 August, 2009) 'Edinburgh TV Festival: David Simon interview in full', available online at: http://www.guardian.co.uk/media/video/2009/aug/29/david-simon-edinburgh-interview-full.

16. Parker, R. (2009) 'Top Gear tops iPlayer chart', *Broadcast*, available online (subscription only) at: http://www.broadcastnow.co.uk/news/multi-platform/top-gear-tops-iplayer-chart/5009261.article.
17. *Ibid.*
18. Sweeney, M. (26 December, 2009) 'BBC shows dominate festive ratings', *Guardian.co.uk*, available online at: http://www.guardian.co.uk/media/2009/dec/26/bbc-wins-christmas-ratings-war.
19. Sweeney, M. (29 December, 2009) 'The play's the thing for 900,000 viewers on Boxing Day', *Guardian.co.uk*, available online at: http://www.guardian.co.uk/media/2009/dec/29/hamlet-david-tennant-ratings.
20. To reach the same audiences for the stage production of *Hamlet* as those who watched the Christmas Day *Doctor Who* would have required David Tennant to have a real-life Time Lordly lifetime of more than 160 years of 'live' performance.
21. See note 11.
22. *Ibid.*
23. Stewart, William G. (16 January, 2004) 'Comment – show some appreciation', *Broadcast*, available online (subscribers only) at: http://www.broadcastnow.co.uk/news/multi-platform/news/comment-show-some-appreciation/1086243.article.
24. The Q Scores Company (2008) 'Press Release – The Q Scores Company Reports Fans of CBS' "Survivor" Franchise Have the Strongest Emotional Connection of Any Prime-Time Series Returning This Fall', Available online at: http://www.qscores.com/pages/Template1/site11/47/default.aspx?ItemID=1.
25. Bell State University Newscenter (2005) 'Average person spends more time using media than anything else', available online at: http://www.bsu.edu/news/article/0,1370,7273-850-36658,00.html.
26. *Ibid.*
27. Ofcom (August 2010) 'The Communications market 2010: UK. Key findings of the consumer's digital day', available online at: http://www.ofcom.org.uk/static/cmr-10/UKCM-1.8c.html.
28. Jones, P. (31 August, 2010) 'TV Nation 2010 – Britain's viewing habits'. *Radio Times*, available online at: www.radiotimes.com/blogs/1028-tv-nation-television-survey-radio-times/.
29. Lawson, M. (2010) 'The way we watch now', *Radio Times*, 4–10 September. pp. 12–14.

# Does More Mean Worse?

## 3

This chapter considers claims that the huge increase in television channels' output has led to a decline in the quality of the output and to 'dumbing down'. In particular it considers:

- How public service broadcasting (PSB) differs in its nature and appeal form other forms.
- A comparison between the levels of audiences for PSB output, especially news and current affairs, in the UK over a thirty-year period.
- Claims that pressures for higher ratings have undermined 'serious' programming.
- Claims that a move away from the dominance of advertising-funded programmes in the USA has improved the quality of television there.
- The importance of children's television and claims that broadcasters have abandoned 'quality' programmes for this age group.

## The continued importance of PSB in the UK

Countries such as the UK with a strong public service broadcasting (PSB) element might be expected to be 'shielded' from alleged trends of 'dumbing down'. Ascribing PSB values and pinning them down to particular channels and types of output is a tricky business, as will be discussed below, but legislation and regulation demands that PSB includes all BBC radio and television. The following definitions are therefore something of a synthesis of these sometimes quite varied characteristics:

1.  Technical coverage: the crucial first requirement for PSB is that it should be capable of being received by all but a tiny minority of citizens in the defined territory – whether that be national, international, regional or

local. Services, such as the BBC, that levy a licence fee on receivers, must levy the same fee no matter what the variable costs are for reaching one person against another.

2.  Should be an integral part or even the focus for national/local/regional life (as appropriate), in particular in its commemorations of key events that helped unite communities, and should help to define and promote the culture(s) of the nations and/or localities which they serve (but see (3) below). In times of emergencies, whether caused by man-made or natural factors, it should provide essential information and advice.

3.  All programmes should be produced without fear or favour of any interest, especially the interests of government and commercial concerns. They should comply with the law of their country and even then there may be a case for challenging or even defying the law if the broadcasters determine that a law is not in the interests of its citizens.

4.  Programmes should, overall, seek to inform, educate and entertain. PSB, nevertheless, has a particular role in informing the public and in debating issues, so as to produce an informed citizenry, which is taken as a necessary requirement for any meaningful democracy. As such, news and current affairs should be a particularly strong feature on PSB services and should report and debate fully on matters concerning politics, economics and international affairs.

5.  The highest possible standards should be attained, whether they be of a technical, editorial, or artistic nature. All staff and contributors should be aware of, and adhere to, a comprehensive ethical and editorial policy covering the whole range and scope of programme making. The highest standards of ethics and integrity must be maintained. PSB should be mindful of taste and decency and should not needlessly or carelessly upset or distress any of its viewers or listeners. When a broadcast is expected to, or might, cause offence or distress, the programme makers should be clear that there is a justification for this, perhaps because of the need to raise a particular issue or a point of view in order to inform and educate.

6.  Programmes should, taken as a whole, cater for all tastes and interests but should, if anything, have a bias towards groups of people and interests who are otherwise under-served and under-represented by other media, particularly the commercial media who, naturally, favour those who are most economically attractive to advertisers. The overall philosophy should be to make the popular good and the good popular.

These principles have, of course, been adapted and developed in various countries and, it is important to remember, not just for those services funded through taxation, licence fee or subscription. The UK's five terrestrial networks all have PSB obligations, even though three of those five are funded through advertising and sponsorship. 'Independent' or commercial radio in the UK also fell under the PSB banner until 1990.

Nevertheless, in Britain PSB is most associated with the BBC, and its dominance in broadcasting was heavily criticised by James Murdoch of Sky Television in the 2009 James MacTaggart Memorial Lecture at the 2009 Media Guardian Edinburgh International Television festival (MGEITF). Murdoch claimed that the reach and spread of the BBC's services had a 'chilling effect' on the private sector. In response, the BBC's Director-General, Mark Thompson, used the following year's same 'keynote speech' slot at the MGEITF[1] to highlight Sky's ever increasing role in British television which, with its media interests in publishing and newspapers, gave it a cross-media presence that would not be allowed in Sky's parent company's two other major markets, the USA and Australia. He also suggested that Sky should increase its relatively small spend in original programme production. Overall though, it was Thompson's defence of the BBC and its importance to the British public that drove his speech's arguments. This was summarised afterwards for *The Guardian*'s media podcast by commentator Steve Hewlett:[2]

> He made the ideological case for the BBC and for public spending … the idea for public investment – let's call it a licence fee – in a public space – let's call it the BBC – in a public space – let's call it Public Service Broadcasting, can have unambiguously positive outcomes. Because fundamentally what James Murdoch said last year was that public investment must always be kept to a minimum because it crowded out private investment, which was morally and in every other way better. So he made the case … and that if you cut back on the BBC you cut back on all sorts of things which the British public at least really value.

## Comparing PSB in the UK over a 30-year period

In 2007, PSB was still dominant and included all BBC Radio (54.4 per cent share) and all BBC TV services, ITV1, Channel 4/S4C and Five (67 per cent).[3] However, whilst in radio the 21st century has, due to the rise of BBC network radio's share, seen a slight increase in PSB listening, TV viewing to PSB channels declined from 78 per cent in 2002 to 67 per cent by 2006. In TV's case the 36.1 per cent share of all 'other viewing' includes some of the BBC's digital TV services, so we can be confident in asserting that, in the first decade of the 21st century, *well over half of all radio listening and at least two-thirds of all TV viewing was to PSB services*. The dominance of PSB is, in reality, greater than even these figures suggest, as they do not, of course, take into consideration the fact that, according to the commercial radio sector's trade body, there is a great deal of PSB content on commercial stations. As discussed later, the licensing process has tended to favour applicants who promise to include significant levels of PSB-type content, and even the non-PSB TV channels are still obliged by law to adhere to some of the principles of PSB of impartiality and objectivity in news output. Against that, it can be argued that at least some of the BBC's output on both radio and TV has a debatable PSB quality or 'flavour'.

This raises the question of the survival of PSB in maintaining a mass audience. In the week reviewed from September in 2007 the highest rated TV news bulletin only just made the top 30 of the overall ratings' chart and the highest position of any PSB programme was at number 18 for *Michael Palin's New Europe*.[4] The ex-Monty Python member had become established for his entertaining and idiosyncratic travelogues.

It is no coincidence that the highest placed current affairs' placing in the same week of the year in 1977 – for *World In Action* – was for a Monday night show on ITV, benefiting as it did from a very strong 'inheritance factor' from *Coronation Street* and a sitcom. In a three-channel universe, a strong lead in the early evening had an enormous effect on later programmes, as viewers were led from one programme to another by skilful continuity and promotion. It must also be remembered (and this is not a trivial point) this is in the pre-'zapper' era: it took some effort to get out of the chair/sofa to physically press the channel button on the TV. Monday night saw three out of the top twelve programmes of the week and *World In Action* was immediately preceded by the number two show. Monday nights have traditionally been the strongest week-night for viewing in the UK and the strongest night of all in the USA. All this helped *World In Action* to an estimated 12.7 million (15.2 million if taking the difference of population during those 30 years into account) viewers; more than twice the number of viewers as the Palin programme in 2007. Furthermore, the audience for the BBC's flagship current affairs programme *Panorama*, then 50 minutes and overlapping all of *World In Action*, was seen by 6 per cent of the population. So, combined with the nearly 11 per cent watching *World In Action*, 17 per cent of the country – nearly nine million viewers – were watching a current affairs programme that night. With the growth of the population this is equivalent to 10.8 million viewers in 2007, which was higher than the most-watched programme of all that week. In other words the *audience for watching a current affairs programme on one night in 1977 was (proportionately) higher than the top-rated programme of all in the equivalent week of 2007.*

By 2007, *World In Action* had long gone, with ITV's peak-time current affairs offerings mostly supplied by the populist *Tonight with Trevor McDonald*, with an almost wholly domestic agenda and dealing with 'human issue' stories (as the name implies, *World In Action* frequently dealt with international stories and issues; it had no on-screen presenter). *Panorama*, after being pushed off to late Sunday evenings, was restored to Monday nights during 2007 but now ran for 30 minutes, not 50, and the 'head-to-head' interviews such as those with the Prime Minister or Chancellor of the Exchequer in the 1960s–1980s were replaced by filmed reports, 'topped and tailed' by Jeremy Vine, who by then was best known for his daily Radio 2 programme. The BBC was boasting about the programme's 3.6 million viewing average in the early part of 2007,[5] which was one million up on the average in the previous year's Sunday night slot and with a drop of 10 years (to 46) in the average age of the viewer. It should also be born in mind that lengthy, head-to-head political interviews still featured on BBC television in other daily and weekly current affairs programmes, such as *Newsnight* and *Andrew Marr Show*, although none of these are in peak time.

## Declining audiences for news and current affairs

The decline of TV news viewing provides a starker illustration of the changes in television consumption. Using the BBC daily viewing barometer figures[6] to expand the rating list beyond the top 20, it is estimated that in 1977 the *9 O'Clock News* on BBC1 was watched by more than a fifth of the population in three nights out of five in September 1977, equating to 10.2–10.6 million viewers; around half a million more than the top-rated overall programme of the same week in 2007, even without taking into account the significant rise in population in the intervening years. On the two nights when it failed to do so well ('the *Coronation Street* effect') on Monday and Wednesday, ITV's *News At Ten* secured a 15 per cent and 13 per cent reach respectively of the entire population. So we can see that *in 1977 between 13 per cent and 20 per cent of the UK population regularly watched at least one mid–late evening news bulletin.*

An even starker picture is revealed by adding up the viewing figures for both of the early evening news bulletins in 1977 on BBC1 and ITV. These bulletins were both 15 minutes in duration and broadcast at almost exactly the same time on week-nights; the BBC's starting at 5.40 p.m., ITV's five minutes later. The BBC's figures indicate that *around a quarter of the entire UK population – over 12 million viewers – was watching one or other of the early evening bulletins each night:* a quite astonishing national, common exposure to national and international news on a daily basis. Because these bulletins followed the respective channels' children's programmes, they also contained a significant number of children and young people.

The decline in audiences to the 'traditional', evening network TV news bulletins is illustrated even more sharply in the USA. In 1980, the three main networks – ABC, CBS and NBC – were each being watched by between 12 per cent and 16 per cent of all households; by 2006 this had dropped to 6 per cent or less.[7] Comparing the 2006 data with figures from 5, 25, and nearly 40 years earlier puts the trend in sharp relief. In 1969, the three network newscasts had a combined 50 per cent rating and an 85 per cent share. In 1980, the year that CNN was launched, they had a 37 per cent rating and a 75 per cent share. As of November 2006, ratings had fallen 64 per cent since 1969, 51 per cent since 1980, and 23 per cent since 2000. Share, meanwhile, had fallen 60 per cent since 1969, 55 per cent since 1980, and 23 per cent since 2000.

It is true that by the start of the 21st century both Britain and the USA had several rolling news channels and the UK also had two additional analogue TV channels, which both carried daily news programmes as part of their PSB brief. But these programmes do not yield the mass audiences of even the BBC and ITV news programmes. Audiences for rolling news channels are tiny compared with the mainstream channels – not just for any particular slot but overall, with Sky News having only 0.5 per cent share and BBC News 24 (later to become the BBC News Channel) just slightly better at 0.6 per cent. The viewing share of entertainment channels has shown steady growth in multi-channel homes.

At this point in the discussion there will no doubt be a cry along the lines of: 'Ah! But you haven't taken into account all the people using the internet for their news – you are taking a 20th century view of what constitutes news and news consumption'. Certainly, as will be explored further in later chapters, the role of the internet working in conjunction with broadcasters is a very significant factor both in the dissemination of news and current affairs and in the agenda-setting process. Furthermore, as will be discussed in Chapter 11, the broadcasters themselves – especially, perhaps, the BBC – sees 'online' as an increasingly important part of their merged, multimedia, news output. However, although the online figures are growing, they are dwarfed on a daily basis by the number that used to watch, as a matter of daily routine, at least one of the major bulletins on the BBC or ITV. Furthermore, there is evidence from both sides of the Atlantic that the types of people who most use the internet to access news and comment about 'serious' issues are broadly the same people who continue to watch TV news. The online viewer may be younger on average than the TV news viewer but they are overwhelmingly better educated and have higher incomes than the national average. The mass TV news audiences in the 1960s to 1980s were also generally slightly more 'up market' than the general audience for TV (especially ITV – hence the premium paid by advertisers for the mid-way commercial break in *News At Ten*, helping to explain the revival of the show in 2008) but the audience was made up of those right across the social-demographic spectrum. Given that in 1977 there was a 'three-channel universe' in the UK and that there were hardly any VCRs, if you wanted to watch television for much of the evening it was hard to avoid a major news bulletin.

If there is an increase in entertainment-led programmes at the expense of public service output, the reason is obvious. Furthermore, the trend to entertainment has also infected the agendas and attitudes in news and current affairs. As Peter Sissons – who, by the time he gave a major public lecture in Liverpool in 2008,[8] had spent nearly 45 years in network television news and current affairs put it:

Now what's driving this? It's the ratings, stupid! In broadcasting, the name of the game is ratings. Forget all that stuff about public service broadcasters not being in the ratings game. It's the first thing they look at when they come into work in the morning. I've worked for ITN and the BBC and there is no discernable difference in their attitude to ratings.

But in the UK another factor and pressure on TV companies has allegedly caused a drive downwards in diversity and a lack of experimentation in programming on the country's foremost commercial TV network, ITV1. Contracts rights renewal (CRR) was introduced in 2003 following the merger of two of the largest groupings into a single company covering most of the UK outside Scotland. To prevent the new company having an unfair degree of bargaining power over commercial rates, advertisers were given certain rights, including a cut in their spending if the channel's ratings dropped, resulting in what is known as commercial impacts. In an extraordinarily candid contribution, Adam Crozier, at that time the relatively new Chief Executive for ITV, told the House of Lords Communications Committee in November 2010 that this had led to a general dumbing down of the channel, depriving it of revenue and forcing it to schedule the tried and trusted ratings hits to the exclusion of almost everything else:[9]

> It has led us to chase higher-rating programmes, things like soaps and what have you. And therefore the diversity of our schedule today is very different from the diversity of our schedule seven to 10 years ago because we have to invest in programmes that drive the biggest audiences, rather than the most unique audiences ... Were we not to have CRR in place [and ITV] not to have to chase volumes of impact that would allow us to have a much more diverse schedule. That is certainly the plan ... Advertisers would like us to target more unique audiences, rather than the same audiences again and again and again but the system works against that.

In the same session, the Company's Chairman, Archie Newman – a former supermarket boss and Conservative MP – was even more explicit about the decline in the channel's 'quality': 'We are driven to look for mass audiences, so it in a sense drives us to the lowest common denominator.'

The decline in the seriousness of television, of programming designed for high social purposes and in developing an informed citizenry, and its apparently unstoppable descent into populist, derivative, frequently sordid and even pornographic output, has been the subject of much anguished hand-wringing. These concerns were articulated in a particularly entertaining manner by the Hollywood actor Tim Robbins in his keynote speech to a joint session of the 2008 annual conventions of the National Association of Broadcasters (NAB) and Radio and Television News Directors Association (RTNDA) in Las Vegas, USA. I was in the hall when he gave his speech and can vouch that most of the 1,400 or so in the audience appreciated his candour and wit, although some did walk out and some others sat with arms folded and had a rather humourless expression. It seems clear that the ferocity of Robbins' critiques and his plea for the broadcasting networks to foreswear some of their profits as a price worth paying for more public service broadcasting caused consternation amongst some important industry figures.

Robbins seemed clear that the television networks were engaged in distracting viewers from thinking about important social and political issues. As he put it: 'Show me *Knight Rider* drunk on the floor and I won't care about a lack of healthcare for my kid.'[10] Robbins joked that the 'Left's obsession with information' was being drowned out by 'Hollywood starlets getting out of cars without any panties on.' He called on 'the leaders in this room' to 'leave the focus groups behind' and look beyond the bottom line, and that 'instead of catering to gossips and voyeurs you can lift us up'. Broadcasting, in Robbins' view, dwells far too much on the negative and sordid aspects of life and should concentrate on citizens' better motives and deeds.[11]

Robbins' views were eerily – and perhaps deliberately – reminiscent of Edward R. Murrow's clarion call to network executives at his so-called 'wires and lights in the box' RTNDA speech in 1958[12] and which begins and ends the 2005 movie *Goodnight, and Good Luck*.[13] That such views could still gain currency half a century later is testament to the fact that, despite all the differences, there is still a strong belief embedded in the culture of the USA, the UK and many other countries that broadcasting has a nobler role than simply producing the largest audiences and the biggest profits.

As discussed in Chapter 2, however, the different economic model of cable channels, such as Home Box Office (HBO) in the USA, has enabled more creativity and a more profound 'message' to be incorporated into the narrative of dramas – which are uninterrupted by commercials. David Simon, creator of *The Wire*, told a session at the 2009 Media Guardian Edinburgh International Television Festival that American television had 'short-changed' itself from the beginning because of its primary motive of selling gods and services to the audience:

> only when television managed to liberate itself from the economic construct of advertising was there a real emancipation of story. American television up to the point of premium cable was all about interrupting every 13 minutes to sell you cars, and ... jeans and whatever else. That was the point of the show, not the s*** they put around the ad's, the ad's *were* the point, so you had to bring the maximum number of eyeballs to that show and that meant dumbing it down, making the plot simple, gratifying people into the hour – more tits, more ass, more blowing stuff up; that was television. So as a storyteller you can't do anything serious. And since my impetus is journalistic, at least it's to argue what is and isn't true about the world ... Once it became 'here's 58 minutes and we're not going to interrupt it to sell any s***, the only thing we're selling is the story', that's the place where I can stand and do something that matters and that's a relatively new situation ... for some people [*The Wire*] is just a gangster story and whether the cops will catch the bad guy, but for us it was 'this is what went wrong in the West in the last part of the last century and the beginning of this one'.

It is ironic then that, just at the point in the 21st century when US television – at least in the cable sector – was becoming more interesting and 'serious', many people in the UK were criticising the BBC, in particular, of dumbing down. Amongst those who have made this accusation are Stephen Fry – the actor, writer, documentary-maker, and host of quiz show *QI* and who in 2006 was voted by readers of the *Radio Times* as 'the most intelligent person on TV' – who accused British TV of 'infantilism' during a question and answer session following his speech at a BAFTA (British Academy of Film and Television Arts) event in June 2010.[14] Whilst Fry's speech could be accused of 'golden ageism' – fondly recalling the breadth and depth of British TV in his childhood and young adulthood – the key factor may be, as television has become so ubiquitous and the number of channels so proliferate since that period (1960s–80s) that the medium (regardless of economic factors) was bound to lose its special place in the lives of citizens. The experience of watching the same programme as half or more of the nation is – as Fry concedes – unlikely to happen again, barring progress by England's soccer team to the finals of that year's World Cup – which didn't happen. Fry argued that:[15]

> television as the nation's fireplace, the hearth and the heart of the country, the focus of our communal cultural identity, that television is surely dead. It seems unlikely ever to return. Instead of being the nation's fireplace, TV is closer to being the nation's central heating. It's conveniently on in every room, it's less discernible, less of a focus, more of an ambient atmosphere.

## Children's broadcasting

Of all the aspects of public service broadcasting only one area excites as much debate as news and current affairs – and that is children's television. The maturing and developing of young minds is often regarded as one of the key elements, and indeed justifications, for the continuance of a non-advertising-funded service. The range and quality of children's programmes on the BBC equates with the best of all its programme output.

Before considering the pressures on continuing wide-ranging children's output in television, it is worth mentioning that the BBC also continues to produce drama, readings, songs and music for children up to adolescents on its digital service BBC Radio 7 – which had a dedicated, daily strand for children. In 2011 this was shifted to an online-only service. However, its weekly programme on Radio 4 was axed in 2009, after it revealed that its average age was a far from youthful 52. That BBC network was the focus of a small but well-organised lobby for a substantial commitment to speech-based children's programmes, but this has not been successful. Various trials and experiments were aired, especially during the school holidays, but controllers argued that, although a vociferous section of middle-class parents regarded such programmes as important and necessary, the hard fact was that by the 1980s, if not sooner, children were far more likely to engage with television than with radio. Campaigners argued that the success of stories and other forms of spoken word on audio-cassettes, CDs and, later, MP3 files, demonstrated that children still enjoyed and were stimulated by the spoken word; it was argued that the screen culture had only become dominant amongst the young because the broadcasters had given up trying to engage children in the radio medium.

A long campaign for dedicated and protected children's services on DAB digital radio has only been partly successful and is only available in some areas. As with so much else, early pledges to use the new medium for minority PSB output were not fulfilled.

Jocelyn Hay is a former Chair, and latterly Honorary President, of the Voice of the Listener and Viewer (VLV) – which, as its name implies, campaigns on behalf on what it sees as the interests of listeners and viewers throughout the country, and the organisation undoubtedly interprets this chiefly in the preservation of public service broadcasting. It is also concerned about the effects of non-PSB broadcasters such as Sky, due to their acquisition of channels and frequencies and the effect on all of this on the overall broadcasting ecology. One of the chief concerns of the VLV has been the withdrawal of funding for the UK production of children's television and, especially, of the non-animation varieties on both BBC and, (in particular) ITV, which, as indicated above, have had a long and glorious tradition of children's broadcasting.

Jocelyn Hay, although clearly sensitive to criticisms that any campaign and pressure for the preservation and even development of PSB and radio (especially radio) children's output is something of a middle-class fixation, argues that there is in fact less need for concern about the middle classes than for those lower down the social-economic scale, as such children may have fewer options for stimulating activities and interests:

> The thing about television is that middle-class children who are affluent have so many alternatives. Their parents spend half their lives driving them to ballet lessons or drama lessons or whatever. Children in poorer homes don't have that opportunity. All they've got very often is the television, that's their only option for seeing life of any kind outside the home. Their parents may well be working and they haven't got the money to take them out anywhere else ... They may be in a tower block in the middle of the city and it's terribly important that those children especially have access to a range of television – however it is delivered – that helps them to learn about the wider world, to see how other families live, to get an introduction to the arts in factual programmes that are made to meet their own needs and interests in their own cultural idiom, in their own language, reflecting their own cultural heritage, their own environment, their own country and reflecting their own values. Children, particularly girls, are being brainwashed by advertising ... into becoming over sexualized and being adult too young. Where is this

coming from? Mostly from the imported American programmes that dominate our satellite and cable channels and for which the main motivations is to treat children as young consumers. (Personal interview, November 2007)

The situation for young and middle years' children then gives great cause for concern. But there is even greater anxiety and frustration in the provision for the crucial years of 12 to 16, especially following the BBC's announcement that it no longer regarded this age group as 'children' and that they were to be catered for by a new brand of entertainment-led shows with, naturally, a great emphasis on, and associations with, a social networking site. The 'Switch' strand[16] is an interactive, multi-platform service, which won plaudits for the imaginative and innovative ways of reaching out to what is generally agreed is the tricky age group of early-mid adolescence.

It is certainly true that many in this age group scorn anything that reeks of 'children' and aspire to adult programming, often being avid followers of continuing series such as *EastEnders*. The development from child to adult in western societies in particular is a tricky one and also a crucial stage of social and psychological development. Of great importance is the adolescents' understanding of adult behaviour and in discovering what are acceptable, or not acceptable, forms of behaviour. Whilst it is true that there are sophisticated barriers and filters in distinguishing between what is 'real' and what is fiction, it is surely not unreasonable to be concerned that the types of behaviour depicted by many of the leading characters in the 'soaps' are providing an unfortunate example to impressionable minds. Long gone are the days when such programmes invariably showed that mean, selfish and violent behaviour would lead to punishment of some kind or another for the protagonists. Many of the story-lines in the 'soaps' revolve around lying, cheating, and general unkindness to others; something that is also certainly true of much of Reality Television – discussed further in Chapter 5. Of course, it is difficult to engage adolescents in 'improving' material, and programmes that showed characters behaving in an exemplary fashion would, to say the least, lack conviction and be sure to be derided by their target audiences. But the BBC in particular has a tradition of walking that difficult tightrope and in producing dramas and other programmes that are realistic and yet provide positive role models.

*Grange Hill*, set in a north London comprehensive school, ran from 1978 but at the beginning of 2008 the BBC announced it was to end. For its first 25 years the show was shot at the BBC's Elstree studios but in 2003 this transferred to the same studios as Phil Redmond's Mersey television's *Brookside* 'soap', which had been broadcast on weekdays on Channel 4 since 1982. Redmond – one of the most important and influential figures in British television since the late 1970s and someone who is certainly not known for being reticent about giving his opinions – became even more forthright and damning about the BBC's treatment of *Grange Hill*. He roundly criticised the BBC's decision not only to end the series from 2007 and to fail to provide a substitute but in the way the show's appeal had changed since he lost control of the production:

> The BBC has abandoned what *Grange Hill* was about in order to attract younger viewers aged 6 to 12, rather than its 13-plus constituency, so there's nothing to celebrate.[17]

Further chapters in this book explore how new technologies and public interaction with broadcasting output are re-shaping audiences' expectations, demands and requirements for broadcasting.

## Notes and references

1.  Robinson, J. (27 August, 2010) 'BBC's Mark Thompson takes aim at Murdoch empire in MacTaggart lecture', *Guardian.co.uk*, available online at: http://www.guardian.co.uk/media/2010/aug/27/bbc-mark-thompson-murdoch-mactaggart.
2.  Guardian Media (30 August, 2010) 'Edinburgh TV Festival 2010', *Media Talk*, available online at: http://www.guardian.co.uk/media/audio/2010/aug/29/media-talk-edinburgh-tv-festival.
3.  Various sources were used for these comparisons, including information in the public domain published by Broadcast magazine, RAJAR audience listening figures and, as acknowledged in note 6, non-published BBC research.
4.  BARB/*Broadcast*, 5 October 2007, p.34.
5.  BBC Press Office (2007) 'Panorama "10 Years Younger" – bringing bigger and younger audiences to BBC current affairs', available online at: http://www.bbc.co.uk/pressoffice/pressreleases/stories/2007/02_february/07/panorama.shtml.
6.  My thanks to the BBC Monitoring Service at Caversham for supplying this data.
7.  *Journalism.org* (2007) 'The State of the News Media 2006 – Evening News Ratings November 1980 to November 2006', available at: http://www.stateofthemedia.org/2007/chartland.asp?id=209&ct=line&dir=&sort=&col1_box=1&col2_box=1&col3_box=1.
8.  'Peter Sissons' Roscoe Lecture' (19 June, 2008) *Liverpool – City of Media,* audio available online at: www.ljmu.ac.uk/MKG_Global_Docs/Peter_Sissons-roscoe_lecture.zip.
9.  Sweeney, M. (2 November, 2010) 'ITV: we're stuck in a ratings rat race', *Mediaguardian.co.uk*, available online at: http://www.guardian.co.uk/media/2010/nov/02/itv-adam-crozier-archie-norman.
10. *TV Newser* (2008) 'Apologies to Bill, Sean and Laura What's-Her-Name', available online at: http://www.mediabistro.com/tvnewser/nabrtnda_2008/apologies_to_bill_sean_and_laura_whatshername_82378.asp.
11. *Huffington Post* (2008) 'The Power and Responsibilities of the Nation's Broadcasters', text and audio available online at: www.huffingtonpost.com/tim-robbins/addressing-the national-a_b_96836.html.
12. RTDNA (n.d.) 'Industry Leaders – Edward R. Murrow Speech', available online at: http://www.rtnda.org/pages/media_items/edward-r.-murrow-speech998.php.
13. Clooney, 2005.

14.  Press Association (16 June, 2010) 'Stephen Fry: Doctor Who is a children's programme', *Guardian.co.uk,* available online at: http://www.guardian.co.uk/media/2010/jun/16/stephen-fry-doctor-who.

15.  *Guardian.co.uk* (16 June, 2010) 'Stephen Fry's BAFTA speech', available online at: http://www.guardian.co.uk/media/2010/jun/16/stephen-fry-bafta-lecture.

16.  Carter, M. (24 September, 2007) 'Teenage Kicks', *Guardian.co.uk,* available online at: http://www.guardian.co.uk/media/2007/sep/24/mondaymediasection.television2.

17.  Walsh, J. (2008) 'Phil Redmond – Man of the People', *The Independent*, 9 February, pp. 44–5.

# Radio: The Chameleon Medium

4

This chapter considers the case for radio being considered as a separate medium, due to its unique appeal and uses by audiences. In particular it will discuss:

■ Arguments that the particular 'uses and gratifications' of audiences in radio listening by scholars means that radio should be treated as a separate field of study.
■ The continued importance of early morning radio and its on-air personalities.
■ Radio's continued importance at times of acute danger to the public.
■ The declining importance of radio as an outlet for music, especially amongst younger listeners.
■ How and why campaigners saved BBC 6 Music from threatened closure.

## Why studio radio?

Except for a few notable examples, the academic community has paid scant attention to radio broadcasting when compared to that afforded to other forms of mass and/or popular media. This is despite the global extent of its reach, despite the eighty and more years that have elapsed since public broadcasting began, despite its continuing importance as the primary medium for most of the world's population.[1]

The above quotation, from the very end of the 20th century, is from the abstract for an article in what was, significantly, the first edition of an academic journal devoted to radio, and encapsulates the continuing frustration and incomprehension by the growing band of scholars interested in research into radio as to why 'their' medium is so neglected in scholarly studies. The majority of books devoted to 'mass communications' and even 'broadcasting' devote little space to the medium, and when it is mentioned it is often only by association and is subservient to other media in the topic being discussed. Barnard[2] points out that radio scholarship – which he notes has been a 'neglected field within Media Studies over the years' – has not developed a distinct theoretical framework of its own. In a book published at the end of the 1980s, Barnard discussed music radio in the UK and bewailed the fact that such academic and critical discussion of the medium that did exist almost wholly ignored the content and style that had grown to dominate radio output.[3]

This was still true well into the 21st century, one of the few exceptions being Gillian Reynolds, who writes on radio for the *Telegraph* newspaper. As a former Programme Controller in UK commercial radio (also the first, and for some time the *only*, female to hold such a post) she also writes authoritatively about the music- and talk-based daily 'sequence programmes' that dominate overall radio output in the UK, as they do in much of the rest of the world.

A 'commonsense' answer to the question as to why radio should have lost its hitherto pre-eminence in broadcasting is that television replaced radio as the main medium for mass entertainment and news in the prime periods for relaxation and domestic gatherings in industrial societies from the early 1950s. TV sets were put in the centre of living rooms, with radio being largely banished to the kitchen, bedroom and car, and returned to being a medium of private consumption, and above all as a mainly daytime medium that accompanied other activities – a 'complementary' or 'secondary' medium.

However, radio has several characteristics that meant that it was able to re-invent itself, not least in its ubiquity and mobility. The relative cheapness of radio receivers means that not only are they within the means of those with very modest incomes – not least in the developing world – but that radio can be listened to in almost every physical environment, including moving vehicles.

Radio is not only inexpensive as a consumer product, it is also relatively cheap to produce and to transmit. This opens up the possibilities for groups that are marginalised economically, socially, culturally, or politically, to be heard through a radio service and for this to be heard over longer distances and in the isolated communities which, for example, would otherwise be hard to reach and distribution of the print media would be both difficult and dangerous. Authoritarian regimes in all parts of the world have discovered to their frustration that it is very hard to prevent clandestine radio broadcasts, or listening to stations outside their territory. This means that radio has often been utilised as a means of mobilising and inspiring opposition to such regimes. At a more specific level, peace activists – such as a women's international radio group, FIRE – have sought to use the medium to counter aggression and conflict in many of the world's trouble zones, as well as against more general issues of violence and human rights' abuses.[4]

One of the key factors in this lack of scholarly engagement with the medium is its largely ephemeral nature. Scholars tend to privilege texts – not least because of the requirement to provide citations for assertions and arguments. Relatively little radio output in the UK is routinely archived. Most radio programmes, for copyright reasons, are available for only seven days after transmission and (contrary to popular belief) broadcasts are not available for public or even scholarly access.

The situation for older archives is even worse and contrasts sharply with the emphasis given to archives of the moving image – film and TV. Although the British Library holds sound archives with limited public access, as do some other centres, these are again mostly for the major award-winning documentaries, dramas, radio talks and news broadcasts. A major exception is that held by Bournemouth University, which has digitised and made available online to universities the archives of LBC (the speech commercial station in London) and Independent Radio News (IRN).

Much of the online archiving of the sorts of radio which millions grew up with, however, is left to amateur sites, often run by radio enthusiasts (referred to as 'anoraks'). In the USA there is an excellent site, Reel Radio,[5] which has archived hundreds of hours of Top 40 radio output from the 1950s–1990s. Other sites make available archive recordings from radio's supposed 'golden age' (1930s–early 1950s). But the USA is far better than the UK in preserving and making available its broadcasting past – radio *and* TV – with major museums in New York and Chicago combining public 'displays' of TV and radio programmes, with further scholarly access to scripts and other materials. No such national museum exists in the UK – in my opinion an almost scandalous omission for a nation that has been such a major influence in the development of broadcasting.

So far as media industries are concerned there can be no doubt that television contains higher prestige, rewards (as well as risks) than radio. The cost per hour to produce the equivalent output is vastly greater on television compared with radio, and advertising budgets – both for production of commercials and the airtime and consequent commission for advertising agencies – is much greater for television, so in the commercial and financial worlds there is little doubt that television is by far the more important of the two media.

Radio's transformation, at least in industrial or post-industrial societies such as the UK, from being a foreground medium – something that demanded the fullest attention of the listener – to being a background medium, which accompanied other activities, has allowed it to integrate with other media in the online world, leading to renewed interest in the use of audio. Undergraduate and post-graduate courses, either devoted to the medium or including it as a substantial element, have been increasing in the UK, USA and many other countries. The amount of space and time devoted to the medium outside the world of academia has also notably increased in the 21st century. Radio scholars, however, have to constantly justify the continued place of radio studies as a discrete form of mass communications – usually in the face of arguments that it is much less significant than television. The next section uses some academic/theoretical terms and concepts in order to try and understand the unique appeal of radio.

## The uses and gratifications of radio

Perhaps the most important of these are its intimacy and companionship. Almost all books and courses for would-be radio broadcasters stress that, however many people may be listening to the broadcast, the broadcaster should always use a 'mode of address' which appears only to talk to that individual listener at that time. Companionship provides an important psychological and cultural need. Radio has long been regarded as being a particularly effective agency for the alleviation of loneliness and boredom. This is often linked with 'familiarity': radio programmers understand that listeners become attached to particular voices and features at certain times of the day and often become upset if schedules and presenters are changed. For example, the departure of Terry Wogan from the BBC Radio 2 breakfast show at the end of 2009 made the front pages of almost every national newspaper in the UK. With the possible exception of the defection of Morecambe and Wise from the BBC to ITV in 1978 there is no equivalent in popular interest in television personalities. And this is not just at the national level; when local radio presenters have moved from one station to the other in the UK this has also led to front-page splash headlines in the regional newspapers. The 'revival' of the New York oldies' station, WCBS-FM in 2007 (after two years as an automated service) was greeted by messages from the city's mayor, the then Presidential hopeful Hillary Clinton and numerous recording artistes. When the offshore 'pirate' radio stations were threatened with closure in 1967 there were protests and demonstrations, and, as discussed below, the planned closure of a digital-only station in the UK prompted a huge (and successful) national campaign; it is highly unlikely that the closure of a TV channel – let alone a schedule change – would provoke anything like that level of interest. This demonstrates radio's ability to insinuate itself into the daily routine of social and domestic life.

Associated very much with this is the concept of 'liveness'. Unlike most television output (aside from news, and even newscasts contain a large amount of pre-recorded material), most of radio in the UK and other territories is 'live'. Part of the listener's engagement with the medium may be ascribed to the knowledge that what they are hearing is created, or at least presented, then and now and, in the case of local stations (the largest single sector in the UK in terms of audience share), from a known and recognisable locality. Of course, nearly all the music broadcast is recorded, as it mostly consists of commercially available recordings. But the actual playing of the music tracks, often with the presenter/DJ talking over at least parts of them and weaving other elements in and out of the songs, represents an engagement with the different programming elements that the listener knows is happening within a fraction of a second of them hearing it. This is linked with an important quality of most radio – that of 'spontaneity'. Clearly, most of the output of the various mass media is the result of careful and sometimes complex production and editorial decisions. Much of radio's output though, whilst produced within a framework that can certainly be both elaborate and precise, contains unscripted and, to some extent, *unmediated* speech. Whilst a great deal of apparently 'ad-libbed' speech may in fact be contrived and even rehearsed, superficially at least the listener is in the position of feeling that 'anything can happen'. It is a commonplace for other media to report instances of presenters 'going too far' in terms of taste, decency or controversial views (see Chapter 6 on the Ross/Brand affair). Indeed, many of the best-known names in broadcasting have built their reputation largely on such instances. The allied ability of listeners to interact with the presenter and the editorial content by means of social networking, blogging, phone calls, emails, text messages and so on – sometimes speaking directly to the presenter(s) off and on air – provides a direct engagement which no other medium can match. The whole area of 'modes of address' is very relevant here. Crucially, we must consider the phenomenon of the disc jockey, someone who is both similar to the intended audience but is also special and different, someone who is a cultural or sub-cultural leader and perhaps leads – is perceived to lead – a rather more glamorous life than the ordinary listener. This relationship between sender and receiver is unique to radio and helps to explain the special attachment and enduring appeal of the medium. Even the more traditional networks, such as BBC Radio 4, with formally trained continuity announcers (linking programmes) and news-readers, have greatly changed their modes of address since the 1960s, when the disc jockey became established in the UK and many other countries as a crucial part of radio's forms of communication. Whereas listeners were formally addressed as a mass, unseen crowd, the techniques developed by Top 40 Radio in particular, led to a more intimate, informal one-to-one mode.

The dynamic and multi-faceted relationship between broadcaster and listener has been highlighted by David Hendy, who considered the global phenomenon of radio.[6] Hendy argues that it is the unassuming and often undemanding nature of radio that, paradoxically, provides its greatest potency and listeners are (to some extent unwittingly) part of this dynamic.

Andrew Crisell has even subscribed a slightly more sinister interpretation on the apparently innocuous nature of much of modern radio broadcasting; that radio might affect the listener in almost subliminal ways.[7]

## The enduring importance of 'breakfast shows' and on-air personalities

In the UK, radio listening exceeds consumption of all other media, including television, up to 1.00 p.m. on weekdays.[8] Most stations' peak audience is in the breakfast 'morning drive' slot, which for a commercial station can account for up to half of all its revenue. But even public service broadcasters such as the BBC place considerable emphasis at this time on all its networks; the breakfast show on BBC Radio 2 alone attracting more listeners than *all* TV viewing in that time slot. Terry Wogan,[9] having hosted the most-listened to daily show in the UK, is in a strong position to reflect on the changing nature of the relationship between broadcaster and listener between the 20th and 21st centuries. At the time of interview (December 2007) he had been broadcasting on BBC network radio and television for over 40 years. He had two periods (or 'incarnations' as he refers to them) of hosting the Radio 2 breakfast show; from 1972 to 1985 (when he left to host a thrice-weekly chat show on BBC television) and then from 1993. Although his presentation is superficially relaxed and good-natured, it can in fact be sharp and, in the broadest sense, political; a style that has been described as 'gently subversive'. Even though he counts many teenagers and those in their early twenties amongst his audience, most seem happy to describe themselves, and be referred to, as Terry's Old Gals/Geezers (TOGs): being a Wogan listener is more a state of mind than of years. Terry Wogan was able to reflect on the changing ways in which his audience interacted with him:

> In the first incarnation it was all letters and cards and I would always try to generate a response, generally offensive banter. So I would initiate something and then I would get a response, maybe two or three days later on, and that was fine. So when I came back for the second incarnation I thought we'll try faxes and that did work very well but then the email started to come in and very quickly my listeners – and given that they're all very well stricken in years – leapt onto the bandwagon and actually bought computers so that they could email me! Most of the contact is now emails and is now from the TOGs website and all the rest of it. You see the great thing about the email is that I can say something at 7.32 after the news and I'll get a reaction at 7.33 and sometimes I feel they are ahead of me! I suppose we'll get maybe 500 to 600 emails overnight and in the course of the programme – as you saw yourself – they are constantly coming in and responding to whatever is being said or whatever occurs to them.

Sir Terry has come to accept – and even relishes – the fact that, however experienced you and your production team are, as a broadcaster it is impossible to predict what will and won't galvanise the audience. He is also acutely aware that longevity on the air-aves does not mean stagnation, for either the broadcaster or the audience:

> I probably have changed and they have changed. People think that because you get such an audience they say: 'oh, it's the same people who've been listening to him for years; it's predictable and it's familiar

and it's a bit like an old piece of carpet that has been there all the time that we can rely upon'. But if you listened to it even as little as five years ago you would find that this programme has changed. And it has completely changed since I came back to do it ... the only constant factor being my voice. It isn't conscious on my part but it has to change and nothing can stay the same. The public's taste is different and email speeds up the reaction. I have become slightly more astringent in my comments about what's happening in the world outside and they respond to that. But you can't always lead them because sometimes you think 'Oh that's a great idea' and they won't react to it at all! Dear old Pauly Walters [the much loved and respected producer of the programme who died in 2006][10] would say something about him having a found a tin of rhubarb over seven years old and having romantic attachments to it and that will get an immediate response! I will seek to lead them but only up to a point. They will choose what they want to respond to and that's really what the whole thing is about.

The often surreal nature of the topics on this show (Sir Terry was succeeded by Chris Evans on the Radio 2 breakfast show in January 2010 but continued to present a weekly 'live' show on Sundays) illustrates the claim that is often made that 'radio has the best pictures' because it is capable of working on the listener's imagination, especially in works of drama and comedy. It is, of course, far cheaper to produce works of those types than, say, for television or movies, or even the theatre. A simple sound effect can transport the listener into a different world and the surrealist humour of one of British radio's landmark programmes, *The Goons*, proved in the 1950s that a cartoon-ish sequence could be created in the mind far cheaper and more vividly than carefully creating 24 images a second for a visual animation work. Radio of this sort requires an intellectual engagement between creator and listener in a way that more visual media do not. The oft-made and seemingly commonsense point that radio is a 'blind' medium is contested by Tim Crook.[11] In the context of discussing radio drama he argues that there is a psychological bond formed between the radio production and the listener; a 'sense of feeling' constructed by the use of techniques in radio drama, especially through the use of music. The fact that everyone 'sees' a character in a drama or a scene means that each listener has a unique and essential role in the creative process. But this is even true of music-led entertainment shows. Chris Evans remarked at a session on creativity at the 2010 Radio Festival in the UK that, as a teenager, he was intrigued by how on his local commercial station, the disc jockeys used to create fantasies that, for example, a programme was coming from a four-poster bed!

> It was all about pictures. When I used to listen to the radio then and listened to Timmy [Mallett, who had presented an evening show aimed at teenagers], all I could see was pictures. (Author's notes)

Another justification for the separate treatment and study of radio is the way that audio can be used creatively and experimentally. In the USA, Chicago Public Radio's *This American Life* features documentaries using imaginatively produced and mixed audio, which have challenged traditional forms of journalism and narratives. In the UK, both BBC Radio 3 and some community stations, such as London's Resonance FM, have broadcast experimental drama and documentaries using traditional forms and structures of the spoken word and have relied heavily on creative mixing of 'real' sounds, and music.

It is also no coincidence that many established TV ratings winners began their life as a radio programme and that writers, actors and other performers have found that radio has provided them with early opportunities to develop their art and craft.

## The declining importance of radio in the consumption of music

Until the widespread availability, at least in developed countries, of online music services, radio was the commonest and indeed most efficient way of exposing music to a mass audience. Because, at least in the popular genres, interest in music tends to peak in early to mid-adolescence, radio establishes itself in those years with each individual – which, typically, in developed countries, are years of anxiety, uncertainty and even trauma – as an important, trusted and valued 'friend'. Furthermore, much of the music on radio in a non-dramatic context is likely to produce this imaginative engagement and most powerfully, perhaps, with 'Gold' music is liable – indeed intended – to provoke nostalgic feelings about events and people. The era of the internet, downloads and seemingly ubiquitous MP3 devices has meant that many millions of people in their teens and twenties are not getting their radio habit in the way that was the case for many previous generations. Although, as discussed in Chapter 2, radio listening in Britain and many other countries seems robust, there are indicators that radio listening in the lower age ranges is in decline. Moreover – as research presented at the 2010 UK Radio Festival revealed,[12] when those same listeners go into the next age bracket (25–34) they are not acquiring the radio habit to the extent of previous generations within that age group. Indeed, they are not even listening as much as *they* did when younger. This might indicate a long, slow death of radio. But the same presentation cited the BBC's 'Share of Ear' survey, which clearly indicates that radio listening continues to dominate all audio listening: 82 per cent in 2010, with only 18 per cent of audio time spent in listening to MP3 players and so on.[13] However, the fact that even FM receivers – let alone digital ones – are not standard in the mobile (cell) phones may also prove to be a major stumbling block in radio's long-term survival as a distinct medium.

A major criticism of radio in the 21st century, especially in commercial music-based radio, is its increasing homogeneity and, in the local sector, abandonment of local news, information and 'live' presentation (see below for potential public safety issues created by this). There are a number of factors at play; as noted in Chapter 1, broadcasting in much of the developed world was de-regulated at the end of the 20th century. In New Zealand, complete de-regulation allowed for the abandonment of any local, or public service content in commercial radio. The situation in the UK was not quite so extreme, but the Digital Economy Act, passed in the dying days of the Labour government in the spring of 2010, allowed for more consolidation of services, leading to the merging or axing of dozens of local services and the creation of a semi-national FM station, as five regional stations with the Smooth Radio brand merged into a single network by the end of that year. The justification for this was the economic pressures on the stations, caused by a general economic downturn, hitting advertising revenues, and competition from other media, notably the internet, both for revenues and consumer time.

## Radio's continued appeal in a 'screen world'

The coverage of news and sports on television clearly has 'added value' over radio – rather than just being an audio witness to events and reports, the television viewer can use both sight and vision. For sports in particular it might have been assumed that, once television cameras were able to show the action, radio would (leaving aside the important issue of the rights for TV coverage, which are far more expensive than for radio) be made redundant. However, radio sports coverage – and above all discussion about sports – still forms a major and popular part of radio output. Despite its increasing mobility, TV is still not as mobile or as accessible as radio – especially, of course, when driving a car. Not only that, but some viewers clearly prefer the radio commentary over that on the TV, even when sitting in front of the TV set. During the 2006 soccer World Cup the BBC provided viewers with the choice of sticking with the 'intended' commentary to the TV coverage of matches, or switching to that provided on BBC Radio 5 Live. By 2009 this approach was extended to coverage of the Wimbledon Lawn Tennis Championships. Although figures on those taking up this option were not available, anecdotal evidence – such as letters to newspapers – indicate that a sizeable minority took advantage of this choice. The radio commentary for England's Cricket Test (international) matches has long been something of a cult and many followers of the game have claimed that, even when they could see a TV set, they still preferred the commentary on the famous *Test Match Special* (*TMS*). Of course, some of this can be attributed to preference for the style and approach of the radio commentators over those for television, but it seems that there is more to it than that: radio has the ability to form a special, intimate bond between broadcaster and listener. In the case of *TMS* there are eccentric and, to those not familiar with the discourse, frequently bizarre and even surreal comments, especially when (as so often happens in England) rain prevents play. Listeners are likely to be regaled with accounts of, for example, a pigeon landing near the commentary box, or a discussion of a cake sent in by a listener. Something very interesting culturally and in terms of 'modes of address' is going on here. Those attracted to the somewhat arcane rules of cricket – in the case of Test Matches the game can last for five days and, after all that, result in a draw – are, perhaps, likely to already feel that they belong to a rather special 'club' and feel drawn to others (the commentators) who 'get it'; in other words there is a shared sensibility that provides a special psychological pleasure. The 'uses and gratifications' of radio seem to be quite distinct from other types of media.

Even for those do not feel isolated or lonely, the particular sensibility that can be gleaned from radio, particularly perhaps in comedy, provides a very enjoyable connection to the unseen millions of listeners. In an increasingly atomized society these connections are perhaps even more necessary and desirable, and although the internet, particularly in social networking sites, may have replaced this function to some extent, there is still a great satisfaction and enjoyment in a shared joke, especially when the audience is required to use their imagination to visualise unseen characters, situations and humour. A good example of this is in the much-lauded BBC radio comedy panel game *I'm Sorry, I Haven't a Clue*. Some thirty series of the show – which is recorded in front of a 'live' audience at different venues around the country (the host's introductory monologue invariably mocks the history and culture of the place of broadcast) – were broadcast from 1972, chaired by Humphrey Lyttleton, who had a preceding and concurrent career as a jazz musician. His urbane, laconic and frequently sardonic and waspish approach to the show's 'games', contestants, audience and locale, seemed an integral part of the programme's appeal. The show's future seemed in doubt when Lyttleton died in April 2008, aged 86. It returned, though, 14 months later, with a different host each week. In welcoming back the show, *The Guardian*'s Sam Leith argued[14] that this programme could only work on the radio – and if you had a particular sensibility.

As noted in Chapter 1, radio's ability to unite people across the miles, especially notable in linking up servicemen with their families and 'ex-pats' in far-flung places has provided enormous comfort, solace and reassurance to millions of people. The 'streaming' of domestic radio services has provided additional links with kith and kin, as well as providing good-natured if gleeful boasting as those in sunnier climes torment the folks back in the UK with the current weather conditions in California, South Africa, southern Spain and so on. But even when the sender and recipient of radio messages are close at hand, radio can be a useful tool to lubricate social and, especially, romantic liaisons, whilst at the same time promoting local music and culture. An example of this – discussed by Ece Algan[15] – is with stations in the Turkish city of Sanliurfa, in the country's rural south eastern region near the Syrian border. The 'messages', contained in the song lyrics and in their accompanying requests assume enormous importance to young people and DJs, and producers had to be especially careful to make sure that the right message went with the right song, or misunderstanding and even serious offence could be caused. In innumerable cases, though, the stations become conduit for messages of love and devotion which the initiators found difficult or embarrassing to express in person.

Commercial radio in particular, however, has to appeal to a mass audience, so all such programmes have to find a 'gratification' for the vast bulk of the listenership who will not – at least in any one programme – be directly involved as the sender or recipient of messages. Of course, they may well like the music but Algan described the intense interest of the listeners in the messages of others. In this way, such radio becomes almost a soap opera, albeit with 'characters' that usually appear only fleetingly and with only tantalisingly small morsels of their 'back stories.'

## Radio's continued importance as a trusted source of news and current affairs

Although, as noted in Chapter 1, due to fear of upsetting the government and other authorities, as well as the powerful newspaper proprietors, the BBC initially did not provide its own news service. However, in other countries, notably the USA, from the very early days of the medium, news was seen as a necessary and obvious element of radio. Even local top 40 music stations (from the late 1950s) regarded a competitive and credible news service as an important selling point for their services, and created the illusion of fleets of radio cars constantly on standby, rather like emergency vehicles, to screech to the latest fire, murder scene or traffic accident. This also assuaged the guilt that listeners might feel of listening to 'trivial' output: they could convince themselves and their peer groups that their main reason for tuning in to such stations was surveillance of the latest local news. This policy was adopted by the American backers of 1960s 'pirate' radio stations aimed at British audiences, such as Radio London, even though in reality they plagiarised the news simply by listening to the BBC's bulletins and re-writing them in a more dynamic style. One of the most successful radio stations in Europe was the 'pirate' Europe 1. Launched in 1955 it made news and information its core appeal; founder, Louis Merlin calling it a 'radiophonic newspaper'.[16] Later, in the student uprisings in Paris in May 1968, when the country seemed on the break of a second revolution, its independent news service was much valued by the protestors and it earned the name (English translation) of 'Radio Barricade'.

For politicians and others concerned with the public sphere however, there is the fact that, in the UK, as in most part of the world, television is the most important news source. According to a survey, jointly conducted by the BBC, Reuters and the Media Center in 2006[17] – one of the largest of its kind ever held, polling 10,230 people in 10 countries[18] – television was the most important news source (55 per cent), followed by newspapers (19 per cent). Radio scored only 12 per cent, with the internet vying to take over, at 8 per cent. Indeed, 19 per cent of younger people (aged 18 to 24) named online sources as their first choice. Although radio may have long lost its position as 'first choice' for news, it is still well trusted. The survey put trust in the news on 'public radio' at 67 per cent, but not as high as national television (82 per cent), or national/regional newspapers (75 per cent) and slightly behind local newspapers (69 per cent).

However, a further survey by the University of Gotenburg in November 2010[19] showed that trust in Sweden's public radio service was higher than for any other media. Research published in May 2010 by UK broadcasting regulator Ofcom[20] also suggested that radio was the most trustworthy source for news in the UK, with some two-thirds of the public saying that they trust what they hear in radio news. This was a significantly ahead of TV news (54 per cent) and news websites (58 per cent).

The strong public service traditions and perhaps a well understood requirement of the broadcasters for accuracy and impartiality in news coverage is reinforced by an evident overall trust in radio. There is, in other words, a set of a cultural and medium-specific factors at work here. Paradoxically, the lack of visual distractions may well work in radio's favour. A public weary of the tricks of visual presentation in screen media, perhaps distrusting their own susceptibility to visual 'cues', may find reassuring integrity in an apparently simple medium. As trust and credibility lie at the heart of the appeal and strength of any news outlet, radio clearly has a unique advantage over other media.

Local radio in particular with its mostly seamless, sequence programmes and therefore flexibility in covering breaking local news, seems to meet the classic requirements for the salience of news, these being proximity (close to the listener's location), relevance (to the listener due to it being 'close to home') and immediacy. In trying to convey the essence of the output and relate it to something listeners would be familiar with, BBC local radio stations often promoted themselves in their early days (from 1967) as 'your local newspaper of the air'. Furthermore, a 2009 government review into UK commercial radio by John Myers, former chief radio executive of the Guardian Media Group, found that radio had a more consistently important role for *local* news cross the age groups than any other medium, including the internet and one which was even more vital, given the decline of staffing and coverage in local newspapers.[21]

## A matter of life and death

As Myers notes, radio is at its most vital in two distinct areas of speech programming. The first, in its ubiquity and flexibility, it can be literally a matter of life and death. As noted in Chapter 1, local radio, in particular, has long played a vital part in emergency planning. In Britain, stations would simulcast information in the event of such a nightmarish scenario,[22] from the BBC's Wartime Broadcasting Service in nuclear bomb-proof studios. Both BBC and, from the mid-1970s, the larger commercial stations, were equipped with additional transmitter sites and standby generators. Radio journalists – I was amongst these – were asked to volunteer to be placed in the wartime broadcasting studios in the alternative regional centres of government. Even if some thought that, given the scale of devastation that would be caused by a nuclear attack, such preparations were futile and may even give a false sense of security, the particular qualities of radio reception – typically over a battery-powered set, less vulnerable than mains-operated equipment – gave the medium a particular role in such circumstances.

The threat to public health and even life when local radio stations are not staffed was demonstrated in the USA in 2002. Eric Klinenberg, Professor of Sociology at New York University, has described the reaction – or, rather, lack of reaction – to a chemical leak in North Dakota in January that year.[23] The confused and fearful residents had tuned to their local stations for information and safety advice. But the town's six non-religious commercial radio stations, all owned and operated by Clear Channel Communications, were broadcasting pre-recorded programmes. Police dispatchers couldn't find anyone in the company's local offices and no-one answered the phones. As Klinenberg put it: 'as one man died and hundreds became ill from inhaling the poisonous gas, the airwaves were filled with canned music and smooth-talking DJs'. The abject and, literally in this case, fatal flaws in local radio coverage, have much to do with economics, regulation and in particular, the consolidation of previously independent radio stations by one, profit-hungry media giant in which the public utility, social purpose of radio, had been lost.

## The successful campaign to save BBC 6 Music – and what it tells us about radio's unique appeal

In February 2010, the BBC's executive body, faced with increasingly shrill criticism about its alleged media domination and profligacy in terms both of pay and on programmes at a time of economic recession, announced a number of cuts to its domestic services, including the digital radio station BBC 6 Music. Defined initially as mixture of archive recordings from the BBC's huge and largely untapped session tapes, concert recordings, and a more 'serious' approach to popular music than is generally supplied by the analogue behemoth services Radios 1 and 2, 6 Music gained a considerable reputation amongst its relatively small but loyal audience and in the music industry itself, especially as an outlet for less commercial, more 'left-field' artistes and albums. The Corporation's managers declared, though, that its audience was not large enough, distinct enough or underserved enough (the average age of the listener was mid-30s) for it to continue and that its audience was in the range most desired by commercial competitors. The £9 million or so spent on the station could, it was argued, be better used elsewhere, by providing more adventurous output on other services.

Some industry observers, however, thought the station was a token sacrifice – it took the heat off the BBC from both commercial and political critics (the announcement came in the run-up to a general election) and that the claim that the station did not provide a unique and much-needed service merely confirmed that most senior executives have 'tin ears' and think that all 'pop music' is pretty much the same. However, under the BBC's governance, the final decision rested not with the executives but with the BBC Trust. A three-month public consultation exercise was announced and a campaign to 'Save 6 Music' launched. This got underway on the day of the announcement and included a direct attack on Channel 4 News from one of 6 Music's presenters, Adam Buxton, to the BBC's Director-General, Mark Thompson – who the presenter insisted on calling 'Tommo' – and whom he challenged to settle the matter by a fight!

The campaign was diffuse in its strategy – involving special pages on social networking sites, all of which provided links to the site for the public response to the closure plans, and the recruitment of high-profile names from the music industry such as David Bowie, Jarvis Cocker and Lily Allen – but was also relatively coherent in its arguments. These were that 6 Music did indeed provide a unique service and one which no commercial operator would provide and therefore was in the finest traditions of BBC public service, and that its closure would be a massive blow to the under-pressure British music industry. It even became an issue during the 2010 general election campaign, with political leaders pressurised to state whether they supported the station: the then Prime Minister Gordon Brown coming out in favour and a Shadow Culture Minister, Ed Vaizey, also voicing support (after the election and now in government, Vaizey pronounced that he was 'over the moon' at the station's reprieve). If the closure announcement had intended to appease the political class it had certainly backfired. It was quickly seen to be distinctly 'un-cool' not to support 6 Music and new methods of campaigning had mobilised public support to an unprecedented level for a media issue. *The Guardian*'s 'Organgrinder' blog[24] argued that in the past a newspaper editor might have started a national campaign, but it could not have engendered the response possible through social media.

The enormous publicity engendered by the campaign naturally alerted a great many people to a station that either they had not heard of, or certainly had not heard. The next RAJAR audience survey[25] showed the station had increased its audience by nearly 50 per cent in just a few weeks, taking weekly listening to over the million mark. On top of that, the station received prizes – as well as very supportive speeches – at the annual Sony Awards.[26]

The announcement by the BBC Trust in July 2010 that it 'was not convinced' by the arguments for closure[27] brought a triumphant response on and off air – with many regarding it as a triumph for the social media or the 'Twitterati'. Other were less convinced; some believing that it was a clever piece of PR and that the BBC had never intended to close the station in the first place, and that the BBC Trust (itself lacking support in the political class, with its demise openly discussed by the Conservatives) was keen to make a popular – even populist – decision. Indeed, I predicted and speculated on these very points in my own blog.[28]

A major factor in the success in the mobilisation of social media was the demographic make-up of the 6 Music audience. The mid to late 30-year-olds, predominantly in the higher social brackets, were also in the peak age and class for social media use and were always likely to get their voice heard more effectively than would be the case for either a much older or much younger audience, and/or one predominating in the lower socio-economic groups.

A digital-only station such as BBC 6 Music of course relies on the public being prepared to invest in digital devices. But the public seems unconvinced – and even resistant to – the idea of ditching its trusted FM radios for its supposed replacement standard in the UK, Digital Audio Broadcasting (DAB). The UK government set a switch-over timetable of 2015 to DAB for most services if, before two years of that date, over half of all listening was being done through digital means, and DAB coverage matched FM's. But by the end of 2010 this target date or 'aspiration' seemed certain to slip and, according to at least one respected analyst, might never be achieved.[29]

Paradoxically, the public has a more intense and personal relationship with radio than any other medium but it does not value it in the same way as television. The British – perhaps in particular, but not uniquely – greatly values, trusts and has a deep affection for its radio services, yet it is unwilling to spend money on receivers and is largely deaf to advocates of alternative, new services. Radio has been compared to a pair of comfy old slippers, while television is a smart new, fashionable suit or dress. Radio is more like an aural comfort blanket; a friend who you always expect to be there and who doesn't require any work or expense to maintain the relationship, whereas television is an exciting and interesting – if familiar – associate, whose new fashions and acquisitions are a constant source of fascination and delight.

## Notes and references

1.  Dolan, J. (1999) 'The voice that cannot be heard – radio/broadcasting and 'the archive', *The Radio Journal – International Studies in Broadcast and Audio Media*, 1 (1), 63–72.
2.  Barnard, S. (2000) *Studying Radio*, London: Arnold, p.3.
3.  Barnard, S. (1989) *On the Radio – Music Radio in Britain*, Milton Keynes: OUP, p.7.
4.  Feminist International Radio Endeavour (FIRE), (November 2009), available at: http://www.fire.or.cr/indexeng.htm.
5.  See: http://www.reelradio.com.
6.  Hendy, D. (2000) *Radio in the Global Age*. Cambridge: Polity Press, pp. 2–3.
7.  Crisell, A. (1994) *Understanding Radio (*2nd edn) London: Routledge, p. 224.
8.  'IPA TouchPoint Hub Survey', presented at the Radio Festival, Salford, UK, October 2010. (Thanks to the IPA for permission to quote this survey).

9.   See the Radio 2 biography of Terry Wogan at: http://www.bbc.co.uk/radio2/shows/wogan/biography.shtml.

10.  See the *Daily Telegraph*'s Obituary of Paul Walters online at: http://www.telegraph.co.uk/news/main.jhtml?xml=/news/2006/10/23/db2302.xml.

11.  Crook, T. (1999) *Radio Drama – Theory and Practice*, London: Routledge, p.61.

12.  'Is Radio Dying?', presented at the Radio Festival, Salford, UK, October 2010. (Thanks to Alison Winter, Research Manager for BBC's Audio and Music department for permission to cite this research).

13.  *Ibid.*

14.  Leith, S. (15 June, 2009) 'If I'm Sorry I Haven't a Clue is such a daring show, why won't they let a woman take the chair?' *Guardian.co.uk*, available online at: http://www.guardian.co.uk/culture/2009/jun/15/sorry-havent-clue-woman-chair-sam-leith.

15.  Algan, E. (2005) 'The role of Turkish local radio in the construction of a youth community', *The Radio Journal – International Studies in Broadcast and Audio Media*, 3 (2), pp. 75–92.

16.  Hedges, M. (2010) 'Post-modern consumers, cultures and media – the six radio brands', Geneva: *Follow the media*. p. 6.

17.  *GlobesScan* (2006) 'BBC/Reuters/Media Center Poll: Trust in the Media', available at: http://www.globescan.com/news_archives/bbc.reut.html.

18.  Brazil, Egypt, Germany, India, Indonesia, Nigeria, Russia, South Korea, UK and USA.

19.  *Follow the media* (15 November, 2010) 'Public radio most trusted'. available online at: http://www.followthemedia.com/index.php#tickle2.

20.  Ofcom (17 May, 2010) *UK Adults' Media Literacy*, p. 74, available online at: http://stakeholders.ofcom.org.uk/binaries/research/media-literacy/adults-media-literacy.pdf.

21.  Myers, J. (April 2009) *An Independent Review of the Rules Governing Local Content on Commercial Radio*, PDF and Word versions available online at: http://webarchive.nationalarchives.gov.uk/+/http://www.culture.gov.uk/reference_library/publications/6053.aspx.

22.  BBC News (3 October, 1998) 'BBC nuclear bomb script released', available online at: http://news.bbc.co.uk/1/hi/uk/uk/7648042.stm.

23.  *Democracy Now!* (25 January, 2007) 'EXCLUSIVE: ... 911 Calls in North Dakota Town |Reveal Dangers of Media Consolidation', available online at: http://www.democracynow.org/2007/1/25/exclusive_911_calls_in_north_dakota.

24.  *Guardian.co.uk* (5 July, 2010) *Organgrinder Blog*, 'BBC 6 Music: is its reprieve a triumph for social media?', available online at: http://www.guardian.co.uk/media/organgrinder/2010/jul/05/bbc-6-music-saved.

25.  *Guardian.co.uk* (13 May, 2010) 'Rajars analysis: BBC 6 Music needed this – but did Radio 2?', *Organgrinder Blog*, available online at: http://news.bbc.co.uk/1/hi/entertainment_and_arts/10106403.stm.

26.  BBC News (11 May, 2010) '6 Music and Asian Network win Sony radio awards', available online at: http://news.bbc.co.uk/1/hi/entertainment_and_arts/10106403.stm.

27.  BBC Trust (July 2010) *BBC Strategy Review – Initial Conclusions*, p.6, available online at: http://www.bbc.co.uk/bbctrust/assets/files/pdf/review_report_research/strategic_review/interim_conclusions.pdf.

28. Rudin, R. (2 March, 2010) *Rudinblog*, 'Why 6 Music may be saved and why the BIG radio story has been missed', available online at: http://rudinblog.typepad. com/my_weblog/2010/03/why-6-music-may-be-saved-and-why-the-big-radio-story-has-been-missed.html.

29. Revoir, P. (30 November, 2010) 'Lifeline for FM Radio as digital switchover is delayed to 2017', *MailOnline*, available online at: http://www.dailymail.co.uk/ news/article-1334250/Digital-switchover-radio-delayed-2017-Ministers-privately-accepted.html.

# Reality Television

5

---

This chapter considers the phenomenon of reality television and then considers wider themes of the representations of Reality Television in broadcasting and the 'negotiations' of it by audiences. In particular it discusses:

- The Reality TV show *Big Brother* and its impact on audiences.
- A classification, with examples, of different types of reality television.
- How all television output has elements of 'fakery'.
- The breaking down of boundaries between comedy and current affairs television.
- Disputed versions and interpretations of 'reality', including the case of reaction to the TV drama *Life On Mars*.

## The life and death of Jade Goody – as seen on TV

When Jade Goody entered Channel 4's *Celebrity Big Brother* house in January 2007 she seemed to epitomize the triumph of celebrity culture: of being 'famous' without having achieved anything of note aside from being herself – famous for being famous. She had shot to fame two years previously in the regular *Big Brother*. There, her displays of ignorance (especially on the geography of her own country, for example thinking that East Anglia was 'abroad' and Cambridge was 'in London') appealed to the apparently large swathe of the nation who could feel simultaneously superior to her whilst at the same time fantasising that they, too, could become rich and famous simply for 'being themselves'. This combination of superiority/emulation, however, was to prove toxic and, as Goody was to find out in the most extreme fashion, public support can be a fickle thing: support, even adulation, when it is based purely on personality, can be inverted into ridicule, loathing and even hatred. When confronted with someone who had achieved fame through talent – as well as undoubted beauty and sophistication – in the form of 'Bollywood' actor Shilpa Shetty, Goody's fragile self-esteem was shattered. She clearly felt threatened and humiliated, and she, her mother and her partner, Jack Tweedy, lashed out with personal and racial abuse. Goody was then portrayed in some parts of the tabloid press and on internet chat rooms as almost worse than evil and 'the most hated woman in Britain'.

The confrontations – also involving other house members – caused an international incident. With exquisitely unfortunate timing, Gordon Brown, who was then Chancellor of the Exchequer and soon to become British Prime Minister, was touring India at the height of the furore and found himself facing a barrage of questions from Indian journalists, not on trade and development but on a Reality TV show back home. The broadcaster found itself at the centre of a media and political storm: this time not because of investigative documentaries or groundbreaking drama, but whether it was correct in allowing an edited version of the programme to include the offending comments. Even worse than questions over the channel's editorial judgement were allegations that, in a battle of the ratings, it had deliberately set up a situation which it must have known would have caused an unedifying confrontation. Not only that, but there were questions of a failure of a 'duty of care' towards individuals who might need protection from themselves.

To some observers, it was all an accident waiting to happen – a demonstration of the cynicism and amorality of much of modern television. In Victorian Britain the public would be invited to the local lunatic asylum in order to jeer at the unfortunate inmates in their cages – perhaps pushing sticks at them in order to goad them into ever greater displays of humiliation and degradation. It is not hard to see Reality Television as the modern, electronic version of this sort of public entertainment; the unseen but omnipresent 'Big Brother' setting tasks and situations that would be sure to prompt the 'housemates' into ever more extreme behaviour. As in those visits to 19th-century Bedlam, the exhibition of anti-social, selfish activity also allows the viewers to congratulate themselves on being morally, intellectually and temperamentally superior to those 'inside'. *Big Brother*'s format also allowed the audience to 'vote off' those housemates who displeased them. Viewers may also have been filled with a degree of self-loathing for having enjoyed and encouraged this spectacle, and this guilt could only be assuaged by the inexpensive action of voting for Shilpa Shetty, who emerged as the clear 'winner' of that series of *Celebrity Big Brother*.

It was both tragic and in some terrible way also fitting that Goody should learn of the cancer that was to kill her 'live' on TV during an episode of India's version of *Big Brother* the previous August. When learning the cancer might be terminal she told a Sunday newspaper:

I've lived my whole adult life talking about my life. The only difference is that I'm talking about my death now. It's OK … I've lived in front of the cameras. And maybe I'll die in front of them.[1]

She had learned only a few weeks before that the cancer had spread to other organs and she had only a short time to live. She then married her boyfriend and tried to secure the future of her young sons in media deals, thought to be worth £1 million. The final days of her life were indeed caught on camera, in an exclusive deal with the satellite/cable channel called – somewhat ironically – Living TV.

The public certainly had strong and diverse opinions about the whole phenomenon of Goody's public life and death. In 21st century Britain you do not have to take difficult and perhaps dangerous actions to demonstrate your morals and values; you can merely take part in a TV phone poll – and of course, let everyone else know you have taken this 'action'. Chat forums, social networking sites and countless thousands of text messages and emails between viewers provide a mutually supportive orgy of self-satisfaction and sanctimony.

But what of the participants? Certainly no one was killed or physically hurt in the *Big Brother* house, but there had been, arguably, psychological damage to individuals and, in the short term at least, to Britain's international reputation.

The series certainly led to debate on questions of the nature of modern British society and the character of its people. The idea of the show had initially struck its eventual British promoter, Peter Bazalgette, as unlikely to appeal to British public taste and he wrote to the programme's Dutch inventor, John de Mol:

> The rats-in-any-cage-who'll-do-anything-for-money is something that I doubt we could sell on to commercial television ... as currently constituted, we feel the show has a narrow market in the UK.[2]

Clearly, Bazalgette had second thoughts and he has defended the show on numerous occasions. He has not been alone in portraying the show as an interesting as well as entertaining insight into human behaviour. The idea of isolating a disparate group of individuals (whether defined as 'celebrities' or not) and compelling them to live together and cooperate – sometimes, in other variants of the genre, to physically survive – certainly has some merit as an anthropological and psychological study. There is undoubtedly a fascination in not only observing the behaviour of others but in identifying with them and their situation and wondering how we would cope and behave. The interest is further increased by the knowledge that, as with watching many fictional dramas, *we* can see everything that is going on and most importantly hear the gossip, intrigue and backstabbing of all the participants, who often remain blissfully unaware of the plotting or scheming, or can only guess at it. As in 'real life' people gain and lose popularity; friendships and alliances are forged and then broken; there is betrayal and rejection, as well as support and affection. Most work and other social situations contain elements of all this but while office politics can be distressing and debilitating to those directly involved, Reality TV allows us to enjoy the spectacle, help determine the outcome (by 'voting off' participants), argue and discuss the individuals and situations both within our social groups and through websites, blogs, etc., without any negative consequences. The dynamics of the group change when individuals leave, either by being voted off by the public, or in some instances of their own accord. This again is similar to work situations, familiar to many.

This is also the very stuff of dramatists, not least those who are involved in writing and producing continuing serials or 'soap operas'. Dramatists, though, have to work at our suspense of disbelief, but the whole point of Reality TV is, of course, that it is real people in real, if contrived, situations and happening before our eyes. There is no script and no knowledge of how it will all end – or, at least, that is what we are led to believe.

The appeal to the public can be measured both in the ratings and by the number of votes cast at the various stages of elimination of the *Big Brother* contestants. In 2001 these had exceeded those for the winning party in that year's general election and six million more than in the previous poll for UK seats on the European Parliament.[3] There was much anguish and hand-ringing amongst the media and political classes and many other parts of society that this demonstrated that the British public had become both infantilised and decadent; or, as explored in Chapter 3, 'dumbed down'. Others countered that, at a time when the major political parties were virtually indistinguishable from each other and when Westminster politicians were unable or unwilling to effect change or make a difference to a world dominated by multinational companies and international politics, it was at least as rational to participate in a *Big Brother* vote as to bother voting for an MP or MEP.[4]

*Big Brother* and its *Celebrity* version are the best-known shows of the genre. For Channel 4 it was also by far the most important in terms of advertising revenue, accounting for about half of the network's annual profits. Therefore, the announcement several months after Goody's death that the next series of *Big Brother* would be the last and that the celebrity version would cease the following year, with the expenditure on these programmes being ploughed into 'serious' drama, seemed to demonstrate that this particular show and its variants had run its course.

But many other formats and series have had 'reality' attached to them. The documentary, too, relies on unscripted programmes featuring 'real' people in 'real' situations, and the 'fly on the wall' technique used in the example of *Airport* (based on the employees and the daily work situations at London's Heathrow Airport) certainly employs techniques of documentary used in its classic form. However, I exclude 'normal' documentary from Reality TV, as, in the classic form of documentary, there is a clear agenda and intention of the programme team to show dramatic events.

Here then is a definition of Reality TV – for a programme to be described as belonging to the genre, it should comply with the following:

1.  It must be primarily devised as, and intended to be, *entertainment*.
2.  It must not be news or current affairs – there must be no 'issue', nor must it inform public policy or debate.

3.  It must be unscripted and feature non-actors, showing 'real' reactions from the participants to the situation in which they are placed.
4.  The main focus and appeal of the programme lies in the interactivity and relationships between the participants.

In addition, we can add two further aspects which are *likely* to form part of the make-up of such a programme:

5.  It is likely to directly involve the viewing public, who are asked to vote on who should 'survive' and who should be eliminated from the show.
6.  It will not be a one-off programme, but part of a series, allowing the audience to form judgements on the participants.

The main genre can then be sub-divided into a number of sub-genres – even if these sometimes overlap – as illustrated in Table 5.1.

The last two examples in Table 5.1 have a definite educational, public-service value, rather than solely entertainment. *The Apprentice* supposedly provides an insight into the skills and qualities that are needed for success in a highly competitive business world and those being sought by leading entrepreneurs, and *Surviving the Iron Age* informs us about the living conditions and material circumstances of pre-civilisation ages (other shows in this genre have followed participants in re-creations of much more recent times, including trench warfare in the First World War, and Britain in the Second World War, with its rationing, etc.).

There are clearly grey areas in my classification of Reality TV as a genre and other forms of television: for example there is a great deal to connect reality talent shows with 'ordinary' talent shows such as *The X Factor* and *Pop Idol*, and I have included one of these shows – *Britain's Got Talent*, because the concentration of the private life and the 'journey' by one individual – Susan Boyle – seems to just cross the line into the 'reality' genre and it would seem that this connection with the individual was at least as important to its ratings success as the 'talent' revealed. The 2009 final of the show, which included Susan Boyle (who was pipped to the prize by a dance troupe) achieved the highest ratings of any TV show broadcast in the UK since England's 2004 Euro soccer match against Croatia and the largest audience for a non-sporting broadcast since an edition of *Coronation Street* in 2003, peaking at 19.2 million viewers – with the average audience of the show comprising two-thirds of all TV viewing.[5] In addition, the show provided an unprecedented lift to viewing of the show on the broadcaster's website – 55 million views from 13 million users.[6]

The phenomenon of Susan Boyle crossed the Atlantic and a clip of her on YouTube had by far the greatest number of downloads of the year – a staggering 120 million worldwide.[7] This quite unprecedented public interest led to the show's broadcaster, ITV1, being criticised by some media analysts for *not* exploiting the material for its own commercial gain. However, the producers

**Table 5.1**  Sub-genres of reality TV programmes

| Type | Example | Description |
|---|---|---|
| **Reality unexpected situation:** Unwitting public is confronted by a contrived, unusual and/or baffling situation or predicament. | *Candid Camera* | A 'classic' format from the early days of network TV in both the USA and UK but which has been revived and adapted to a number of much later shows, either as 'stand alones' or as segments of entertainment programmes; concealed cameras. There is no direct 'voting' and the participants are unaware of being filmed, so the appeal of the show is that they are seen acting completely naturally; this distinguishes this sub-genre from all the others below, but the appeal to the viewer is similar – how they react to it and imagining how they would react in the same situation. |
| **Reality human behaviour:** Confined, isolated and observed participants in normal domesticity. Viewers vote off the participants until only one is left and declared the 'winner'. | *Big Brother* | A group of disparate individuals is confined to a particular location, cut off from the outside world but otherwise in a normal, domestic situation; the viewer observes almost all of their activities (and even when sleeping). The main interest is the viewer watching their interactivities and evolving relationships and in how they discuss other participants, both with different members of the group, and in isolation in a 'confession' booth. |
| **Reality challenging situation:** Participants are isolated in challenging, unusual situation/location. Viewers 'vote off' participants, as above. | *I'm A Celebrity ... Get Me Out of Here!* | The disparate group are confined to a challenging environment, such as the Australian jungle, and obliged to find and cook whatever food is native to the location, construct their shelter, etc. They may be further stretched by other challenges, especially activities to which they are known to have a natural disinclination, e.g. those prone to vertigo being compelled to climb high structures. |

*continued overleaf*

**Table 5.1** *continued*

| Type | Example | Description |
|---|---|---|
| **Reality skills-acquiring shows:** Participants learn a skill that is outside the abilities for which they are known. | *Dancing On Ice* | The appeal is to see the frustration, frequent humiliation, and ultimate triumph of, for example, rugby players learning how to dance on ice skates to a professional standard. |
| **Reality talent shows:** The viewer follows the participants as they compete for a specific prize which will enable them to be transformed into a major star. | *Britain's Got Talent* | One of the oldest genres of radio and TV entertainment – with its roots in vaudeville – is given a new twist by showing the 'behind the scenes' preparations for the contest and the 'normal' lives of the participants and in monitoring their reaction as other contestants are eliminated and they head towards the prize – usually a record contract, 'season' at a major 'live' entertainment venue. |
| **Reality career competition:** Participants are competing not just for general, public popularity but to specific audience/adjudicators, for a specific purpose. | *The Apprentice* | Contestants vie to be given a contract to work with a leading company/entrepreneur, such as Donald Trump or Alan Sugar. They are set tasks which are designed to demonstrate their individual and relative (to the group) initiative, entrepreneurship, group/social skills and business acumen. |
| **Reality re-creation:** Participants are observed attempting to live in the physical and economic circumstances of earlier generations, or to achieve a specific accomplishment using the materials, etc., only available at the time. | *Surviving the Iron Age* | Appeal of the show is in observing how those used to 21st-century comforts survive in primitive conditions. |
| **Reality documentary:** Has at least as much in common with soap opera as with 'classic' forms of documentary, in that the audience is engaged with the lives of 'ordinary' people, either in 'normal' work or domestic situations. | *Airport* | Distinguished from 'normal' documentary as there must not be any 'news' or 'current affairs' value in the work: the participants must not be in particularly unusual situations or with specific and dramatic events. |

were attacked by others for allegedly exploiting her personal circumstances – in particular, her learning difficulties and for her lack of sexual experience (it was said she had barely been kissed; in the sex-obsessed culture of 21st century Britain this was regarded as freakish, rather than, as it would have been in the not so distant past, a mark of self-restraint, or at least a purely private matter on which it would be unkind and disrespectful to comment).

Following the series finale a number of instances of bizarre – even disturbing – instances led to criticism that the broadcaster had failed to fulfil its duty of care towards her. Once again, it seemed that there was collusion with the public to exploit a 'freak show' element in the life of a contestant. An unhealthy mixture of admiration and pity/mockery seemed to define the response with little, if any regard, for the damage it was doing to the individual.

If there was a carefully orchestrated PR campaign to crank up the programme's ratings' success then it must be said that the British press (and not just the 'red top' tabloid sector) were more than willing to be 'exploited' and the amount of 'chatter' on social networking sites certainly indicated a huge public fascination with Boyle. Naturally, the show's producers and judges denied that they had failed to consider Boyle's health and well-being; any problems, they argued, were the result of the quite unexpected and unprecedented press and public interest. Nevertheless, the contestants for the following series of *The X Factor* (also on ITV1) were provided with greater psychological checks and counselling.[8]

A final main strand of criticism – although less relevant to the discussion in this chapter – was that such talent/reality shows distort the music industry (already under pressure because of the download phenomenon), with 'real' recording talent, finely honed and developed over the years, being pushed aside in a giant marketing frenzy.

## When is 'real' really real?

The more fundamental, if perhaps more esoteric or existential, question arises as to what is 'reality' so far as TV is concerned? The whole of the medium is based on artifice: every shot, every angle, every representation is selected, whether it be for factual programmes, or drama and comedy. Almost everything is scripted and relatively little of the output outside these programmes is 'live'. All sorts of contrivances and conventions are utilised to represent reality. Anyone who has been involved in an interview or 'package' outside the studio environment will be aware of at least some of the 'tricks' that are used to make 'better television'. Participants are filmed entering doors and buildings, or in offices that they never normally use, because the journalist or producer decides that these look more like the 'real thing' – that they conform to the expectations or prejudices of the viewer, or they just 'look better'. So what we are often watching, even in – *especially* in – types of output which depend on the viewer expecting accuracy and truthfulness, are in fact constructed from deceptions of various kinds. Does any of this matter though? The broadcasters argue that not only do such contrivances help to explain the story and engage with audiences but are insignificant in terms of the veracity of the piece. Editing and production devices are inevitable in most forms of factual output and what matters is representing the views of the participants truthfully and fairly and in conveying often very complex and multi-faceted stories effectively within a short timeframe. So long as there is no attempt to mislead the viewer from the essential 'truths' of the story or misrepresent the views of participants, then all is justified. However, editing can mislead: in 2007, the Controller of BBC1 (television) Peter Fincham resigned over the production and promotion of a documentary about the making of a new portrait of the Queen. The promotion wrongly showed Her Majesty apparently storming off in a 'huff'. In fact, the documentary – made by an independent production company – had edited together several sequences from several days' filming.

Broadcasting, and in particular television, is especially potent in building narratives and none more so perhaps than sport. As discussed in Chapter 1, nothing beats 'live' sport in terms both of ratings and as a mass, social experience. In many respects broadcasting and sport are the most natural 'fit': the ability to bring the action 'live' and simultaneously to a mass audience, with viewers and listeners not only able to follow the triumphs and defeats of teams and individuals – there is nothing more 'real' than the unarguable fact of a match result – but to become engaged in the dramas both on and off the pitch, court, etc. Sports' writers in the press had long been able to provide background articles and interviews but to be able to see and hear the participants, including conflicts between, for example, managers, board members and players, provides a narrative that absorbs many.

Furthermore, the public recognizes that much of what it sees in the supposedly factual realm is contrived and part of a complex artifice. Some of the most popular television shows, such as *It'll Be Alright on the Night*, have exposed and even celebrated journalists, presenters and actors having to 'retake' their material. Increasing numbers have direct experience not only in participating in television but of actually making it, so that they 'know' about the 'grammar' of television – editing, framing pictures and so on. Conversely, broadcasters seem ever more willing to let reality intrude into drama output. Most major BBC series now include a programme or feature about the making of the programme and going 'behind-the-scenes', interviewing the actors and production staff about how they achieved the period look or effects. Sometimes, as with *Doctor Who*, these programmes are more than half as long as the episode itself. The DVDs of such programmes, such as with the release of feature films on that format, contain a host of 'extras' and there is little doubt that many viewers love to feel that they have been 'on the inside' of the respective shows. Rather than reducing the dramatic appeal of the shows and compromising the suspense of disbelief, they appear to add to the attraction of the show and engagement by the viewer. Most viewers, then, are able to be engrossed and involved when watching drama programmes, whilst at the same time 'know' that they are carefully crafted pieces of fiction. Yet this increased media literacy does not prevent the most astonishing collisions of fantasy and reality.

## Reality, perceptions and comedy – when fake becomes more 'real' than real

In the 1960s, the TV newscaster and journalist Walter Cronkite had been awarded the title of 'the most trusted man in America'. As noted in Chapter 1, his assessment in 1968 that the USA was losing the war in Vietnam and could not win it, led to the then president, Lyndon Johnson, deciding not to run for a second full term in office.[9] A few days after Cronkite's death in 2009, the news magazine, *Time*, asked its readers in an online poll who they thought was now the country's most trusted journalist. The number one position by some margin was not one of the nation's most experienced and respected print or broadcast journalists, but Jon Stewart, the host of the cable nightly *The Daily Show*.[10] The show mixes monologues, a satirical take on the day's news, including audio and video clips of politicians and celebrities saying and doing unfortunate things, with semi-serious interviews with leading public figures, including Barack Obama, Bill Clinton and Tony Blair, as well as those – in traditional chat-show style – who are there to promote their latest book, movie etc. It is regularly viewed by some 16 per cent of Americans, equivalent to the figures for the established news and talk shows, but its influence is even greater than suggested by the ratings.[11] The show's appeal to younger viewers has been credited with increasing political engagement in the young, especially increasing turnout in the Primaries for the 2008 US Presidential election.[12] For many, it seems, the version of truth by Stewart and his contributors on politics, society and culture is more profound than that presented in the traditional TV output, which is 'framed' as serious reporting and commentary. As one viewer, a 36-year-old teacher of astronomy, put it:[13]

> *The Daily Show* is probably more reliable for news than anything on TV except PBS (Public Service Broadcasting). It stands apart from anything else because it unspins the news. It frankly points out how ridiculous the 24-hour news networks are – mostly gassing away by unqualified 'experts' filling the hours.

Towards the end of the campaign for the US mid-term elections in 2010, Jon Stewart organised a rally in Washington DC in October 2010, to counter the rallies of the populist Tea Party movement, which was fervently backed by Fox News's Glenn Beck. The title of the march alone – 'Rally to Restore Sanity and/or Fear' – suggested a confused, or at least diverse, approach.[14]

The battle of ideas and 'truth' must never have raged so hard than over the effectiveness and general conduct of the US-led operation in Iraq, and here the clash between comedy and journalism reached a peak, when the 'whistle-blower' organization WikiLeaks made available pictures of a machine-gun attack by an Apache helicopter on part of Baghdad (killing over a dozen people, including two Reuters' journalists), which were then widely re-broad-cast on the mainstream channnels.[15] WikiLeaks had called the attack 'collateral murder' – thus challenging the usual interpretations – or spinning – of unintended deaths of civilians as 'collateral damage'. From the audio of the conversations between the marines, there appeared a ruthless, and – at the very least – careless attitude to those they had killed. Stephen Colbert, formerly of *The Daily Show* but by then with his own satirical show, *The Colbert Report*, dropped his normal on-air persona when he interviewed WikiLeaks founder Julian Assange and accused him – through the description of the attack as 'collateral murder' and an introduction to the video of a quotation from George Orwell – not of leaking, but editorialising.[16]

Addressing serious issues in a humorous way, sometimes in order to get around rules and laws made by the power elites in order to prevent criticism of themselves and their actions, has a long tradition. In the UK, the weekly, live, Saturday night show *That Was The Week That Was*, or *TW3* (BBC TV, 1962–3), hosted by the then TV newcomer David Frost, provoked outrage among some of the elites and vociferous criticism by some politicians in and outside Parliament because of its mixture of satire and hard-hitting interviews.[17] Jon Stewart, in a perhaps half serious comment in a 2008 interview, said that he and his production team had regarded Frost as a role model and that they wanted to have the same sort of impact in the 21st century that Frost – who took his show to an American network after the BBC dropped the programme – had achieved in the mid- to late-20th century.[18] Meanwhile, on the UK's Channel 4, the impressionist Rory Bremner, along with John Bird and John Fortune, had mixed satirical 'takes' on the week's news with a rigorous analysis of key issues, in *Bremner, Bird and Fortune*. Some of the sketches were set up as private scenes between, for example the Prime Minister and his political advisers, supposedly caught on closed-circuit cameras, with the picture degraded to make the studio-produced work seem more 'real', and Bremner had once even fooled a government minister into thinking he was the (then) Prime Minister, although UK rules on the use of deception on TV in the UK prevented the interview from being broadcast.[19]

Mocking the conventions and pomposity of television (especially its news coverage) reached a new creative height with *The Day Today* on BBC TV (which developed from a BBC Radio 4 comedy *On The Hour*). In the show, absurd stories were treated to the full 'news effect', the immense self-belief and absurd pretensions of correspondents – as well as graphics, set design, lighting and camera angles – was ruthlessly satirised, not least in its coverage of a 'war', which the fictional TV channel itself was seen to provoke.

One of that programme's creative forces, Chris Morris, went on to develop *Brass Eye* on Channel 4. In this, the 'hands over your face' moments markedly increased as Morris demonstrated how far celebrities and politicians (increasingly indistinguishable) would spout complete nonsense if they were told that it was in a 'good cause', especially over any new scare or moral panic involving young people. One episode, on a fictitious drug called 'Cake', led to an MP, who was filmed being 'briefed' on the drug, raising the 'issue' in the House of Commons. But the show's most controversial programme was a 2001 episode on paedophiles.[20] Morris had been increasingly appalled by the hysterical and gratuitously lavish coverage of attacks on children by strangers – in fact, a very rare event in the UK (children are most at risk from sexual and other physical and psychological abuse by members of their own family in their own homes), causing unnecessary anxiety and fear amongst both parents and children. He was also angry at the media hypocrisy over children – treating them as innocent angels one moment and, once in their mid-teens if not earlier, as sex objects. There was particular fury in sections of the press and some politicians about a sequence in which Morris pointed to a six-year-old boy in the studio who he said was his son, and asked a 'paedophile' if he wanted to have sex with him. To Morris's apparent annoyance, the 'paedophile' replied: 'no'. Morris asked him why not, to which came the reply: 'I don't fancy him'. When condemned for using a young child in this way, Morris – demonstrating how easy it is to fake television – said the boy had never been present in the studio during this interchange but electronically superimposed at a later date.

Channel 4 went on to develop the *Da Ali G Show*, which featured the comedian Sacha Baron Cohen in the guise of a non-black male from an English suburb who, finding his own background and culture distinctly 'uncool', develops a new more 'street cred' persona, incorporating the *patois* and attitudes of Jamaican black culture. In this guise Ali G interviews a number of politicians and personalities, from intellectual heavyweights such as Noam Chomsky, to David and Victoria Beckham. His technique is to play on his interviewees' liberal 'instincts' to engage with a 'black' representative of young British people, and to goad them to agree – or at least to not vociferously oppose – outrageous, ignorant and politically incorrect statements and attitudes. The character and show has been criticized by some commentators and comedians, including Felix Dexter of *The Real McCoy*, who said:[21]

> I feel that a lot of the humour is laughing at black street culture and it is being celebrated because it allows the liberal middle classes to laugh at that culture in a safe context where they can retain their sense of political correctness.

The 'mockumentary' technique was taken even further by the director and writer Armando Iannucci in his BBC TV satire *The Thick of It*,[22] which centred on the 'spin machine' surrounding the then Prime Minister, Tony Blair, and his Head of Communications – or chief 'spin doctor' – Alastair Campbell, discussed in Chapter 6. The idea was developed into a movie, *In The Loop*, which depicted a fictional version of the political and military machinations on both sides of the Atlantic which had led to the invasion of Iraq. The narrative in both the TV series and the movie seemed so close to reality that they had the feel of documentary rather than a TV comedy programme. Indeed, when the Labour party left office in May 2010, the subsequent outpouring of diaries and memoirs from former ministers and 'spin doctors' made it appear that the comedy if anything under-played the frequently bizarre but grim reality of decision making at the highest level which had profound life and death consequences. It is scarcely any wonder then that the audience seem confused about what is fact and reality, or rather, perhaps, are able to see that the lines between fact and fantasy are blurred – or even more intriguingly, that what is true and what is in the realm of imagination cannot easily be separated and distinguished.

This question leads to complex ideas about relativism, interpretation, representation, structure and language, developed by the philosopher Jean Baudrillard[23] and others. This clash or confusion was highlighted by the TV coverage of the first Iraq war in 1991. The CNN coverage – transmitted by other broadcasters, including the BBC – showed to western viewers what looked like a spectacular computer game, full of fireworks and explosions, as missiles rained down on Baghdad. What was not shown were the terrified families on the ground and the death, distress, grief, destruction and terrible injuries caused by the bombardment. So what was seen was *one* truth, but the deeper and, in humanitarian terms, far more profound truth, was not. Baudrillard even argued that at one level the Gulf War did not take place.[24]

It must be concluded that the 'simple truth' is that there is *no* simple truth – rather there are different layers and perspectives, which the audience must constantly negotiate in their psyche and which are largely determined by culture, background and experience – as well as how those who control the images and the output choose to select and represent events. Furthermore, the psychiatrist Dorothy Rowe (emeritus associate of the Royal College of Psychiatrists), has concluded that none of us sees 'reality' directly. Each of us 'guesses' and interprets what is going on and this is partly determined by our past experiences. As Rowe puts it: 'Since no two people ever have exactly the same neuroanatomy or experience, no two people ever interpret anything in exactly the same way.'[25]

The most significant aspect so far as broadcasting in the 21st century is concerned is that 'truth' and 'reality' are contested and negotiated by audiences in new and challenging ways. The following case study concerns the intriguing relationship of the audience to what was 'meant' to have happened in a TV fictional show.

## Life on Mars

*Life on Mars* was an independent production for BBC television, running through just two series of eight episodes each, originally broadcast in 2005 and 2006. A less successful (at least in ratings' terms) adaptation for the USA was made by that country's ABC network and ran for just one season from October 2008 until April 2009 (the following discussion pertains to the UK version, although many aspects of the story-line and 'issues' raised by the series are common to both). Australia screened both versions, albeit on different networks.

At the centre of the drama is Sam Tyler, a police officer who apparently finds himself transported from 2006 to 1973. The first episode of the first series begins with him being hit by a car and, as the opening titles of each episode ask: *is he mad, in a coma, or dreaming?* He is still a police officer in 1973 but finds the methods and attitudes of his fellow officers very different from those in the 21st century. Much of the dramatic interest centres on Tyler's clashes with his superior officer, Detective Chief Inspector Gene Hunt, who believes that 'roughing up' the suspects is not only legitimate but the only effective way of extracting information and obtaining confessions. The forensic methods used – or, rather, the lack of such methods – also appals Tyler, as bodies and scenes of crime are hopelessly contaminated by, amongst other things, cigar ash and egg yolk. The contrast between life in Britain in the 1970s and 21st century are constantly demonstrated, including attitudes towards women, ethnic minorities and sexual orientation. The consumer goods at the time and other technological changes – not least in broadcasting – are also intrinsic to the drama. As with many narratives – sci-fi and thrillers in particular – everyday, bland features of life take on a malevolent form. In *Life on Mars,* the test pattern card – which used to be shown for the purposes of alignment of sets by television engineers and depicts a young girl and a stuffed toy 'playing' noughts and crosses on a blackboard – becomes a sinister feature.

An episode in series two opens with a TV animation based on the characters and, mimicking the style of a children's series from the 1970s, showing Gene Hunt beating up a 'nonce' – slang for a paedophile – with the narrator speaking directly to Tyler through the TV set. (The animators later confirmed they were paying *homage* to the children's programme, as well as the original animators.)[26] Naturally, the soundtrack features plenty of pop and rock from the 1973 to 1974 period and, equally inevitably, some of these tracks were released on a successful compilation CD. The title of the series itself comes from David Bowie's 1973 hit of the same name and the connection with Orson Welles' 1938 radio production of *War of the Worlds* – when, as discussed in Chapter 1, many listeners were convinced they were hearing news accounts of an invasion from Mars – provides a clear reference point, for the idea is about what is true and what is fiction.

The resolution of the mystery about the 'true' state of Tyler's existence and world, in *Life on Mars,* became a matter of intense interest and speculation amongst viewers, TV critics and within the 'blogosphere'. Although the show's creators and producers have insisted that they intended to bring the narrative to a clear and fairly unambiguous close, many viewers were clearly confused or at least uncertain about what was 'supposed' to have happened. Indeed, judging from the numerous blogs, websites and letters to the national and regional press, a significant part of the enjoyment of the series was in guessing what was 'true' and what was not – with discussion of clues and references inserted by the writers in order to confuse or mislead the viewer. The viewer is aware of these contrivances and techniques, and part of the enjoyment of such programmes is in trying to second-guess the writers' intentions and ignore the narrative 'traps'.

This debate on the intentions of the writers – in what we were, as viewers, 'supposed' to believe had 'really' happened – continued for some months after the transmission of the final episode. Some bloggers were convinced that, in fact, aside from a very brief return to consciousness, *all* of the narrative – the parts depicting 1973 and 2006 – was supposed to have been induced by the coma, and it was not until an interview was published with one of the show's writers and creators, stating that in fact *only* the 2006 scenes were supposed to be 'real', that the bloggers were forced to abandon this interpretation. Nevertheless, myths surrounding the processes of the production continued to abound: the most striking was that, in order to avoid the details of the ending leaking out, the producers shot several alternate endings. Several versions of the supposed false or alternate ending were posted on YouTube. Intriguingly, even some of the cast thought that there had been a (benign) conspiracy amongst the writers and directors to keep the actors guessing as to which would be used in the final 'cut'. As the production crew also made clear though, even if the *dénouement* was settled quite far in advance of its shooting, there were many aspects of the narrative and production that were being debated far into the filming – in at one least case literally up to the point when the final shot was 'locked' – and some elements, including soundtrack, were still being debated in post-production.[27]

It is also significant that the hardware of broadcast receivers – the TV and radio sets – as well as the programmes that emanate from them, are an important part of the appeal of the programme, further emphasising the point that our memories of consumption of broadcasting are often bound up with memories of both our personal lives and outside events.

## Notes and references

1.  Percival, J. (22 March, 2009) 'Jade Goody dies of cancer;, *Guardian.co.uk*, available online at: http://www.guardian.co.uk/media/2009/mar/22/jade-goody-dies.
2.  Cited in Sparks, C. (9 April, 2007) 'Reality TV: the Big Brother phenomenon', *International Socialism*, issue 114, available online at: http://www.isj.org.uk.php4?id=314&issue=114.
3.  Morrison, J. (29 July, 2001) 'Big Brother: now for the interactive, online soap opera', *Independent.co.uk*, available online at: http://news.independent.co.uk/media/article235932.ece
4.  Member of the European Parliament.

5. *Broadcast* (1 June, 2009) 'Britain's Got Talent triumphs with 19.2m', available online at: http://www.broadcastnow.co.uk/ratings/britains-got-talent-triumphs-with-192m/5001995.article.
6. Barnett, E. (2 June, 2009) 'Britain's Got Talent boosts IT.com traffic', *Telegraph.co.uk*, available online at: http://www.telegraph.co.uk/technology/news/5430050/Britains-Got-Talent-boosts-ITV.com-traffic.html.
7. *Techworld* (16 December, 2009) 'Susan Boyle is most watched YouTube video', available online at: http://news.techworld.com/security/3208868/susan-boyle-is-most-watched-youtube-video/.
8. Holmwood, L. (18 August, 2009) 'X Factor contestants to face judgment on their mental health', *The Guardian.co.uk*, available online at: http://www.guardian.co.uk/media/2009/aug/18/x-factor-contestants-mental-health.
9. Leopold, T. (19 July, 2009) 'Former CBS anchor 'Uncle Walter' Cronkite dead at 92', *CNN.Com*, available online at: http://edition.cnn.com/2009/US/07/17/walter.cronkite.dead/index.html.
10. Riggio, R.E. (24 July, 2009) 'Why Jon Stewart is the Most Trusted Man in America', *Psychology Today: Blogs – Cutting-Edge Leadership*, available online at: http://www.psychologytoday.com/blog/cutting-edge-leadership/200907/why-jon-stewart-is-the-most-trusted-man-in-america.
11. Pew Research (8 May, 2008) 'The Daily Show: Journalism, Satire of Just Laughs?', available online at: http://pewresearch.org/pubs/829/the-daily-show-journalism-satire-or-just-laughs.
12. Bowlby, C. (27 August, 2008) 'The most trusted man in America?', *BBC News – World – Americas*, available online at: http://news.bbc.co.uk/1/hi/world/americas/7582521.stm.
13. Smith, D. (14 September, 2008) 'How a satirist became America's most influential TV personality', *The Observer*, available online at: http://www.guardian.co.uk/media/2008/sep/14/television.television.
14. Rohrer, F. (31 October, 2010) 'What was Jon Stewart's rally all about?', *BBC News, US & Canada*, available online at: http://www.bbc.co.uk/news/magazine-11656214.
15. WikiLeaks (5 April, 2010) *Collateral Murder*, available online at: http://www.collateralmurder.com/
16. Kennedy, D. (27 July, 2010) *Guardian.co.uk-Comment is free*, available online at: http://www.guardian.co.uk/commentisfree/cifamerica/2010/jul/27/why-wikileaks-turned-to-press?&.
17. BFI Screenonline (n.d.) *That Was the Week That Was (1962–63)*, available online at: http://www.screenonline.org.uk/tv/id/583651/.
18. Whitlock, S. (28 August, 2008) 'Matt Lauer lauds liberal Jon Stewart: "respected and listened to"', *NewsBusters*, available online at: http://newsbusters.org/blogs/scott-whitlock/2008/08/28/matt-lauer-lauds-liberal-jon-stewart-respected-listened.
19. Deacon, M. (1 November, 2008) 'Bremner, Bird and Fortune: Silly Money', *Telegraph.co.uk*, available online at: http://www.telegraph.co.uk/culture/tvandradio/3562776/Bremner-Bird-and-Fortune-Silly-Money.html.
20. Ferguson, E. (5 August, 2001) 'Why Chris Morris had to make Brass Eye', *The Observer*, available online at: httpl://www.guardian.co.uk/uk/2001/aug/05/news.film.
21. Gibson, J. (11 January, 2000) 'Comics find Ali G is an alibi for racism',

*Guardian.co.uk*, available online at: http://www.guardian.co.uk/uk/2000/jan/11/race.janinegibson.

22.    Moran, C. (24 October, 2009) 'Is The Thick of It the best TV show ever made?', *The Times Online*, available online at: http://entertainment.timesonline.co.uk/tol/arts_and_entertainment/tv_and_radio/article6880814.ece?token=null&offset=0&page=1.

23.    European Graduate School (n.d.) *Jean Baudrillard. Integral Reality*, available online at: http://www.egs.edu/faculty/jean-baudrillard/articles/integral-reality/.

24.    Poole, S. (14 March, 2000) 'Meet the David Bowie of philosophy', *Guardian.co.uk*, available online at: http://www.guardian.co.uk/books/2000/mar/14/artsfeatures.davidbowie.

25.    Rowe, D. (21 June, 2010) 'Liar, liar: Why deception is our way of life', *New Scientist*, issue 2765, pp. 28–9.

26.    Kudos (2007) 'Behind the Scenes of Episode 5 – Camberwick Green', *Life on Mars – the complete series two. Disc 3 – episodes 5 & 6*, Contendor Home Entertainment.

27.    Kudos (2007) 'The End of Life on Mars', *Life on Mars – the complete series two. Disc 4 – episodes 7 & 8*, Contendor Home Entertainment.

# Truth and Trust: Broadcasting's Greatest 'Weapon'

6

This chapter considers the importance of, and challenges to, broadcasting's importance due to its reputation for telling the truth and being trusted by audiences. In particular it discusses:

■ Claims that broadcasting has had mixed success in reflecting the lives of 'ordinary' people.
■ The 'Gilligan Affair' and how this impacted on the relationship between the BBC, its audiences and government.
■ The so-called 'Sachsgate' affair and how this crystallised tensions between different public attitudes to 'risky' broadcasting.
■ Revelations of financial and banking problems and whether this suggests there can be too much 'truth'.

## The 'voice of the people'

Much of this chapter discusses examples of conflicts between broadcasters and others over the truthfulness of their output, but having excluded documentaries from the definition of Reality TV in the previous chapter, this one begins with a discussion about attempts to show *real*, real life. Broadcasters have often been criticised for failing to show and discuss the reality of most people's lives. Whilst the BBC has always made efforts to include the public in its programmes, to many observers its TV and radio programmes mostly consisted of one kind of elite or another talking *at* the public, rather than *to* them, or reflecting the lives of so-called 'ordinary' people. When the public were allowed to intrude, they were often patronised and certainly carefully controlled. The rhetoric of ITV's approach, explicitly in the official book commemorating its half-century – *ITV: The People's Channel*[1] – was that the commercial network was far more in tune with 'ordinary' people. This claim can of course be examined and criticised but can be seen to have manifested itself in a wide variety of programme genres. First, and most obviously, through the inclusion of *Vox Pops* or 'street interviews' on ITN and regional news programmes; second, and rather more contentiously, by the predominance of quiz shows and quiz elements within variety programmes, notably *Sunday Night at the London Palladium*; this and most intriguingly, in documentary programmes. One of the most fascinating and long-lasting examples of these are in Granada TVs *Seven Up* programmes, which were an offshoot of *World In Action*, discussed in Chapter 3. The idea was to illustrate and demonstrate the continuing significance of class and social upbringing by filming and interviewing a group of subjects from wide social backgrounds at, and from, the age of seven. The programme was produced by Michael Apted, who, despite subsequently going to Hollywood, has returned to Britain every seven years to direct each of the programmes, with *49 Up* being shown in 2005. These programmes constitute one of the most remarkable and arguably most moving pieces of television ever produced.

But it is interesting how little of even 'serious' television current affairs concentrate on the lives of supposedly 'ordinary' people. One of the exceptions was made in 1971 by John Pilger, a journalist who was to become much better known for investigative reports on the US military and sponsorship by western countries in genocide and dictatorships. *Conversations With a Working Man* was a very different type of documentary but in many ways just as radical.[2]

As well as this celebration of 'ordinariness', Pilger is adding to the arguments developed from the 1970s by academics such as those in the Glasgow Media Group and their *Bad News* series of critiques on the way that television journalism in particular 'frames' news stories – at a time of great industrial strife the academics were particularly interested in how strikes and other forms of labour disputes were reported. Theirs is a complex and well-researched critique that deserves further study but, at the risk of oversimplification, one of their main observations was that, whilst the workers were invariably portrayed as unreasonable and even threatening – usually filmed during robust mass meetings and their leaders shown in an aggressive and uncompromising manner and context – the bosses were almost invariably portrayed as the voice of of calm authority, and filmed in reassuring locations such as an office. The labour force was seen as a mass rabble – not consisting of mainly hard-working individuals living in, at best, modest circumstances and struggling to feed their family and generally 'make ends meet'.

## The Gilligan Affair

When it comes to credibility, however, it is clearly essential for broadcasters to have the reputation of being truthful and being an 'honest broker'. The BBC has a long – and one might even say noble – history of confrontations with the government of the day, often as a result of their different claims to 'truth'. Indeed, the Corporation to some extent prides itself on these rows, as it feels it shows the world that it is independent of government. In the past, the disputes have mostly either been because news and current affairs programmes had been seen as disloyal or even traitorous to the country, often because they gave voice and dignity to those identified by the government of the day as 'terrorists'. This especially applied to coverage of 'The Troubles' in Northern Ireland, which spilled over into the British mainland in the early 1970s, and to dramatised documentaries, such as 1965's *The War Game*, which had depicted in all too graphic detail the impact of a nuclear attack on Britain and which, following pressure from the government, was banned by the BBC for some 20 years.[3] The tone and language of news broadcasts had also been criticised, but the truthfulness and accuracy of the BBC's journalism had never before been so questioned as in the Gilligan Affair. Andrew Gilligan, a reporter for the daily breakfast-time Radio 4 programme *Today*, took part in a line rigged up to a makeshift studio at his home for an unscripted 'live' two-way (a type of interview with the presenter of a programme interviewing a fellow journalist), about the evidence the government had used for justifying the invasion of Iraq the previous month – an invasion which had failed to produce the weapons of mass destruction (WMD) that the UK government had, at least in part, used as its justification for joining the US-led invasion in 2003:

*Today* programme, BBC Radio 4, 29 May, 2003[4].
**John Humphrys:** The government's facing more questions this morning over its claims about weapons of mass destruction in Iraq. Our defence correspondent is Andrew Gilligan. This in particular, Andy, is Tony Blair saying they'd be ready to go within 45 minutes.
**Andrew Gilligan:** That's right, that was the central claim in his dossier which he published in September. The main case, if you like, against Iraq and the main statement of the British Government's belief of what it thought Iraq was up to. And what we've been told by one of the senior officials in charge of drawing up that dossier was that, actually the government probably knew that that 45-minute figure was wrong, even before it decided to put it in. What this person says is that a week before the publication date of the dossier, it was actually rather a bland production ... and Downing Street, our source says, ordered a week before publication, ordered it to be 'sexed up', to be made more exciting and ordered more facts to be, to be discovered.
**Humphrys:** When you say more facts to be discovered, does that suggest that they may not have been facts?
**Gilligan:** Well our source says that the dossier, as it was finally published, made the intelligence services unhappy ... because it didn't reflect the considered view they were putting forward – that's a quote from our source – and essentially, the 45-minute point was, was probably the most important thing that was added ...

**Humphrys:** Does any of this matter now – all these months later – the war's been fought and won?

**Gilligan:** Well the 45 minutes isn't just a detail, it did go to the heart of the government's case that Saddam was an imminent threat and it was repeated four times in the dossier, including by the Prime Minister himself in the foreword. So I think it probably does matter. Clearly, you know, if it was wrong – things are got wrong in good faith – but if they knew it was wrong before they actually made the claim, that's perhaps a bit more serious.

The fall-out from the broadcast was to lead to the death of a government scientist (the source of the story) and the resignations of Gilligan, the Chairman of the Corporation's Board of Governors and its Director-General (editor-in-chief). As can be seen from the transcript, the dispute came down to a simple question of whether the government – and the Prime Minister in particular – had lied, or at best exaggerated, the intelligence reports on the weapons and other military capabilities of the previous Iraqi regime in order to convince the public and parliamentarians that it was necessary to join the USA in an invasion of the country. A secondary but very important factor was the BBC's relationship with the Prime Minister's Director of Communications, Alastair Campbell, who was angry at what he saw as a consistent 'anti-war' bias across BBC journalism. This in turn had galvanised the BBC's senior editorial figures – not least the editor-in-chief himself, the Director-General, Greg Dyke – to clearly resist pressure from the government to adopt a more compliant and supportive line. Dyke was perhaps a uniquely popular figure among BBC employees, mainly because he was seen as such a doughty defender and supporter of his staff.

So, when Alastair Campbell reacted with fury over the Andrew Gilligan report, the response from the BBC at its highest level was not to question or investigate the sources, the wording and the overall accuracy and veracity of the report, but to dig in its heels and engage in full-blown 'trench warfare' with the government and its infamous 'spin machine'. Once the Corporation had refused to countenance any criticism or accept that there were any flaws in the Gilligan story as broadcast it had set itself up for a fall when the enquiry under Lord Hutton concluded that the government had *not* lied or exaggerated in its presentation of the intelligence briefings and, furthermore, that the Gilligan report lacked journalistic rigour. One of the issues that Hutton seemed unable to comprehend was that very often the BBC, along with all other types of journalistic outlets, report what *others* have told them, but that it is easy in a 'live', unscripted broadcast to forget to emphasise this, so that it appears that the BBC *itself* is making such claims. Furthermore, Hutton seemed incredulous that the BBC would put out such claims – which would be bound to be highly contentious – in a 'live', unscripted broadcast.

The convention of the 'two-way' – which forms the basis of most of the first 40 minutes or so of the *Today* programme – is a useful way to achieve the programme's 'agenda-setting' role and previewing what seem likely to be the day's main stories. The preparation for such broadcasts usually involves the reporter briefing the presenter or editor as to what she or he thinks is the main story and the presenter then effectively feeding questions to the reporter – rather as in the comedy duo the 'straight man' feeds lines to the 'funny man' – so what is presented as a spontaneous piece of radio is in fact carefully prepared. However, to prevent this contrived conversation sounding too stilted, it is normal not to precisely script the questions or answers. There is clearly, then, an inherent danger that what eventually is broadcast does not have the same rigour or preciseness of a well-crafted and fully scripted report. The fact that Gilligan rarely visited the newsroom at Television Centre – and indeed on the fateful morning, as with many other occasions, filed his report from home – may also have been a factor. The BBC Governors' official report,[5] following the affair, recommended that:

> While two-ways from home are acceptable, in the normal day-to-day output, they should not be the natural transmission source for contentious stories or stories involving serious allegations where preparation in the production office with the editorial team is essential.

The questions of truth, location and 'liveness' then are clearly linked. Had the enquiry by Lord Hutton and another by Lord Butler found that the Prime Minister had indeed knowingly deceived the British public then it would almost certainly have led to his resignation and probable electoral defeat for the Labour Party at the next general election.

So, the stakes were high in the battle over who was telling the truth. The BBC's credibility as an impartial and accurate purveyor of news was, of course, also at stake and ultimately it came down to a simple question: whom do you trust most, the government or the BBC?

There is little doubt of the public's view: a number of surveys into public attitudes were held in the year or so following the Hutton report, which were collated and discussed in an article by Barrie Gunter in 2005.[6] This included a YouGov poll in 2004, conducted shortly after the Hutton report was published, which showed that 67 per cent trusted the BBC a 'great deal' or a 'fair amount', compared with trust in the Labour government at just 31 per cent. In fact, with the exception of the 'red top' tabloid newspapers, trust in all the main journalistic outlets was greater than that for the government. One survey from the British Life and Internet Project[7] asked a sample, amongst other things, whether they thought that the BBC had been irreparably damaged by the criticisms contained in the Hutton report. Nearly three-quarters thought it had *not* been and a clear majority regarded the Gilligan episode as an untypical lapse in editorial standards. Even more significantly, 71 per cent in the same survey thought that, despite the journalistic shortcomings of Andrew Gilligan's report, the potential importance of the story was so great that it was right that it should be broadcast. Greg Dyke must have felt vindicated that two-thirds of respondents thought that it was not justified that he should have lost his job, and opinion was pretty evenly split as to whether Andrew Gilligan should have remained in post.

When the public was asked which TV news services it trusted the most, well over half named one provided by the BBC – with a third nominating BBC1 alone. Other services were named by only single figure percentages with, rather surprisingly, the US-based CNN being nominated more than the UK's ITV1 or Channel 5, and only just behind Sky News.

## 'Sachsgate'

The provenance of the second incident, some five-and-a-half years later, was even more bizarre – the transmission, on a Saturday night programme on BBC Radio 2, of a series of messages from two of its star presenters to the answer-phone (voicemail) of Andrew Sachs (an actor, then 78, best known for his portrayal as the hapless waiter Manuel in the classic 1970s sitcom *Fawlty Towers*). This led to the suspension of both presenters as well as the resignation of the station's Controller and several other BBC staffers.

The pairing of Russell Brand, who was certainly known – indeed was perhaps *best* known – for his 'edgy' style on TV, with his guest that fateful week, fellow *enfant terrible* Jonathan Ross (who was no longer so *enfant* and perhaps increasingly anxious to seem *terrible*, especially in the company of a presenter who had somewhat eclipsed him in broadcasting and who even had a movie career) should have set off 'alarm bells'. Against that, it was a show with a distinctly off-peak slot and relatively small audience and was often pre-recorded (as in this case), so allowing for content to be checked and, if necessary, 'referred up' to senior management before transmission:

> *Russell Brand Show*, BBC Radio 2, 18 October, 2008[8]
> (JR=Jonathan Ross; RB=Russell Brand)
> [To Andrew Sachs's answerphone]
> JR: [interrupting] He f****d your granddaughter!' (laughter) ... I'm sorry I apologise. Andrew I apologise ... I got excited, what can I say. It just came out.
> RB: Andrew Sachs, I did not do nothing with Georgina – oh no, I've revealed I know her name! Oh no, it's a disaster ... Abort, abort ... Put the phone down, put the phone down, code red, code red. [In 'Manuel' accent] I'm sorry Mr Fawlty, I'm sorry, they're a waste of space ...
> JR: ... the poor man sitting at home sobbing over his answer machine ... If he's like most people of a certain age he's probably got a picture of his grandchildren when they're young right by the phone. So while he's listening to the messages he's looking at a picture of her about nine on a swing.
> RB: She was on a swing when I met her. Oh no!

JR: And probably enjoyed her.

(The answerphone message plays again).

JR: (as the message plays): She was bent over the couch ...

RB (singing): I'd like to apologise for these terrible attacks –
Andrew Sachs. I'd like to show contrition to the max, Andrew Sachs.
I'd like to create world peace, between the yellow, whites and blacks,
Andrew Sachs, Andrew Sachs.
I said some things I didn't of oughta, like I had sex with your grand-
daughter.
But it was consensual and she wasn't menstrual.
It was consensual, lovely sex. It's full of respect. I sent her a text. I've
asked her to marry me ...
Oh Andrew Sachs, will you marry Jonathan? It sounds like he wants
to now.

JR: This has made it worse, I feel it's made it worse, you've trivialised the whole terrible incident. It started fine and then you went on about nonsense.

RB: You said you wanted to marry him ...

The offending section occurred because there seems to have been a lack of communication between members of the production team (the first of many in the various stages of the saga) over the booking of Sachs as a studio guest, who was expected to promote a forthcoming TV documentary, but who failed to turn up. The fact that the show was recorded more than 48 hours before transmission made the lack of judgement by various BBC staffers, including the Controller, hard to fathom, especially as the privacy of both Sachs and his granddaughter had clearly been breached, and there was, to say the least, a lack of clarity and transparency as to whether Sachs had given permission for the calls to be broadcast. Still, the fact that it received only two complaints from the public must have given all concerned hope that a major row had been avoided. Brand referred to the calls again during the following week's show, broadcast 'live', during which the control room staff were told of the content of the front-page splash story on the following day's *Mail On Sunday* (which, with its sister paper the *Daily Mail*, has been one of the Corporation's most vociferous critics). It was this story which then triggered the thousands of complaints from people, the vast majority of whom hadn't heard the original broadcast.

The Director-General was forced to abandon a family holiday and to fly back to London – it later transpired this was at licence-payers' expense – to deal with the ever deafening clamour, not least from the tabloid press, including demands for the sacking not only of the presenters but senior executives in the Corporation, even including the Director-General.

Reaction from the public, however, showed a generational divide. Producers on the Radio 5 Live phone-in noted that younger people were generally forgiving and had found the calls and the 'apology song' funny; older listeners were more critical. This split was also demonstrated on two sets of *vox pops*, recorded before the presenters' suspensions, and shown on TV news bulletins and on the Corporation's website. The first set came from mostly middle-aged to elderly people, who were queuing outside a studio to be in the audience for a recording of a BBC show:[9]

1. I think it's disgusting ... Jonathan Ross has got a mouth like a sewer.
2. ... should be sacked, the amount of money they get is ridiculous to talk like that.
3. Andrew Sachs deserves a lot more respect than that ...
4. It shouldn't have been let out, not if it was recorded ... the people above them should be done, because they were the people who let it go out.

But students at a college, aged about 16 to 18, generally had a much more relaxed attitude:[10]

1. ... I don't think there was a problem with what he did. I think it was quite funny and everyone should just lighten up.
2. I think it's been blown up out of all proportion. I think it started out as a joke and went too far. I think an apology should be sufficient.
3. They know what Russell Brand is like ... so why take it so seriously? It must be just his sense of humour.

After the resignation of Lesley Douglas, the Radio 2 Controller, the station's presenters were 'door-stepped' by BBC TV news as they left or arrived at the studios. They demonstrated a mixture of anger that a clearly much respected Controller had been lost and anxiety that the affair would damage the station's relationship with the public:[11]

> **Terry Wogan** (the then Breakfast Show host): The media's indulged in a feeding frenzy. The whole thing was really blown out of all proportion. Of course it was reprehensible ... let Radio 2 and my public and everyone else's public get back down to business now and let's raise some money for 'Children in Need' (the BBC's annual telethon and radio and telethon appeal that was to take place several weeks later).

> **Jeremy Vine** (host of weekday 12.00–2.00 p.m. slot which mixes current affairs, consumer advice and music): It'll be interesting to see how he [Ross] manages, given the damage done to this radio station ... we've lost a great Controller. I hope he's apologised to her.

> **Chris Evans** (the then host of the network's evening 'drive-time' show): We understand the seriousness of what's gone on. We all do, Jeez ... it shouldn't have happened. Andrew Sachs ... he doesn't want to be 78-years old and remembered for this ...

Both the presenters also left the Corporation's airwaves; Brand 'resigned' from his TV and radio work, saying he would not work for the BBC again as he was upset that the incident had made people 'unhappy', and Ross had his freelance contract suspended for three months. Fans of Ross and Brand fought back against the 'sackings'.[12] Over 4,000 signed an online petition asking the BBC to give the presenters back their jobs as the stunt was 'only intended as a joke', and on Facebook more than 7,500 people joined the group 'Reinstate Ross and Brand – Need over 18,000 to join'. Ross's TV chat show returned in early 2009, as did his weekly Radio 2 programme, but several months later – following complaints that he had made a 'homophobic' remark on his 'live' radio programme – BBC bosses decreed that in future it would have to be recorded, so that producers could check that the output was fully 'compliant'. Some critics believed that the knowledge that the show could be censored meant that it had lost its 'edge' and the feeling of 'live' unpredictability – one of the attractions of the show – had been lost and listening figures took a significant dip in the 'recorded era'.

## How could this crisis have happened?

The first significant factor was that those at the very top of the BBC did not have an entertainment programming background and therefore thought that editorial practices on entertainment-led radio networks were unlikely to be problematic. There were other factors that created the 'perfect storm' at the end of 2008: most significant of these was the public disquiet, again stirred up by the newspapers, of the pay given to the Corporation's star presenters. Reports that Jonathan Ross was paid £6 million for each of the three years of his contract to present a weekly Saturday morning programme on Radio 2, as well as his TV chat shows and movie review programmes, had not been denied. Worse, when it was pointed out that the fees paid to Ross would fund the salaries of around 1,000 journalists at a time when the Corporation was cutting back on its news staff, Ross countered that he was 'worth' such a sacrifice.[13] Such comments were hardly likely to endear him to the BBC's journalism corps and there is some anecdotal evidence that, following this, some of the journalists were waiting for the moment in which they could strike back. If so, the journalists were likely to find support and encouragement – as well as willing outlets – from their counterparts in other media. Part of the British press, and indeed other sections of the media, were becoming increasingly hostile to the BBC. This was partly because of its engagement in areas which were thought to be damaging to commercial media. Also, at a time when most of the media were under pressure because of falling advertising revenues – due to both an economic recession and structural changes caused by the rise of the internet – the BBC's secure licence fee income enabled the Corporation to be characterised as bloated, and insulated from the realities faced by the general public and media companies alike.

Finally, it was clear that the Corporation's 'stars' had succeeded in shifting the balance of power from BBC producers and managers to themselves and their agents. As the official report from the BBC Trust noted[14], the *Russell Brand Show* had originally been produced in-house, but from April 2008 was made by an independent production company – Vanity Projects – that was owned by Brand and some of his associates. Indeed, a BBC staff producer was 're-employed' by this production company and therefore had a conflict of loyalties and in line management.

In hindsight, this series of factors meant that a 'car crash' was waiting to happen. So far as fellow Radio 2 broadcaster Paul Gambaccini was concerned, it was entirely predictable: Brand's 'edgy' and unpredictable style and the power that he wielded – seemingly unchecked even by senior BBC staff – meant that sooner or later there would be disaster for the whole network.[15] Indeed, on the announcement that Brand would be presenting a weekly show, he had given such a warning in a note to Controller Lesley Douglas. The affair had significant consequences – not least the loss of an evidently much-loved Controller – and, perhaps, above all, by the effect the whole business had on the image of the station and its relationship with the listeners. The BBC Trust singled out the incident(s), which it called 'a spectacular own-goal', for special opprobrium in its next annual report.[16]

The BBC, as with other broadcasters, had long been used to controversies caused by swear words and other forms of discourse that self-appointed moral guardians deemed to be offensive and unacceptable. In the previous year or two there was also a series of (by global standards) minor deceptions of the public, including 'fake' competition winners in radio quizzes, in the telephone voting for winners of TV awards (this also including a Ross-hosted event on the main commercial channel) and, perhaps most shockingly, on the much venerated children's magazine programme *Blue Peter*, which had also been subject to a somewhat bizarre and unlikely scandal involving the public's vote on the name of one of the programme's resident pets.

These were hardly issues on which the fate of nations rests and – in comparison with the very real battles over what was true in matters of war and peace, discussed above in the so-called Gilligan Affair – of no significance in the public sphere. But, in matters small and great, the almost sacred covenant of the BBC with its audience had been broken and its reputation tainted. In July 2008 the Corporation was fined a total of £400,000 by regulator Ofcom over a string of such incidents between 2005 and 2007.[17]

At the end of 2008 the Corporation launched a major survey of public attitudes towards taste and decency, including swearing and invasions of privacy. The report, published in June 2009,[18] unsurprisingly stressed that broadcasting which involved humiliating and intrusive 'stunts' should play no part in the Corporation's output, and re-emphasised the generational gap in attitudes.

The ramifications of the affair continued throughout 2009. Charles Moore, a former editor of a conservative newspaper, the *Daily Telegraph*, and by then a columnist for both that paper and the right-of-centre weekly magazine, *The*

*Spectator,* was so enraged by Ross's behaviour and the Corporation continuing to employ him, that he engaged in a very public defiance of the television licence authorities, announcing that he would refuse to buy a licence until Ross was removed. He provided regular updates to his readers on what he regarded as the bluff and bullying of the licence collectors. Moore seemed to be frustrated that the authorities did not prosecute him, denying him the chance to refuse to pay the fine, which would normally result in a prison sentence. His apparent determination to be a TV licence martyr was frustrated by the authorities, who pointed out in letters to Moore, which he reproduced in his columns, that they had no control over the content of BBC broadcasts.

The wider context of this public spat was that there were increasing signs in this period that the then Conservative opposition would end the licence fee if it came into government. Trust in the BBC was undermined in late 2009 and early 2010 not only because of the scandals described above but because of the severe criticism and even outrage when the salaries and expenses of senior executives were revealed. Although the Corporation sought to defend these, utilizing a similar argument that it had employed over the fees paid to Ross and other stars – that they earned less than those in equivalent positions in the commercial sector – this approach was greatly undermined by the recession and consequent belt-tightening in every other area of broadcasting. The BBC's Director-General, Mark Thompson, sounded increasingly flustered on the issue when challenged on the *Today* programme by the crime novelist, P. D. James (who is also a Baroness and a former Governor of the BBC) on the day of her 'guest editorship' of the programme.[19]

The *dénouement* of the 'Sachsgate' affair, however, did not occur until shortly after that interview, in early January 2010, when, to the surprise of all but a few senior managers and intimates, Ross announced that he would not be seeking a further BBC contract when it expired in July of that year. Ross made no reference to 'Sachsgate' in his statement and also said that his decision was not due to dissatisfaction with the widely publicised policy of the BBC to offer its stars much lower fees when it came to renewing their contracts. Indeed, the Corporation confirmed that it had not even begun contract negotiations, so there was much speculation about the reasons behind this decision. It was a development that certainly caught the attention of the media. For a time, in a period which had seen a challenge to the then Prime Minister's leadership and when the country was in the grip of its worst winter for about 30 years, the story even led national news broadcasts, including BBC Radio 4's daily late afternoon current affairs programme, *PM*. The presenter, Eddie Mair, told listeners that the 'Sachsgate' issue had generated more comments on the programme's blog than any other story before or since. The programme[20] included an interview with Charles Moore, who seemed less than satisfied about the announcement. The interview by Mair with the BBC's Creative Director, Alan Yentob, starkly exposed the gulf between the mindset of one of the Corporation's senior executives and one of its most prominent conservative critics. The following extract provides a flavour of this revealing encounter:

> **Mair:** Charles Moore ... thinks there's something a bit whiffy about how all of this has come out today – he thinks it's a bit of a stitch-up.
> **Yentob:** (sarcastically) Oh, does he now? Oh golly, I have to worry about what Charles Moore thinks, don't I? Why doesn't he just get on and pay his licence fee, or stop listening to Radio 4 and Radio 3 and all those others things for which he's bound to pay.

When Mair upbraided Yentob for his attitude towards what he called: 'a respected journalist ... who has a very public platform and who has had reason to criticise the BBC', Yentob reiterated the steps taken by the Corporation, both in the immediate aftermath of the 'Sachsgate' incident, and then in reviewing its taste and decency guidelines. Concluding that the BBC had not taken it lightly he stated that he didn't feel: 'the need to be lectured to by Charles Moore, no'.

It is possible that Yentob's attitude was untypical of the BBC's senior exec-utives, but it seems unlikely. This interview exposed a gulf in attitudes between the 'two Britains' outlined by Andrew Marr in Chapter 7 and not just between two sections of the media. The online comments on national newspaper sites revealed very starkly divided viewpoints on Ross's departure. (Moore announced in July 2010 that he had resumed paying his TV licence following Ross's final TV and radio shows for the BBC; Ross was signed to present a new chat show on the commercial network, ITV1, from the autumn/fall of 2011 and in November 2010 it was announced he'd made a deal with Endemol, the independent production company that had made *Big Brother*, to make programmes for Channel 4).

What is interesting about the 'Sachsgate' affair is that in an age of supposed fragmentation of audiences in a multi-channel, multimedia world, specific programmes and personalities can still be a cause of such national soul-search-ing. This point is further explored, but by a very different programme and for very different reasons, in the next example.

## Can there be such a thing as too *much* 'truth'?

The demands and expectations on journalists working in the 24-hour world of broadcast news and supporting websites have led to inaccurate stories, and claims that journalists often 'hype up' the mundane in order to create a feeling that the viewer must stay tuned or they will miss something of vital importance. Specialist journalists, who nurture contacts and receive many 'off the record' briefings often get the first inkling of the story long before it hits the airwaves. Sometimes these stories can have a profound effect in a country and even inter-nationally. This is particularly true of stories on finance and business. In the

1960s and 1970s, journalists were under almost constant pressure not to report speculation about possible devaluations of the British pound, as such talk could be a self-fulfilling prophecy. Speculation that a company is in financial difficulties, whether true or not, can easily lead to panicky selling of its shares, thus turning speculation into reality.

In 2007 and 2008, as the western world's financial system faced collapse, the BBC's Business Editor, Robert Peston, found himself accused of being instrumental in directly causing the first run on a British bank in 140 years.[21] In September 2007, Peston broke the story that the Northern Rock bank was asking for emergency funding from the government. Within hours, queues had formed at the bank's branches, with anxious customers desperately trying to withdraw their deposits and savings. Just over a year later, Peston broke the even more sensational story that the UK taxpayer was to bail out large chunks of the British banking sector, which would otherwise collapse. The Royal Television Society named Peston TV journalist of the year.[22] The judges said he:

> owned the story of the credit crunch and its impact on the whole economy ... produced probably the most sustained run of scoops and exclusives in the history of broadcast news in the UK. It would not be an exaggeration to say that a large part of the nation hung on the winner's words every night; he personally revived appointment to view.

Naturally, Peston's honours and fame provoked some jealousy amongst his rivals, with some later claiming that they had also received indications of severe problems in the banking sector but had decided not to publish or broadcast them. But later Peston told a Treasury select committee that he had acted responsibly. Peston's scoops on what is certainly one of the most significant stories, and one with immense ramifications, of the early part of the 21st century, raises questions about ethics in journalism and the pressure on journalists to produce exclusives. These questions are even more pertinent when they apply to a country's leading public broadcaster, when it could certainly be argued that such an organisation has a greater responsibility to consider the effects of its journalism and programmes than would be the case with other media organisations. However, the alternative – that Peston learned of these developments but decided not to broadcast them – would also have had consequences, possibly attracting much greater opprobrium. For example, had he known that Northern Rock was about to collapse and the government had decided not to intervene and the bank *had* collapsed, tens of thousands of depositors and savers could have lost their money and would no doubt be angrily demanding why the BBC had not warned them. There is a broader question about the public's right to know about government policy and discussions, especially considering the some £850 billion of taxpayers' money that was to be put at stake in order to rescue the UK banking system.

There is also the factor that if the public were to believe that certain dramatic events were happening behind-the-scenes, but journalists had agreed not to reveal them, all sorts of damaging rumours would be likely to gain credence, which would otherwise likely be quashed by government denials. In other words, if the public has faith that journalists, especially in the broadcast sector which, in the UK at least, is required to be accurate and impartial, are constantly 'on the case' they may feel assured that all is well unless and until they hear and see to the contrary. Indeed, it can be argued that far from Peston being irresponsible in breaking these stories, the real criticism for journalists in all media was that they did not highlight the dangerous levels of public and private credit and debt which were building up in the UK, USA and many other industrialised countries. It is also fair to say that the small number of politicians who did raise these concerns, notably the then finance spokesman for the UK's Liberal Democratic Party, Vince Cable, did not find much interest from journalists and their editors.

## Notes and references

1.   Cherry, S. (2005) London: Reynolds & Hearn.
2.   *Ibid.*, p. 276.
3.   Watkins, P. (2009) *The War Game*, Peter Watkins Films, available online at: http://pwatkins.mnsi.net/warGame.htm.
4.   BBC News (2003) *Full text: Gilligan's Today reports*. 24 July, 2003, available online at: http://news.bbc.co.uk/1/hi/uk_politics/3090681.stm.
5.   BBC Board of Governors (2004) *The Neil Report*, available online at: http://www.bbc.co.uk/info/reports/pdf/neil_report.html.
6.   Gunter, B. (2005) *Trust in the news on television*, Centre for Mass Communications Research, University of Leicester, Leicester, UK.
7.   British Life and Internet Project (2009), available online at: www.britishlife project.co.uk/hutton.doc.
8.   Times Online (27 October, 2008) *Transcript: 'offensive' Russ and Brand calls,* available online at: http://entertainment.timesonline.co.uk/tol/arts_and_entertainment/tv_and_radio/article5023135.ece.
9.   BBC News, UK (29 October, 2008) 'Jonathan Ross has "a mouth like a sewer"', available online at: http://news.bbc.co.uk/1/hi/uk/7697598.stm.
10.   BBC News, UK (29 October, 2008) 'It's been blown out of all proportion', available online at: http://news.bbc.co.uk/1/hi/uk/7697622.stm.
11.   BBC News, UK (31 October, 2008) 'Radio 2 DJs react to calls row', available online at: http://news.bbc.co.uk/1/hi/entertainment/7702825.stm.
12.   McMahon, K. (31 October, 2008) 'Fans rally behind Ross and Brand', *Broadcast,* available online at: http://www.broadcastnow.co.uk/news/multi-platform/news/fans-rally-behind-ross-and-brand/1912462.article.
13.   Holt, R. (6 December, 2007) 'Jonathan Ross "worth 1,000 journalists"', *Telegraph.co.uk,* available online at: http://www.telegraph.co.uk/culture/film/3669730/Jonathan-Ross-worth-1000-BBC-journalists.html.
14.   BBC Trust (November 2008) *Editorial Standards Findings: Appeals and editorial issues considered by the Trust's Editorial Standards Committee,* available online

at: http://news.bbc.co.uk/nol/shared/bsp/hi/pdfs/21_11_08_brand_ross_moyles. pdf.

15.  Plunkett, J. (31 October, 2008) 'Paul Gambaccini in tirade against hiring of "timebomb" Russell Brand', *Guardian.co.uk*, available online at: http://www. guardian.co.uk/media/2008/oct/31/russell-brand-lesleydouglas.

16.  BBC Trust (June 2009). *Annual Report and Accounts 2008/09. Part One: BBC Trust's Review and Assessment for 2008/09: 4*, available online at: http:// downloads.bbc.co.uk/annualreport/pdf/bbc_trust_2008_09.pdf.

17.  Parker, R. (30 July, 2008) 'BBC fined £400,000 over phone-in fakery', *Broadcastnow*, available online at: http://www.broadcastnow.co.uk/news/multi-platform/news/bbc-fined400000-over-phone-in-fakery/1769209.article.

18.  BBC Trust (June 2009) *Taste, Standards and the BBC – Public attitudes to morality, values and behaviour in UK broadcasting*, available online at: http://www.bbc.co.uk/info/running/reports/pdf/taste_standards_june2009.pdf.

19.  The programme had established a tradition of inviting prominent figures in the arts, politics and other areas of life to edit the programme during the normally quiet period of news between Christmas and New Year.

20.  BBC Radio 4 (7 January, 2009) *PM*.

21.  Gerard, J. (21 November, 2008) 'Robert Peston: we should teach our children finance', *Telegraph.co.uk*, available online at: http://www.telegraph.co.uk/finance/financetopics/financialcrisis/3496037/Robert-Peston-We-should-teach-our-children-finance.html.

22.  Digital TV Blog (27 February, 2009) 'Robert Peston leads triumphant BBC at RTS awards', available online at: http://www.digital-tv.co.uk/blog/robert-peston-leads-triumphant-bbc-at-rts-awards.html.

# Broadcasting Bias

7

This chapter considers the question of bias in broadcasting; political, cultural and in the subjects debated. In particular it discusses:

- Competing claims that broadcasting and broadcasters serve the interests of the powerful and, alternatively, is part of a liberal–left 'conspiracy'.
- The pressures on broadcasters to remain impartial after the inconclusive 2010 UK general election.
- Clashes over the inclusion of the British National Party on the BBC's *Question Time*.
- The style and influence of Talk Radio and 'shock jocks'.
- Broadcasting's alleged poor coverage of science.

## Creatures of the dominant ideology, or part of a liberal–left conspiracy?

As we saw in Chapter 1, from its beginnings, broadcasting has been attacked from both the left and right of political views. This chapter explores both sets of claims.

Many on the left have accused mainstream broadcasting of being tools of the powerful elites in society. In this perspective, broadcasters do not need to be told which views and attitudes to promote they do it 'voluntarily', not even realizing what they are doing. Others, notably Herman and Chomsky developed the 'propaganda model' – the mass media provides a uniform, partial interpretation of events, in the interests of powerful forces in society. The political economy theory states that the mass media works with political forces in the interests of, specifically, the major economic interests, notably the corporations. Others, such as the sociologist Paul Lazarsfeld in his hugely influential works from the 1930s, argued that it is not a simple matter of a sender (the mass media) sending a message, which is then picked up on by the receiver (the listener/viewer). There were many other influences in society, including those regarded as better informed than most, who would interpret and then pass on their interpretation to others; the so-called 'two-step flow'.

One of the main problem, and disputed, areas is in the field of current affairs broadcasting. Whilst it is relatively easy to achieve balance and due impartiality in news – at least within a straightforward party political context – by giving equal time and weight to opposing views, it is much more difficult in a programme which, by its nature, needs a thesis; an idea or theme which directs the narrative and the selection of material and how 'evidence' is used. Such programmes, many programme makers and critics agree, are inevitably going to be biased. Michael Green, a former producer of the intellectually rigorous BBC Radio 4 current affairs strand *Analysis* (and who was later Controller of the network), said in an edition to mark the programme's 40th birthday:[1]

All programme making is subjective. That's the nature of it. It's somebody sitting in front of a microphone and saying: 'I've been out, I've talked to a lot of people and this is my assessment of the evidence I can bring before you. You make your own judgements, but this is what I think'.

Furthermore, Michael Green believes there is little doubt that the BBC in the 1970s was left-wing:

I think if you were to describe in a thumbnail the ethos of the BBC at that time it would be sort of liberal–left progressive … Thinkers of the right were relatively hidden, they didn't appear much in broadcasting.

But it was *Analysis* that broke that consensus, to such an extent that questions were asked in Parliament, with one Labour MP accusing the producer of being a danger to society. Former producer Fraser Steel told the anniversary edition:

There was certainly a purpose to go beyond the *bien-pensant*[2] agenda. The default position was post-war consensus … the class of '68 by the time I came on board had made its way through the education system and into … positions in the media and in academe. For a time, it seemed that there was no such thing as conservative thought … any critique of received ideas or established ideas which wasn't explicitly from an explicitly Marxist perspective … was … suspected of being right-wing.

Hugh Chignell, Associate Professor of Broadcasting History at the University of Bournemouth, who has studied the programme in depth[3] said in the anniversary edition that although it did have right-wingers amongst its staff and contributors, they were also very professional:

> They believed passionately that it was important that news and current affairs were impartial. However with hindsight … you can detect the right-leaning nature of the programme and in particular a sympathy for the ideas that subsequently became known as Thatcherism.

Critics of the BBC's political approach would certainly say that this was an exception, and one which, moreover, was contained in the somewhat rarefied atmosphere of a rather 'heavyweight', evening programme on a speech network. The main strand in all these criticisms (similar to Marxist critiques from the other end of the spectrum) is not that the BBC staff deliberately attempt to deceive the audience or propagandise – in fact they are usually convinced that they are being unbiased. Rather, it is their background, often from a very narrow social, educational and even geographical range, and the fact of course that they work for a public sector institution, not a commercial enterprise, which leads to a personal mindset and group culture that takes it as 'read' that certain positions are correct and even 'good', whilst others are simply wrongheaded and even dangerous. In the past, the BBC argued that as it was attacked from the right and the left, it must be unbiased; failing to acknowledge that what has been called the 'soggy centre' is in itself a bias. Furthermore, the political centre of gravity has moved markedly rightwards since the late 1970s but the associated ideas for smaller government and greater free enterprise seem to have passed by the majority of the Corporation's employees.

This critique found an especially vocal ally with former BBC journalist Robin Aitken, who worked for the Corporation for 25 years, across many different levels, from local radio to the *Today* programme. His 2007 book[4] provided accounts of BBC liberal–left bias and of a culture that rejects, and ostracises and marginalises anyone who fail to 'sign up' to these values. Aitken provides many examples of his encounters with senior BBC staff in his efforts to at least prompt some genuine self-examination of the alleged bias. Robin Aitken argues this bias was particularly evident in the Corporation's coverage of the European Union. The reason for paying particular attention to the 'European question' in terms of BBC impartiality is not only that there are 'pro' and 'anti' camps to be found in both the Labour and Conservative parties, which makes the normal balancing act of political coverage unusually tricky, but that it is one of the few instances where the accusations of bias come from only one direction – those who are 'Eurosceptic'.

A cross-party think tank, Global Britain, employed a research organisation to look at the BBC's coverage of the announcement of the Labour government's sudden reversal of its policy over a referendum on the planned European Constitution. Minotaur Media Tracking selected the six most important BBC news outlets over a 27-hour period. The findings were summarised as there being a 'consistent imbalance of 2:1 in favour of the Europhile perspective'.[5]

But this bias in favour of the Euro-enthusiast/Euro-tepid approach was not confined to this single issue. As Aitken notes, over five years Minotaur analysed more than 2,000 hours of radio and television and produced 15 separate reports, all of which were sent to the BBC. Their main conclusions were that there had been:

- An overall bias towards Europhile speakers in the ratio of 2:1.
- An untoward emphasis on Conservative Party divisions over Europe and an under-representative of Labour Eurosceptics.
- Scant analysis of the Eurosceptic alternatives such as renegotiation or complete withdrawal.
- Poor journalistic standards where erroneous information favourable to the Europhile position had gone unchallenged.

In 2005 the BBC governors published a report from a committee it had set up under Lord Wilson, which specifically tackled the persistent allegations about this bias. The committee was balanced between known pro and anti-EU members and concluded (in part) that:[6]

> while we have found no evidence of deliberate bias in BBC coverage of EU matters, we have found that there is a widespread perception that it suffers from certain forms of cultural and unintentional bias. It is striking how much agreement there is about this among groups who otherwise disagree passionately about almost everything else to do with Europe. We think there is substance in their concern ... it seems to be the result of a combination of factors including an institutional mindset, a tendency to polarise and over-simplify issues, a measure of ignorance of the EU on the part of some journalists and a failure to report issues which ought to be reported, perhaps out of a belief that they are not sufficiently entertaining. Whatever the cause in particular cases, the effect is the same for the outside world and feels like bias.

Aitken went 'head to head' with the BBC's then Head of News, Peter Horrocks, at a public meeting in 2007. This in turn prompted Horrocks to note in his BBC Editor's blog that, although there was widespread public trust in the BBC, including readers of right-of-centre newspapers, establishing and maintaining true impartiality was becoming increasingly complex.[7]

But Horrocks's blog also highlighted another, and in many ways more problematic, issue for the BBC – its operation 'within the parameters of formal politics'. The new media poses a challenge to all the established institutions because it bypasses the tried and tested (perhaps to destruction) routes for political activism of representative democracy: the raising of concerns via Members of Parliament or other representatives and the mechanisms of political parties in forming manifestos and fighting elections on a broad policy offering, which could be accepted or rejected by the electorate at the mandated time. But new media does not accept these procedures: it is more ragged, more diffuse and much less respectful of individuals, institutions and processes. The BBC is in a particularly difficult position in all this, being a creature of Parliament and operating under a Royal Charter. Can it both reflect, let alone facilitate, the so-called 'new politics', whilst maintaining its position as part of the broad establishment?

Aitken's allegations of bias have been supported, directly or indirectly by a number of other BBC journalists, notably Andrew Marr, the Corporation's former Political Editor and a man with impeccable liberal credentials, being a former editor of the liberal–left newspaper *The Independent*. In his historical account of journalism, *My Trade*, Marr[8] explains the bias of the BBC as due to complex but readily observed factors, mainly to do with the Corporation's place as a public service institution and the make-up of its staff.

Marr includes Northern Ireland in his examples, and Aitken devotes a chapter of his book to allegations that the BBC's Northern Ireland journalists were culpable in not just bias but outright censorship (of beatings and shootings by Republican groups) in order that the 'peace process' not be jeopardised. Taken together, this evidence is damning of the BBC of both conscious and unconscious bias – including subjects of the most fundamental importance to British citizens. The BBC Trust has defined this problem[9] in the broad terms of impartiality and has suggested a simile, whereby the constituents that make up impartiality can be contained in a number of 'bottles': Accuracy, Balance, Context, Distance, Evenhandedness, Fairness, Objectivity, Openmindedness, Rigour, Self-Awareness, Transparency and Truth. Noting that the original meaning of partial was *in*completeness, the report suggests that Completeness be the thirteenth constituent – in other words, all points of view must be considered. Crucially, the BBC Trust is adamant that impartiality cannot be found by locating the centre ground – the old nostrum that if you are offending both the right and the left of the political spectrum then you are probably getting it right – is no longer sufficient.[10]

This was put to the test during the extraordinary, dramatic period following the UK's inconclusive 2010 general election, in which no one party had gained an overall majority. The five days of fast-changing post-election negotiations between the three parties – unprecedented in post-Second World War British politics – was, of course, ideal for the rolling TV news channels. UK broadcasters have to be politically impartial at all times, but never are they more scrutinised for this than during election campaigns. In this strange period *after* the campaign, however, the strain in maintaining impartiality seemed to tell on Sky News – the biggest shareholder of which at the time was Rupert Murdoch and his family, whose UK newspapers fully supported the Conservatives. In this interregnum, Sky News's Kay Burley had a hostile encounter with protestors outside the Liberal Democrat HQ, who were urging the party leader not to give up his demands for electoral reform as the price for any coalition deal. This led to an effective social media campaign, with protestors quickly armed with new posters – and slogans – urging: 'Sack Kay Burley, watch the BBC!'

During this fraught and fast-moving period there was also an on-air spat between the famously combative former Communications Director for the Labour government(s), Alastair Campbell, and Sky News Political Editor Adam Boulton, who were both being interviewed by Sky News presenter Jeremy Thompson:[11]

> **Campbell**: Adam, you're obviously upset that David Cameron is not Prime Minister.
> **Boulton**: I'm not upset …
> **Campbell**: You are, you probably are.
> **Thompson**: [laughs]
> **Boulton**: [voice raised] Don't keep casting aspersions on what I think. I am commenting … don't keep saying what I think.
> **Campbell**: This is live on television – dignity, dignity.
> **Boulton**: Don't keep telling me what I think. This is what you do, you come on … you say no one won the election. I'm fed up with you telling me what I think …
> **Thompson**: Alastair, you are being provocative and unnecessarily so …
> **Campbell**: Me?
> **Boulton**: Yes.
> **Campbell**: And you are elected are you?
> **Boulton**: No, but …
> **Thompson**: Gentlemen, gentlemen.
> **Boulton**: You are the one who has cooked this up with Peter Mandelson [Cabinet Minister, former EU Commissioner, and regarded as one of the architects of 'New Labour']
> **Campbell**: Oh my God, unbelievable. Adam calm down, calm down. [camera pans away]
> **Boulton**: [out of vision] I actually care about this country.
> **Campbell**: You think I don't care?
> **Boulton**: [inaudible]
> **Campbell**: Adam, you are a pompous little arse.

## Bias in wider cultural/societal attitudes

Conservative critics in the UK have also long had the BBC in their sights for, in their view, actively undermining respect and deference in society and under-mining family life with, they claim, clearly demonstrated negative conse-quences. Whilst the liberal–left may have been forced to give up their campaigns for a socialist society, given its clear rejection by the electorate and the collapse of communist states in Europe, the 1960s generation had, it was claimed, won the so-called 'culture wars'. This victory, runs the argument, was one not primarily in news and current affairs – where blatant propaganda could be more easily detected – but in the broad run of dramas, comedies and other forms of culture. It certainly tends to be the case that, artistic types working in the culture industries do not tend to be of a centre-right conservative disposition and it is very hard to find centre-right viewpoints expressed in comedy programmes in the UK. Since the alternative comedy movement in the 1980s, the viewpoint of comedians and comedy writers on weekly comedy panel shows such as BBC TV's *Have I Got News For You?* has been almost exclusively left of centre and one with an almost identikit set of predictable views on a wide range of topics.

When an 'old school' entertainer, Bruce Forsyth, the then 82-year-old host of the Corporation's hit TV show *Strictly Come Dancing* made comments in support of a professional dancer who had made an off-air comment widely perceived to be racist, he was met with howls of protest. A bewildered Forsyth said that the offending word – 'Paki' – was surely just a shortened form of Pakistani and urged the nation to have a sense of perspective.[12] However, although he argued that the comment used in this context was different from when the word was used with 'malicious intent', he perhaps failed to fully appreciate that it was often used by violent racists, who talked of, and sometimes used it as a prelude to, 'Paki bashing.' This seemed to be a clash of experiences and culture; Forsyth is perhaps more used to the golf courses of the leafy suburbs of England than the modern, metropolitan-urban 21st-century Britain of a multicultural, younger generation, which is sensitive to perceived insults to minorities of all types.

The context of the Forsyth incident was that earlier in 2009, Carol Thatcher, the daughter of the former Prime Minister and winner of the fifth series of the Reality TV show *I'm a Celebrity …*, had been sacked from the Corporation's daily TV magazine programme *The One Show*, for – again – a comment made off-air, this time about one of the show's guests, a black, African–French tennis player, whom she likened to a 'golliwog'. This was the name of a favourite toy for many generations of British children, which was also the symbol of a brand of jams and featured in many children's stories, but came to be regarded as an offensive image, with imperialist and racist overtones. Again, Carol Thatcher complained that she had meant no offence in using the term, pointing out that it had been used in a private situation (in the 'Green Room' after the broadcast) and, had offered a 'fulsome apology'.[13]

## America, too!

Complaints that Britain and other parts of Europe are overly influenced by American culture and values is, rather perversely, reflected in a similar argument about liberal–left bias in the USA. In an eerily similar diatribe to Aitken's on the BBC, former staff journalist at CBS News, Bernard Goldberg, has written an excoriating account[14] of his experiences at the organisation and observations about how certain are stories never reach the network newscasts because, he alleges, they run counter to the liberal view of life and the world.

An example of this is the claim that those American schoolchildren (and by extension we could apply this to British children) who do relatively poorly in educational terms and indulge in negative, antisocial and generally unfortunate forms of behaviour, do so largely because both parents (if there are two parents present) are out at work. As Goldberg puts it, the journalists in network TV news fail to 'connect the dots'.

There is little doubt that in Goldberg – an Emmy award-winning journalist – touched a nerve with his book and the public appear to have been voting with their feet as they desert the main newscasts on the three original networks and migrate to Fox with its right-wing, populist approach. By the end of the 'noughties' this network was more trusted than the longer established networks, some 50 per cent ahead of the next most trusted network, CNN and over three times as trusted as any of the 'big three' networks – NBC, CBS and ABC.[15] Fox was, however, recognised by the survey as having a conservative bias. The public broadcasting system (which the Fox network and its co-riders in the right-wing syndicated talk radio shows would describe as irredeemably liberal–left) believed that Fox News, especially its talk shows with Glenn Beck, became enormously influential in public perceptions of President Obama.[16] The relentless tirades against the President resulted in an increasing number of US citizens believing that Obama was not born in the USA (a constitutional requirement for Presidential office) and that he was a Muslim.[17]

## Impartiality and the limits to 'free speech'

In October 2009, the limits of free speech and the requirements of impartiality by public service broadcasters in the UK produced a further, 'perfect storm', that caused the BBC to be roundly condemned by senior members of the government party of the day, as well as other commentators and public figures. The source of this furore was the appearance as a panellist on the Corporation's weekly TV current events discussion programme, *Question Time*, of Nick Griffin, the leader of the British National Party (BNP), widely viewed as a racist organization, due to its stated policy of returning Britain to what it termed its indigenous – by which it seems to mean exclusively white – peoples.

Thanks to a collapse in the Labour vote and a proportional representation closed party list system, rather than any significant increase in support, the BNP had made an electoral breakthrough in that June's elections to the European Parliament, gaining nearly a million votes and two candidates elected as MEPs – including Griffin, who topped the BNP list in north-west England. The BBC said they were obliged to offer the party a place on a panel in order to comply with the Corporation's obligations to 'due impartiality'. The mainstream parties lifted their previous 'no shared platform with the BNP' policy and Television Centre in west London was besieged by anti-fascist protestors – some of whom managed to storm the security gates. The Centre went into 'lockdown' but the recording of the programme went ahead and the broadcast gained the largest audience, eight million, in the show's 30 years' history (this is remarkable, considering that, when it started, there were just three TV channels, compared with today's 300 plus). The programme also became one of the most viewed programmes of the year on the web catch-up service, the iPlayer.

The main arguments against Griffin's appearance were twofold. One was that the BNP was not a normal political party, as it was the only party of any significance which had a racist policy and it should not therefore be treated in a similar way to other minority parties who had also gained seats in local councils and in the European Parliament. To do so, ran the argument, was to risk normalising what, to most people, was a very objectionable approach to politics and one which, furthermore, would almost certainly lead to increasing attacks on ethnic minorities. On the day of the broadcast, the former Mayor of London, Ken Livingstone, warned the BBC that it would be morally responsible if there were such a 'spike' in attacks, which, he claimed, had been identified on previous occasions when anti-immigrant views had been expressed in the broadcast media. The other main objection was that, whilst it might be acceptable to subject Griffin to rigorous interviewing by the likes of John Humphrys (on Radio 4's *Today* programme) or Jeremy Paxman (on BBC 2 television's *Newsnight*), it was another to include him on a programme in which he could both make statements, unchallenged by a professional interviewer, and where he would probably be asked to opine on less contentious areas, articulating views that might be supported by moderate voters. But the BBC protested that it was not within its powers to make fine judgements of that sort. If Parliament wished to ban a party from the airwaves then it should do so and of course the BBC would comply with such an order, but if the party was allowed to contest elections and received a certain level of support it could not deny it the opportunity to participate in a range of current affairs programmes.

In the event, almost all the programme was devoted to an examination, and mostly condemnation, of the views of Griffin and his party. This allowed him to complain the following day that he had been subjected to a 'lynch mob' outside the Television Centre, whilst at the same time boasting that the programme had been the party's best ever recruitment drive, with a least 3,000 people pledging their support online during the programme. Polls taken in a daily or two after the broadcast seemed to indicate that there *had* been an increase in support for the party, albeit from a low national base, and a further fifth of voters said they would 'seriously consider' voting BNP.[18] However, polls also showed that over two-thirds of the public supported the BBC's decision to invite Griffin on to the programme. It seems as if the British public's respect for the importance of free speech and open discussion trumped any queasiness over Griffin and his policies.

The row continued over the next few days in most of the media, and two weeks later the Cabinet minister Peter Hain – who had campaigned against South Africa's apartheid in the 1970s – appeared on the programme and rounded on the BBC and the programme's presenter and chair, David Dimbleby, saying the Corporation should 'hang its head in shame' for giving the BNP a platform. Certainly, Griffin did not appear to give the Corporation any credit for his invitation, condemning it as 'part of a thoroughly unpleasant ultra-leftist establishment which, as we've seen here tonight, doesn't want the English to be recognised as an existing people'.[19]

Many of the comments on the blog of the programme's executive editor, Gavin Allen, were to some extent sympathetic with Griffin's complaints against the BBC – especially that the audience had been packed with liberal, metropolitan and untypical representatives of the British population – the top posting reading:[20]

> Seems to me that the BBC must have used the Lib Dem party membership list to select the audience – Yes, I'm afraid the bias was that obvious.
>
> As for the 'rent-a-mob' outside the BBC, well how ironic that they were claiming to be pro-democracy but were trying to stop AN ELECTED MEP from stating his parties [sic] views on OUR PUBLIClY [sic] FUNDED PUBLIC SERVICE BROADCASTER paid for by everyone in the UK (but treated by the loathsome Peter Hain as his personal property). That is called facism [sic] when other governments do it – but not apparently [sic] in PC UK.

The limits on free speech and the responsibility of broadcasters not to stir up hostility to minorities, whilst at the same time exposing and discussing legitimate public concerns, has resulted in a number of highly debated cases. One of the most extraordinary was in 2007, when the UK's Channel 4 used secret filming in mosques around Birmingham to produce a programme in the *Dispatches* strand called *Undercover Mosque*. Viewers were exposed to highly inflammatory and hate-filled statements and speeches against women, homosexuals, Jews and indeed those of any faith other than Islam, some of which were made in a mosque which was a self-proclaimed centre for moderation, and as such received public funding. It might be presumed that, having seen the programme and viewed its transcripts, the focus for concern and action by the local police would be to seek out and prosecute those who appeared to have grossly violated laws designed to prevent speech and behaviour likely, or calculated, to incite hatred and violence. However, to the shock and dismay of many broadcasters, politicians and others, West Midlands Police instead referred the *broadcaster* to the prosecuting authorities, on the basis that the transmission of such views was likely to incite hatred against Muslims. When the prosecutors decided there was insufficient evidence to produce a conviction, the police were undeterred and tried another tack by referring the programme to the regulator, Ofcom, to see if the broadcast had broken *its* rules. In November of that year Ofcom rejected 364 complaints from viewers, as well as that of West Midlands Police, concluding that.[21]

> *Undercover Mosque* was a legitimate investigation, uncovering matters of important public interest. Ofcom found no evidence that the broadcaster had misled the audience or that the programme was likely to

encourage or incite criminal activity. On the evidence (including untransmitted footage and scripts), Ofcom found that the broadcaster had accurately represented the material it had gathered and dealt with the subject matter responsibly and in context.

Nevertheless, the fact that the police had pursued the broadcaster with such apparent zeal continued to alarm many, with broadcasters talking about a 'chilling effect' on future investigations and that the ten months of inquiry had raised the sinister image of the police 'sitting in the editing booth'. This was a point taken up vigorously by the then Conservative spokesperson on Home Affairs, David Davis, who challenged the complaint to Ofcom from the police, which had said that some of the comments of the Muslim preachers 'had been taken out of context'. Davis retorted[22] that, for example, there was no context in which advocating the beheading of British soldiers could be acceptable. Nevertheless, the fact that the police's attempts for both prosecution and censure/fine against the broadcaster had failed and resulted in them receiving such opprobrium, helped to confirm that programmes, which many found uncomfortable or even objectionable, could be defended on public interest grounds. The UK situation, though, has to be seen in the context both of a strong culture and history of public service broadcasting, including requirements for fairness, accuracy and impartiality, especially in controversial matters but also one which operates in a legal framework of very tough libel and other laws which have certainly tended to limit free speech.

## Talk radio

Building on the success of music-led formats and the powerful relationship between listener and broadcaster, came the phenomenon of the talk-show host and its demotic child the 'shock-jock'. Both popular music and populist talk genres rely on a term which might appear to be an oxymoron but describes the often intense level of communication – the 'public intimacy' between listener and broadcaster. The general association with phone calls is of a one-to-one mode of communication and where intimate thoughts and emotions can be expressed. The vast bulk of the audience, who are not contributing to the phone-in are in the position of talk radio voyeurs.

Several radio personalities claim to have invented the genre and role of 'shock jock', notably Dan Ingram on WNBC in New York, but the most famous – or infamous – must surely be Howard Stern, not least because he immortalized himself and his career in the movie *Private Parts*.[23] Both in the movie and his radio shows, Stern is self-portrayed as something of a heroic figure, battling against stupid or venal station executives, humourless and dictatorial regulators and less talented professional rivals. This 'one man against the system' approach is a potent and frequent discourse by journalists and broadcasters but it is hard to take at face value the idea of Stern and his ilk as being 'on the side of the angels' when their 'heroic' battles consist mainly of trying to establish the right to use unlimited obscenities, and terms and references which many find derogatory to individuals or groups, or even inflammatory. Nevertheless, there can be no doubt that in a period when many working-class or blue-collar men and indeed male teenagers have felt threatened and even emasculated by a more assertive and clearly competent female half of the population, Stern's programmes have, at the very least, provided a safety valve for their insecurities. Stern and other shock-jocks have been likened to creating a broadcast version of the male locker-room, with its testosterone-filled discourse of sexual jokes, bragging and teasing. For example, Stern says his obsession with the allegedly (small) size of his penis began when he attended a school with a large proportion of African–Americans – rather weirdly, in the movie he plays himself at many stages in life, including a scene as a teenager in the school locker-room, casting envious glances at his naked classmates – playing to a rather wearisome belief about physical differences between races and an age-old fear by white males of the virility and general physical confidence of African–Americans. This 'small penis complex' has resulted in (no doubt profitable) book spin-offs. But Stern is clearly onto something in making such a claim about such a personal matter – it means that his male listeners can then both feel superior to this radio superstar, or feel empathy with a fellow 'sufferer', and in any case are emboldened by a man breaking a previous taboo subject on the airwaves and feel they can, therefore, talk about any matter.

Stern's approach to broadcasting may have caused him to fall foul of the US broadcasters' regulator, the FCC, but he found his home on the unregulated (because it is only available to the public via subscription, rather than free over the air broadcasting) Sirius satellite broadcasting system. This earns some $100 million a year – a figure which dwarfs the paid for British broadcaster Jonathan Ross, discussed in Chapter 6.

Here, radio's intimacy is used to reduce inhibitions to the normal restraints. Radio phone-ins are a potentially democratic form of communication where every caller could be treated with equality and legitimacy and without being edited and framed in a particular context. The much discussed 'gatekeeper' role of the media in the form of managers, editors, etc., is greatly diminished. In its purest form, there is no filtering of calls and although the presenter has, of course, the ultimate control of having his or her finger on the switch and volume fader, they do not have control over who is ringing and on what subject.

The BBC, unlike commercial radio in the UK, does not employ a delay system, which allows the presenter and/or producer to cut off a caller before reverting to 'real time'. In the 1970s and 1980s, a tape-loop system was used and a seven-second jingle played in when a caller made an objectionable comment, which allowed the tape-delay system to kick back in. From the late 1990s, however, digital systems imperceptibly 'stretched' the delay time so that it is not so obvious when callers have in fact been cut off. Despite the absence of a 'pure' kind of talk radio in the UK, there is no doubt that phone-ins – which became a staple diet and a cheap way of providing public service radio – have allowed a much greater range of voices, opinions and topics than was the case before the late 1960s.

Britain, though, has had an ameliorated version of the US 'shock jock' phenomenon. Most of the best-known phone-in hosts come from print journalism rather than, as in the United States, from a music presentation background. Unlike in broadcasting, there is no requirement in the UK print medium for balance and impartiality so it naturally provides a good 'training ground' for opinionated hosts. Nick Ferrari on London's LBC and Jon Gaunt (respectively, formerly of BBC local radio and the national commercial station talkSPORT) are two of the best-known presenters of this style of radio in the UK. Jon Gaunt's approach seems to confirm the view that there is no greater adherent to a philosophy than a convert. In a newspaper interview[24] he described how he had been part of the metropolitan liberal–left elite, who had written much-lauded plays for the left-wing theatre, but had come to despise this particular version of 'reality'.

In 2008, Gaunt fell foul of the UK regulators after describing a councillor from a local authority which had banned couples who smoked from fostering children 'a Nazi' and 'an ignorant pig'. Although Gaunt apologised and said his attitude had been inflamed because the councillor implied his response was due to the fact that he had himself been put into social care as a child, the station dismissed him and an investigation by Ofcom upheld complaints against him over the broadcast. Gaunt appealed against this and was supported in his High Court action by the human rights group Liberty – an unexpected liaison, given that Gaunt had once described the organisation's Director, Shami Chakrabarti, as a danger to the country.

Liberty believed though that Ofcom's ruling ran counter to Article 10 of the European Convention on Human Rights, which is supposed to guarantee freedom of expression. One of the High Court judges, Sir Anthony May, found that the broadcast was both offensive to the individual and could have offended the broadcast audience and was 'gratuitous, having no factual content or justification'.[25] However, after the hearing Gaunt claimed that the ruling, although apparently a defeat, had in fact established an important principle that 'political speech' *was* protected under law. This view was supported by Liberty's legal officer Corinna Ferguson, who told BBC radio[26] that it was only the offensive and abusive language used when Gaunt had lost control of the interview and attacked the councillor – because of a perceived personal insult – that was ruled to be unacceptable. In her view the judgment marked a very important clarification of legal protection for UK broadcasters expressing controversial views in robust terms.

By this time though Gaunt had left broadcasting completely and joined a new online radio station run by the (in)famously populist tabloid newspaper, *The Sun*, which was also broadcast on FM to British ex-pat communities in Spain and the Canary Islands. To Gaunt, the internet makes radio redundant, certainly in the areas of 'free speech'. The *Media Guardian*'s blog[27] reviewed Gaunt's first programme on SunTalk, which featured an interview with the then Conservative Leader of the Opposition, David Cameron.

Following the High Court ruling over Gaunt's talkSPORT interview there were rumours that News International – believing that the case meant that controversial and partisan style of talk radio was now allowable in Britain – had decided to bring the service on to conventional broadcasting and that it was seeking a slot on the commercial national DAB multiplex. However, in a quite spectacular turnaround in fortunes for Gaunt, not only did this rumoured plan not come to fruition but the SunTalk 'station' was closed down within days of the High Court hearing,[28] News International citing 'business reasons', despite only weeks before being confident and bullish about the service's future.[29] It seems that legal protection is not enough to bring the sort of polemical and robust style of talk radio, so common in much of the developed world, to the UK. Cultural factors and the dominance of the BBC in speech radio at both the local and national levels and its public service approach, including editorial requirements of impartiality and balance, might have too strong a grip on radio audiences.

## Pay attention … here comes a bit of science

In addition to allegations of both specific and general bias in politics and culture, scientists have long complained that their areas are either ignored by broadcasters (and the wider mass media) or, if covered, are trivialised or sensationalised. These criticisms do have substance: one of the problems is that relatively few people working in broadcasting have scientific training or experience at a post-school level, as the industry naturally tends to attract those with an arts or humanities background, so there is genuine ignorance about much of science. Second, broadcasters – particularly those working in news and current affairs – tend to be much more interested in sudden and dramatic events: war, murder, disasters (natural or man-made), politics and various other aspects of human drama. Even coverage of the arts is usually focused on newness and novelty – the latest play, movie, recording, TV series, etc. – all of course supported by a huge public relations and marketing industry, with spokespeople trained and experienced in dealing with media interest. Science, on the other hand, tends to develop in small, incremental steps, which are then verified and repeated by other scientists, before being published in peer-reviewed journals. Furthermore, science rarely provides definitive answers to specific questions, such as which foods are likely to increase the risk of cancer. The further up you go in scientific hierarchies, the more specialist is the knowledge and the more arcane the terminology. Scientists don't usually have access to much in the way of public relations expertise and are notoriously bad at communicating their complex knowledge into simple, layman's terms, often objecting that to do so over-simplifies the topic to the point of it being misleading. All these factors tend to militate against science playing a prominent part in mainstream broadcast output.

The difficulty for broadcasters in reflecting scientific developments is perhaps a more subtle critique, but nevertheless one of great importance. A study by George Mason University[30] showed that only 10 per cent of the TV newsrooms in the USA had a dedicated science correspondent (compared with the much larger number employing full-time entertainment correspondents) and many seemed proud that they were covering at least one science story *a month*.

This ignorance of scientific thought and development is regrettable, given the impact of science in so many aspects of daily lives, not least in perhaps the most crucial question of the age – the influence of human activity on the climate – which requires at least a measure of engagement by the public in scientific process and data if they are to have a hope of understanding the claims and counter claims on this topic. If nothing else, public spending on developing 'green' technologies and the financial impact on regulations on public and private enterprises is going to have a massive impact on the national economy.

Theories and claims about man-made climate change had been around since at least the 1970s but, for the majority of mainstream politicians and others in public life, it was a few years into the 21st century when such theories seemed to develop into established 'facts'. This settled and apparently incontestable view was achieved, however, without any significant public debate in the broadcast media, at least in Britain. By the time contrary views were broadcast on the Channel 4 programme, *The Great Global Warming Swindle*, in March 2007, those who were, at the very least, sceptical about the effect of so-called 'greenhouse gases' on the climate were cast as heretics, fools, and certainly irresponsible. The programme investigated what it claimed was misleading data about changes in the climate and accused some of the advocates of man-made (anthropogenic) climate change of bad faith, in particular those scientists who were seeking research funding. There were interviews with some significant figures from the scientific world in support of its case, as well as others from public life, including the former British Chancellor of the Exchequer, Nigel Lawson. However, one of those interviewed, Carl Wunsch, Professor of Oceanography at the Massachusetts Institute of Technology, stated after the programme that he strongly disagreed with the programme's conclusions and the way his interview material was used. Professor Wunsch's complaint was just one of many that were subsequently investigated by the broadcast regulator Ofcom, which in July 2008 ruled that,[31] although it was of 'paramount importance' that broadcasters such as Channel 4 explored controversial subject matters and that the programme was clearly identified as a 'polemic', it had breached the regulations on impartiality. This was because it did not reflect contrary views on a matter of public policy and was unfair to Sir David King – the UK government's former Chief Scientific Advisor – the Intergovernmental Panel on Climate Change (IPCC) and Professor Wunsch.

Following the ruling, views contrary to claims that the climate was indeed changing – and not in a good way, and that these changes were largely the result of man's activities and consequently steps needed to be urgently taken to reduce 'greenhouse gases' – were hardly ever aired on the main UK broadcasters. However, this uniformity of view is not shared by many other sections of the British media, notably several national newspapers, which almost daily poured scorn on claims by the so-called 'warmists'. Public opinion seemed to be out of kilter with the broadcasters, with one survey at the time of the Copenhagen conference in December 2009 (held to try and agree on a coordinated international effort to curb 'greenhouse gases') indicating that only 41 per cent of the public believed that it was an established scientific fact that climate change was largely man-made.[32] This might indicate the British public is foolish, wilfully ignorant, even perverse, in refusing to accept overwhelming agreement among scientists, or it may be that they have spotted flaws and inconsistencies in these claims, which the newspaper industry has been far more astute in teasing out. It would also seem to give strength to those who argue for a liberal–pluralist perspective on the media, as even when all the broadcasters follow the same line on a major policy issue, the public is subjected to, and responds to, contrary information and arguments.

Only when leaked emails from researchers at one of the major institutions investigating climate change seemed to indicate a wilful suppression of contrary data, did the BBC's flagship radio current affairs programme *Today* acknowledge that the science was not 'settled' and that there was further debate to be made as to how much effort and money should be spent on trying to limit 'greenhouse gas' emissions and how much on mitigating the effects of climate change, whether man-made or not. The *Today* debate,[33] between Philip Stott, Emeritus Professor of Biogeography at the University of London – an anthropogenic climate change sceptic – and environmentalist Jonathon Porritt, provided a rare example of a well-mannered, respectful and informative discussion on the issue. Perhaps if the BBC had produced a major debate in peak time television in 2008, at the time the Climate Change Bill[34] – with its enormous implications for public finance – was going through Parliament and allowed all major viewpoints and claims to be examined and tested in a calm but rigorous manner, the public might have been better informed.

The fall-out from all of this was that the BBC's updated Editorial Guidelines, published in October 2010, mandated the Corporation's editors, producers and presenters to reflect, at least on occasion, the views that were contrary to the supposed consensus on man-made climate change.[35]

## Science lacks the 'fizz' demanded of news 'events'

On the rare occasions when there does seem to be a genuine scientific news event, it often disappoints. A classic example of this was the start of the experiments with the Large Hadron Collider (LHC) – essentially a long tunnel running underground on the French/Swiss border – which was being used to propel tiny particles at great speed, in an attempt to recreate the conditions immediately after the 'Big Bang' and was part of the CERN (European Organisation for Nuclear Research) project. Some scientists and commentators excitedly talked about finding the 'God particle' – the element which could unlock the great secrets and mysteries of the universe. The start of this experiment seemed to be a programme editor's dream: a hitherto semi-secret, somewhat mysterious underground lair, with shades of a James Bond movie, a dramatic countdown to the start of the experiment, and the much discussed (if fervently refuted) claims that, as this had never been done before, it could result in a gigantic 'black hole' which would suck in the earth's matter and therefore result in the end of all life. This experiment therefore posed interesting questions concerning not only of science but of religion and metaphysics. Determined (in true public service broadcasting style) to engage with as wide an audience as possible, the BBC designated the date for the 'switch on' – 10 September, 2008 – as 'Big Bang Day' and commissioned a raft of programmes,[36] including a radio drama, *Lost Souls*, a spin-off from the TV drama *Torchwood*, itself a spin-off from *Doctor Who*. The drama was written by Joseph Lidster, who managed to achieve a rare collaboration between science and the arts.[37]

The BBC, along with many other broadcasters around the world, went 'live' to the control room of the LHC at the appointed time and waited for, well, something to happen. Needless to say, nothing of a televisual nature did happen and many commentators and presenters were left looking both perplexed and somewhat embarrassed. Shortly afterwards, a fault meant that the LHC was closed down for some weeks and, although it was restarted, coverage of the experiment almost disappeared from the mainstream media. The LHC had failed to deliver a dramatic, televisual moment, equivalent to the Apollo craft landing on the moon nearly 40 years earlier. There was no 'one small step for man' speech, no scientists were engaged in a perilous journey to the dark side of matter. The earth wasn't being sucked into a black hole. A particle proving – or disproving – the existence of God had not been discovered. It was just the same old scientific story: a slow, meticulous process of experiment and observation, resulting in articles in peer-reviewed journals, written in (to the layperson) impenetrable, specialized language. It just wasn't 'fit' for broadcasting.

## Notes and references

1. *Analysis* (25 October, 2010) 'The Secret History of *Analysis*', BBC Radio 4.
2. From the French, as being one whose 'world view' is that of the conventional wisdom of the time and/or group; often associated with being self-righteous, smug and/or arrogant.
3. Chignell, H. (2006) 'The Birth of BBC Radio 4's *Analysis*', *Journal of Radio Studies* 13 (1), 89–101.
4. Aitken, R. (2007) *Can We Trust the BBC?*, London: Continuum.

5. Gyngell, K. and Keighley, D. (2004) 'Blair's EU-Turn: A Case Study in BBC partiality', *Centre for Policy Studies,* available online at: http://www.cps.org.uk/cpsfile.asp?id=124.

6. BBC Governors (2005) *BBC News Coverage of the European Union*, available online at: http://www.bbcgovernorsarchive.co.uk/docs/reviews/independentpanel report.pdf.

7. Horrocks, P. (23 February, 2007), available online at: http://www.bbc.co.uk/blogs/theeditors/2007/02/23/index.html.

8. Marr, A. (2004) *My Trade: A Short History of British Journalism*. London: Macmillan.

9. BBC Trust (June 2007) *From Seesaw to Wagon Wheel – Safeguarding Impartiality in the 21st Century.*

10. *Ibid.*, p.6.

11. Transcript from *Adam Boulton v. Alastair Campbell: what they said*, available at: http://www.guardian.co.uk/politics/2010/may/10/adam-boulton-alastair-campbell-transcript.

12. Simpson, R. and Revoir, P. (2009) 'Brucie blasts the PC brigade in Strictly race row (and infuriates his BBC bosses in the process)', *Mail Online*, available online at: http://www.dailymail.co.uk/news/article-1218955/Strictly-Come-Dancings-Bruce-Forsyth-says-nation-sense-humour-defends-Anton-Du-Bekes-slip-up.html?printingPage=true.

13. Foster, P. (2009). 'Carol Thatcher's golliwog remarks 'made eyes roll in the green room', *Times Online*, available online at: http://entertainment.timesonline.co.uk/tol/arts_and_entertainment/tv_and_radio/article5671863.ece.

14. Goldberg, B. (2002) *Bias – An Insider Exposes How the Media Distort the News*, Washington, DC: Regnery Publishing.

15. Sacred Heart University (2009) *SHU National Poll: Trust and Satisfaction with the National News Media*, available online at: http://www.sacredheart.edu/pages/30046_shu_national_poll_trust_and_satisfaction_with_the_national_news_media.cfm.

16. PBS Newshour (30 August, 2010) 'Charting Glenn Beck, Tea Party Influences on U.S. Electorate', available online at: http://www.pbs.org/newshour/bb/politics/july-dec10/glenn_08-30.html.

17. Pew Research Center for the People and the Press (19 August, 2010) *Growing Number of Americans say Obama is a Muslim*, available online at: http://people-press.org/report/645/.

18. Prince, R. (23 October, 2009) 'One in five "would consider voting BNP" after Nick Griffin Question Time appearance', *Telegraph.co.uk*, aAvailable online at: http://www.telegraph.co.uk/news/newstopics/politics/6417906/One-in-four-would-consider-voting-BNP.html.

19. Groves, J. (23 October, 2009) 'BNP's Nick Griffin jeered on BBC's Question Time', available online at: http://www.dailymail.co.uk/news/article-1222424/BNPs-Nick-Griffin-jeered-BBC-Question-Time.html.

20. Allen, G. (23 October, 2009) 'Nick Griffin on Question Time', *Editor's Blog*, available online at: http://www.bbc.co.uk/blogs/theeditors/2009/10/nick_griffin_on_question_time.html.

21. Ofcom (19 November, 2007) *Broadcast Bulletin Issue Number 97*, available online at: http://www.ofcom.org.uk/tv/obb/prog_cb/obb97/.

22. BBC Radio 4 (19 November, 2007) *PM*.

23. Thomas, B. (1997), more details online at: http://www.imdb.com/title/tt0119951/

24. Burrell, I. (28 January, 2008) 'Jon Gaunt: "I'm the voice of ordinary folk"', *Independent.co.uk*, available online at: http://www.independent.co.uk/news/media/jon-gaunt-im-the-voice-of-ordinary-folk-774802.html.

25. Robinson, J. (13 July, 2010) 'Jon Gaunt loses high court case over 'gratuitous' interview', *Guardian co.uk*, available online at: http://www.guardian.co.uk/media/2010/jul/13/jon-gaunt-talksport-high-court.

26. BBC Radio 4 (14 July, 2010) *The Media Show*.

27. *Media Guardian* (20 April, 2009) 'Sun Radio goes live with Jon Gaunt and David Cameron', available online at: http://www.guardian.co.uk/media/organgrinder/2009/apr/20/sun-radio-live-jon-gaunt.

28. Hyslop, L. (19 July, 2010) 'SunTalk radio shuts down;, *Telegraph.co.uk*, available online at: http://www.telegraph.co.uk/expat/expatnews/7895403/SunTalk-radio-shuts-down.html.

29. News International (25 May, 2010) 'Sun Talk plans ahead after successful first year', available online at: http://www.newsinternationalcareers.co.uk/news/222028/SunTalk-plans-ahead-after-successful-first-year.

30. Maibach, E., Wilson, K. and Witte, J. (30 June, 2010) *A National Survey of News Directors About Climate Change: Preliminary Findings*, George Mason University – Center for Climate Change Communication, available online at: http://www.rtdna.org/media/TV_News_Directors__Climate%20Change%281%29.pdf.

31. Ofcom (21 July, 2008). *Broadcast Bulletin, No. 114*, available online at: http://www.ofcom.org.uk/tv/obb/prog_cb/obb114/.

32. Riddell, P. and Webster, B. (14 November, 2009) 'Widespread scepticism on climate change undermines Copenhagen summit', *Times Online*, available online at: http://www.timesonline.co.uk/tol/news/environment/article6916510.ece.

33. BBC Radio 4 (4 December, 2009) *Today*, available online at: http://news.bbc.co.uk/today/hi/today/newsid_8394000/8394501.stm.

34. Department for Environment Food and Rural Affairs (2008) *Implementing the Climate Change Act 2008*, available online at: http://www.defra.gov.uk/environment/climate/legislation/index.htm.

35. Midgley, N. (13 October, 2010) 'BBC told to balance coverage on climate change', available online at: http://www.telegraph.co.uk/culture/tvandradio/bbc/8060211/BBC-told-to-ensure-balance-on-climate-change.htmlelegraph.co.uk.

36. BBC (7 August, 2008) 'Press Releases – Radio 4 has exclusive access to CERN's Big Bang experiment: programming for Big Bang Day', available online at: http://www.bbc.co.uk/print/pressoffice/pressreleases/stories/2008/08_august/07/cern2.shtml.

37. Wright, M. (10 September, 2008) 'Torchwood – Lost Souls', *The Stage/Blogs: TV Today*, available online at: http://blogs.thestage.co.uk/tvtoday/2008/09/torchwood-lost-souls/.

# Moving Time

8

This chapter considers the significance of removing previous restrictions in time in broadcasting's output, consumption and funding. In particular it discusses:

- The importance of utilising time and its associated 'liveness' in broadcasting.
- The significance of time in the cost and placing of broadcast commercials.
- The timeless but changing appeal of 'pirate' radio.
- The issues surrounding the use and availability of archive recordings, including the case of *Kenny Everett's Radio Days*.

## Free at last!

An important aspect of the 'golden ages' of radio and television was the dictation by the programme schedulers of the consumption of programmes. Before the advent of audio magnetic reel-to-reel tape (invented in Germany in the mid-1930s and widely used by radio stations from the 1940s) and then reel-to-reel video tape (widely used from the late 1950s) most programmes were broadcast 'live'. Film was sometimes used but it was expensive and took time to process and edit. Early BBC dramas, first screened at the weekend, were even repeated 'live' mid-week: the performers simply performed the play again, rather as they would have done in repertory theatre. The pressure to remember lines and not to fall over the scenery when there was an audience of millions must have been very great!

In the 21st century, the occasional 'live' edition of a drama – often to mark a landmark anniversary or number of programmes – is a major event, attracting widespread publicity, adding a *frisson* of excitement for both audience and performers/directors, all of whom know that if something goes wrong the show will have to, somehow, go on. Even when video-tape became commonplace from the late 1950s it, too, turned out to be an expensive option and editing was clumsy compared with audio tape, so even when programmes were recorded they were often done with minimal 're-takes'. The cost of the tape also meant that many programmes which are now regarded as classics were simply wiped after transmission and re-used; after all, why would anyone want to watch a comedy, drama or 'pop' show decades later? Television was regarded as largely ephemeral and unlikely to gain status as part of a country's social and cultural history. Public appeals from the BBC and the British Film Institute's 'Missing Believed Wiped' initiatives have resulted in many now valued (even iconic) programmes being retrieved from listeners' and viewers' personal collections; others from filmed versions that were exported to overseas broadcasters; and a few others were even retrieved by an employee from a skip outside BBC studios.[1]

Before domestic recordings became commonplace in the late 1970s, listeners and viewers had no choice but listen/view the programmes at the times they were broadcast over the air. This had major social implications: outside the workplace lives were to a great extent organised around the schedule: mealtimes and other social activities were subservient to, first the radio, then the television, programmers. When a particularly popular programme was broadcast, pubs and restaurants would be empty, dinner parties cancelled and children would pester their parents to stay up late. In the 21st century, the only type of output that is likely to have that effect is 'live' coverage of major sporting events – but now this is more likely to fill the pubs and bars, as like-minded supporters gather for a communal, social experience of watching the triumph or defeat of their team on large, plasma television sets, or huge outdoor screens in public places, increasingly in high definition (HD) and also 3-D(imensional). On these occasions, television has in fact reverted to the ways in which it was originally viewed – albeit then due to the expense and rarity of receivers – of communal viewing and social interaction with the content.

Chapter 2 discussed the importance of time in determining – and manipulating – audience ratings. The positioning of the audience around time and timings was crucial in the development of broadcasting. This was linked to the work and social routines that were largely determined by the patterns common to the majority of the audience: the shift times at factories and other workplaces; clocking on and off; overtime; dinner-time, and so on. Those producing and presenting daily, 'live' sequence programmes on radio or TV need to remember that – especially during the breakfast/morning 'drive' period – the audience will be relying on particular fixed points or junctions to inform them whether or not they are on time for their daily routines ('if I am not leaving the house when the sports' news comes on, I am late'), so every effort needs to be made to ensure timings are kept to almost military precision. The Greenwich Time Signal (GTS), commonly known as 'the pips' remains the almost iconic indication of the time – so it becomes *time* for the news; *time* to go over to the weather centre, and so on. Programmes often had 'time' in their title. These included a variety show from a different works' canteen at lunch-time for *Workers' Playtime*, (BBC Home Service, then Light Programme, 1941–64), to the weekly television current affairs discussion programme *Question Time* (1979–). In the first instance the BBC thus indicated that they were integrating their scheduling with the perceived likely routines or availability of their audiences for a certain type of activity, but in the second dictating that a particular time period was to be allocated for a particular type of programme.

The federal nature of the British ITV network meant that definite 'clock starts' were required for their programmes, as they switched (manually to begin with) between programme output from different regions. This meant that ITV programmes tended to have much more rigid programme lengths – generally half an hour or an hour – whereas the BBC output, nearly all of it played out from a central presentation suite, could start programmes late and accommodate 'odd times' of programmes. This is not a trivial point: a comedy such as *Fawlty Towers*, for example, might require an extra five minutes to a total of 35, rather than a neat 30, in order for the narrative and comedy to work. An ITV comedy, soap opera or drama not only had to fit a commercial half-hour (usually about 26 minutes of actual programme time) but had to have a narrative 'hook' to keep the audience through the mid-way commercial break. In the original UK legislation commercials were confined to 'natural breaks' in programmes, e.g. between scenes in the narrative, so as not to be too intrusive on the action. In an hour's drama these would generally be around the 20 and 40 minute mark. However, the easing of restrictions on both commercial minutage and the timing of commercial breaks in the 21st century resulted in the introduction of an additional fourth break per hour. So, when dramas from the earlier period are repeated there is often a jarring cut of scenes into and out of the breaks.

The extent to which the broadcasters adhere to the published schedule is an indication of how 'commercial' the programming is designed to be. For example, due to a number of imperatives, not least the precise timings of commercials, the cost of which is to a large extent determined by their broadcast time, the moving a commercial break even by a few minutes can make a big difference to the listening or viewing audience, so commercial broadcasters have to be virtually obsessive in keeping to the times scheduled and paid for by advertisers. These breaks are now computer-controlled and 'live' output such as rolling news channels have to structure their output round the advertising breaks. The most noticeable element in the gallery (control room) at Sky News is a big digital clock showing the time left to the next commercial break – if a news presenter or contributor is talking at the scheduled break time, they are liable to be cut off in mid-sentence. The difficulty of melding computer-controlled systems with 'live' output was exemplified in June 2010, when viewers to the first England game in the FIFA World Cup on ITV1's new HD channel missed the first goal by England as a computer cut to a commercial.

In US television programmes, the convention has long been to have a break following an initial scene in a comedy or drama, before the opening titles, so the first scene had to build up suspense or comedic tension to lead the viewer through the commercials and be hooked into the programme. Programmes made in the UK, but with the US market in mind, adopted this technique, even though in Britain there would be no commercial break. Similarly, US dramas and comedies would have a break before the final scene and 'end titles', so there had to be a 'pay off' scene after the main drama had been resolved to keep the viewer tuned through the commercials.

However, output which is of 'high culture' is usually much less tied to exact timings. BBC2 television in Britain, for example, which was designed as an alternative to the mass appeal (although still public service) of BBC1, was notorious for starting programmes late. Discussion programmes and concerts of all types, but particularly featuring classical music, often overran, leading to a cumulative impact on the start times of subsequent programmes. Perhaps the greatest example though is of the BBC's Radio 3 network, which broadcast mostly 'serious' music and talk from its launch in the immediate post-war period (originally 'The Third Programme') and is designed to be at the apex of the pyramid of taste and culture in the portfolio of BBC radio networks. The attitude of the broadcast staff and managers is clearly that programmes should, within reason, run for as long as is thought desirable. It is still is regarded as extremely vulgar to curtail a discussion programme merely because the clock indicated that its allotted time was up. Even more objectionable – in fact unthinkable – would be the cutting of a 'live' classical music concert before its end.

There are clear links with social classes here: working-class life was and still is very much dictated by the clock in terms of shift times, literally 'clocking on' and 'clocking off' at the factory or other workplaces and work and leisure time clearly delineated; whereas the life of the upper classes and even the *bourgeoisie* do not have such rigid demarcations and obligations. Working-class culture was, and remains, much more commodified and part of that commodification is in terms of strict structures and timings, for example the length of the average popular song is around three minutes – this being about the maximum time that a recording groove could be stamped onto a 45 r.p.m. disk without there being a distinct loss of sound quality. The Top 40 radio format was in fact not just, or even mainly, named after the Top 40 bestselling discs of the week but the number of such records that could be played in a typical three-hour DJ-led programme. Time is also related to copyright restrictions in broadcasting. In the UK, the Musicians' Union, in combination with the owners of the recording copyrights, combined to restrict the amount of 'needletime' that could be played by licensed radio stations until the 1990s; in Canada 'Canadian content' rules meant that a certain percentage of recorded music broadcast had to have at least some input from Canadian citizens.

Time is also connected to the 'dumbing down' issue, due to the much shorter scenes and reduced length of individual shots in every genre from news to drama, which in turn has been linked to the effect of pop videos and their effect on the so-called MTV generation with their supposed shorter attention span, and a tendency to 'zap' between channels if something does not immediately engage and entertain. The news on British commercial radio and the length of individual reports within bulletins has certainly been greatly reduced since the 1970s. Then, a typical voice report on the national news provider's service would be between 30 and 40 seconds; by the early part of the 21st century these had been reduced to 10 to 15 seconds and in fact are rarely voiced reports as such but 'soundbites', usually taken from a longer report broadcast on the sister TV news service.

A further aspect of this time/length issue, highlighted by – appropriately enough – the chief writer for a series about a Time Lord, *Doctor Who*. At the 2010 Media Guardian Edinburgh International Television Festival, Steven Moffatt announced that, from the following year, the normal 13-week series/season run would be split into two in the first showing in the UK; seven in the normal spring period, followed by a summer break, returning in the early autumn.[2] The split would mean that child viewers would have grown during the break and would also reduce what, to a child was, up to that point in the show's 21st century revival, a very long time between series:

> What I love about this idea is when kids see *Doctor Who* go off the air, they will be noticeably taller when it comes back. It's an age for children. With an Easter series, an autumn series and a Christmas special, you are never going to be more than a few months from the new series of *Doctor Who*.

An important feature of 21st century broadcasting is the availability of output to be listened and viewed again at a later date/time – and indeed on a myriad of devices, discussed further in Chapter 11 – which aid the engagement of the audience with the programme. A podcast of a radio programme can be heard at the optimum time and place for the listener; particularly important with more demanding, speech-based content. The public radio programme *This American Life*, created by Ira Glass, is an example of this 'listen at your leisure' elimination of the time and spatial restrictions of radio listening in the 21st century which also enables radio to move from background listening to the foreground. It is something that listeners clearly appreciate, as Jad Abumrad who, with reporter Robert Krulwich, produces the innovative *Radiolab* programme on the US public radio network NPR, attested in an interview for a feature in the New York Review of Books, which lauded public radio:[3]

> 'I remember when the show began, I'd get this comment all the time: "I really can't wash the dishes when I listen to you guys," ' says Abumrad. Meaning, there's an expectation that when the radio is on you're only using a quarter of your brain. But now that we've got podcasting, people will put it on iPods or whatever. People will listen to it many times, will

appreciate the layers and the details. Before it was hard for us to justify the amount of labor we put into it. Because it was disposable, just out there in the world and then gone.

## The timeless appeal of 'pirate' (unlicensed) radio

Chapter 1 mentioned the influence of the European offshore pirate radio stations in the 1960s and this phenomenon continues to be fictionalised and romanticised in the 21st century. Radio personnel have a particularly strong sense of the medium's history and in romanticising its past, and this is, seemingly, enjoyed and supported by many listeners. In Easter 2004, a BBC local station re-created the sound of the mid-1960s offshore pirates and broadcast from a Lightship just off the Essex coast on the 40th anniversary of the start of Radio Caroline.[4] The station employed many of the original DJs and similar station identification jingles, and so on, as well as using some younger station personnel who weren't even alive during the original period. This novelty service was deemed a success and another set of broadcasts was aired in August 2007, to commemorate the dramatic and tearful ending forty years earlier of most of the stations as the Marine (etc.) Broadcasting Offences Act came into effect, making it illegal for UK citizens to work for, supply, assist or promote in any way unlicensed stations. Through broadcasting on the internet, these novelty stations reached many more listeners outside the AM listening area of the Essex station and numerous emails declared it far superior to current commercial radio, with the latter's restricted formats and more anodyne presenters.

An even larger and wider audience was 're-tuned' to the pirate phenomenon via the 2009 movie *The Boat That Rocked*, directed by Richard Curtis.[5] This movie presented itself (through the use of 'fact' captions at the film's beginning and end) as a fictionalised, but also accurate, account of the stations that did indeed help bring about a very significant change in approach and availability of certain types of radio services in the UK and some other European countries. However, the movie depicted both the managers and the DJs as rebellious figures, who broke taboos about swearing on radio and were part of the counter-culture movements of the 1960s. This is in fact a gross distortion, suggesting that pirate radio was more akin to the underground FM stations in the USA of the late 1960s, which perhaps was deliberate, so that the movie would appeal to the vital US market (where it was re-titled *Pirate Radio*). The reality of the European pirates was both more prosaic and more dramatic than this fictionalised account.

For many, the short-lived *Perfumed Garden* programmes by the DJ John Peel in the spring and summer of 1967 on Radio London ('Big L'), typified their memories of the output. But these 'memories' are unreliable and demonstrate the power of myths, forged and consolidated over long periods of time. In fact, Peel developed the show, which featured album tracks for West Coast

(American) bands. He ditched the usual Top 40 music format, jingles, etc. only slowly, and after realising that most of the station's management were unlikely to be listening during the show's post-midnight slot. The first the 'suits' heard of it was when The Beatles manager, Brian Epstein, rang Radio London's boss to congratulate him for permitting such an experimental format!

The influence and motivation of land-based pirate radio in Britain is even more contested. Such stations sprang up from the late 1960s and perhaps reached their peak in the 1980s, mainly in urban areas, and were mostly run by disaffected African–Caribbean youths. They regarded the licensed stations as inadequate and part of the corporate establishment. Mainstream radio failed to play 'their' sort of music, or put on air the newly emergent style of DJs, who did more than just present the tracks but themselves became *part* of the music as it was mixed and sampled – all of which formed a vital part of alternative cultures and lifestyles.

As commercial radio was expanded from the early 1990s and included niche format stations, many of the pirates went legitimate and gained licences. Those that didn't continued to play a cat-and-mouse game with the authorities, as they found ever more ingenious ways of disguising their locations and transmitters – mostly in tower blocks in deprived inner cities.

In July 2010, Trevor Nelson, a former pirate radio DJ but by then a presenter on BBC network radio, narrated a Radio 4 documentary that considered the appeal, motives and claims and counter-claims about the urban pirates.[6] Unfortunately, Nelson began the programme by repeating the myth that the 1960s offshore pirates were music stations run for and by young music fans, and even that The Beatles could not be heard on the BBC – whereas in fact the 'Fab Four' had gained a great deal of exposure on BBC network radio and recorded many sessions and interviews, some of which have since been made available on commercial CDs. But Nelson convincingly argued that the urban pirates of later years had been influential in developing many forms of music:[7]

> Rinse FM ... has been running for 15 years and it's been instrumental in developing youth music movements like Grime, Dubstep and UK Funky ... and it's making a lot of money for the UK music industry. Pirates like Rinse, Flex, Flava, Rude and Kool FM have helped launch the careers of many artists. Recent successes like Dizzee Rascal, Chipmunk and Tinchy Stryder wear their pirate pasts like a badge of honour ... they've had seven number ones between them. Every time I go to a school or a community centre in the inner cities and I ask the kids what they want to do, most of them say 'I want to be an MC' or 'I wanna be a DJ' and the way they think they can do that is through pirate radio.

In the same programme, Ras Kwame, one of Nelson's fellow DJs on the BBC's national digital Urban Music station 1Xtra, argued that, despite all the fascination with internet-delivered services, there was something very important and special about the connection made by a listener to a pirate FM radio station:

Pirates are still popular because they offer a more specific choice, for me musically, and in terms of what they broadcast, and I think the raw essence of a guy playing a record and speaking to you in a way that's only familiar to you and your neighbourhood, that will always appeal to people.

Opponents of pirate radio then and now have justified their hostility in part by claiming that behind the innocent face of the stations lie criminals, who are using them as cover for their nefarious activities. The main claims against the 1960s offshore pirates and their more recent, urban manifestations, are remarkably similar and vary only because some of the 'moral panics' about youth have shifted, but include:

- The stations ignore the copyright in recordings and so deny the producers of the work their due payment, which is both immoral and compromises an important, creative industry.
- Their transmitters use unauthorised frequencies which interfere with legitimate stations, causing upset and annoyance to those stations' listeners (and not only in the same country – AM radio waves can travel great distance, especially after dark when the upper atmosphere cools, and in the 1960s the UK government received complaints from several European countries that licensed stations were being interfered with by the offshore pirates).
- That, because the transmitters are often poorly made and positioned, they interfere with emergency services and so endanger lives.
- That criminals use the stations as a 'front' for various rackets, including the buying and selling of drugs and the promotion of illegal or at least unauthorised, entertainments, such as 'raves'.
- More generally, that the continued existence of such stations in defiance of the law undermines the very rule of law and the peace and stability of society.

In reply to these allegations, pirate operators and supporters argue, as noted above, that far from stifling the music industry they are a vital element of it, providing exposure for artists and producers ignored or at best marginalized by authorised stations. They contend there are in fact plenty of spare frequencies and that they take care not to interfere with authorised stations, and especially emergency services – most of which, in any case, now broadcast on a separate part of the radio spectrum. They say that the allegations of criminal involvement are grossly exaggerated, and often reflect a dislike, even fear, of anything that challenges the conventions and assumptions of 'straight' society, of youth in general and of particular youth cultures, especially those popular with recent immigrants to the country.

However, the stations often *are* intimately connected with the music business and club scene. These are unconventional businesses, for which huge profits can be made, but often only for a short time, as particular styles of music and venues come in and out of fashion, and which tend to attract, at the very least, unorthodox methods and 'characters'. So it is probably this relationship with the rather 'shady' sides of the entertainment business that produces the criminal link, rather than the stations themselves being run by criminals.

Perhaps most importantly, pirate station advocates and defenders point out that every new artistic development in music and fashion starts on small, backstreet locations, which in turn become adopted and adapted by the mainstream, and that unlicensed stations provide a vital outlet where new talent and music forms can receive their first break and be tried out; supplying a constant refreshment to creative development.

The offshore pirates continued to be heard online and occasionally, over the air, in Britain using short-term AM licences. In August 2010, for example, Radio Caroline, by then operating as a Trust and mostly surviving on funds raised directly from supporters and from the sale of merchandise, broadcast (legally) on AM over parts of south-east England, on its usual slot on the Sky TV satellite and to the world online, from the *Ross Revenge* ship. This had been Radio Caroline's home on the high seas in the 1980s but was by then moored near London. The station's twin slogans (broadcast amongst the music, DJ chat, listeners' memories, and an online auction of items rescued from the original Radio Caroline North ship, the *Mi Amigo* – which had sunk in 1980 – and promotions for the Loving Awareness philosophy), were: 'real radio, real people', and 'same ideology, new technology'. More than 46 years since its first broadcast and after a quite extraordinary and dramatic history, with the station being revived from seemingly fatal blows and relentless and vociferous attempts by successive governments to suppress it, the station – and the concept of 'free radio' – had survived and adapted to the 21st century.

## Kenny Everett's Radio Days

Kenny Everett is routinely cited by fellow broadcasters and critics as the most creative and original disc jockey Britain has ever produced; inspiring countless others to go into radio. Born into a working-class home in Liverpool in 1944 and dying from an AIDS-related illness in 1995, he established his career, and his reputation as an innovative and maverick disc jockey on the offshore 'pirate' radio station, Radio London in the mid-1960s. When it was clear that the government was intent on forcing the shutdown of these stations Everett literally jumped ship and joined the BBC's Light Programme, in preparation for the launch in September 1967 of what became the Corporation's rock and pop music network, Radio One.[8]

His genuine friendship with many luminaries in the music industry, most notably The Beatles – also, of course, from Liverpool and whom Everett had accompanied on a tour of the USA in the mid-1960s and was given access to their recording sessions and private homes – provided him with a unique status on British radio. His much publicised 'sacking' by the BBC in the summer of 1970 – supposedly for making a potentially libellous joke about the wife of the then Transport Minister bribing the examiner of her Advanced Driving Test, but really because he had broken a written undertaking not to talk to the press without formal permission from the BBC – only added to his reputation as a lovable maverick.

In 1972 Parliament passed a new act which led to the setting up of the first legal commercial radio stations in the UK and Everett was contracted to present weekend shows on the new Capital Radio in London. Initially these were recorded, but the station's management persuaded him to move back to London to present shows 'live', at first presenting the breakfast show but later, following a suicide attempt – partly caused by the strain of a daily performance – back to the weekends. Everett had his own TV series on both BBC and the main commercial network in the late 1970s and much of the 1980s. These were both ratings and critical successes. He also guested on many TV comedy quiz shows. His life and work continue to be celebrated and commemorated well into the 21st century, with numerous TV documentaries and radio specials, including two on Britain's most listened-to radio station, BBC Radio 2, over Christmas 2010, by which time a drama-documentary on his early life was being finalised for broadcast on BBC television.

*Kenny Everett's Radio Days* was commissioned and broadcast by BBC Radio 7 (BBC7 at the time of the broadcasts of these programmes, and referred to as such for the rest of this chapter; the station was further re-branded in April 2011 as BBC Radio 4 Extra), one of the Corporation's digital radio networks, which mostly features BBC archive comedy, drama and readings, and produced by Creation Productions, then the production arm of the now-defunct GCap radio group. Due to the nature of its output, BBC 7's programmes are available on the internet on the 'Listen Again' service for up to seven days after the original broadcasts. Some programmes have at least as big an audience again through 'Listen Again' as heard when originally transmitted.[9]

The inspiration for Mary Kalemkerian, Head of Programmes at BBC7, to commission *Kenny Everett's Radio Days*, was a query from a listener on the station's Message Board (personal interview, March 2007). The listener had been watching a TV tribute programme to Everett and wondered if suitable archive material was available from his radio days. In a previous role with BBC Enterprises, Mary Kalemkerian had put together a double audio cassette titled *Kenny Everett at the Beeb* but for copyright reasons this could not be broadcast, nor could any other BBC material in the form of a 'clip show' – unless it had already been broadcast in that format. However, the agreement with the Writers' Guild did not extend to commercial radio archives. She initially commissioned four half-hour programmes. These proved popular and a second series of one-hour programmes was commissioned – these included about 50 per cent music, selected from the tracks played in the original shows. Mary Kalemkerian, although a 'BBC person' believes that Everett's best radio work was done at Capital Radio. She contends that the station gave him more freedom then he had had at the BBC and it was at Capital that he produced the 'spoof' space adventure serial *Captain Kremmen* – the only 'built' (scripted and pre-recorded) part of his shows, which were to form a major part of *Kenny Everett's Radio Days*. Both she and Creation producer Howard Shannon – who was tasked with selecting the clips from hundreds of hours of tapes – agreed that it was important the shows reflected the 'dailiness' and contemporaneous and ephemeral nature of the original broadcasts. With the exception of the *Captain Kremmen*, the material used in *Kenny Everett's Radio Days* was never intended or expected to be re-broadcast. Furthermore, the shows were not archived in any methodical way. This programme presented a unique challenge to the programme editors and producer!

Although the whole reason for choosing Everett's material was that he was much more than a 'time and temp' DJ, even his weekend shows, from which most of the material was gathered, contained many of the routine elements of 'live', commercial radio. One of the most popular features of Everett's shows in this period – *The World's Worst Record* – led to two special programmes comprising the 'Bottom 30'. Everett's humour was often of the 'schoolboy' variety – women's breasts and other 'naughty bits' (as Everett would describe them), *risqué* jokes, *double entendres* and the like. Most of these, if sometimes sexist and almost always unsophisticated, did not pose a problem for the archive compilations. However, some, although perhaps acceptable in the 1970s, are now regarded as decidedly politically incorrect. Howard Shannon decided that although some of this material could have been broadcast on a commercial station, would certainly fall foul of the BBC's own Editorial Guidelines, although he maintains that the use of ethnic and national stereo-types was necessary for the jokes to work (personal interview, March 2007). Mary Kalemkerian was determined that no material should go out that would provide unwarranted offence, especially as the context for the material was from a sequence show, rather than a 'built' programme and Everett's programmes were more recent than *The Goons* and *Round The Horne* – some programmes of which have also been edited for broadcast on BBC7.

Everett's politics – like every other aspect of his personality and beliefs – were complex. One comment which survived the 'self-censorship' by Howard Shannon at Creation was Everett's musings on East Berlin, which the DJ had recently visited. Everett opined that if 'those who thought Communism was a groovy new religion' would be disabused of their views if they visited the divided city, 'and Maggie [Margaret Thatcher, then Prime Minister] would be queen for ever'. Howard Shannon said he pondered about that one for a while but reasoned that as Communism was long gone, it would not be offensive to any current political thinking:

> That was the closest I was prepared to let him express his right-wing views. I left it in because it was one of the few insights where you actually had him off his guard and sailing a little too close to his own views.

Not only were there issues over taste, decency and politics, but editorial decisions also had to be made about Everett's jingles and constant references (in true commercial style) to Capital Radio. In the first series of half-hour programmes, in deference to the fact that Capital Radio still existed and remained a commercial rival to the BBC in the London area, the jingles were excised to omit any references to the station. However, this made for very obvious and crude edits and, for the second series of one-hour programmes, Mary Kalemkerian told Howard Shannon to include some of the original jingles:

> I said be judicious about it. Because I thought we can't be blatantly play-ing Capital Radio jingles ... The network has changed now so it doesn't matter, it was almost advertising a defunct network.[10]

It seems unlikely that, although the already produced *Kenny Everett's Radio Days* will be repeated[11] (the agreement for commissions is for a total of seven transmissions for each programme) there will be more from Everett's Capital Radio days. A further programme, featuring his work for BBC local radio following his 'sacking' from BBC Radio 1, was aired on BBC7 over Christmas 2006, but this had already been broadcast on some BBC local stations. Howard Shannon has already produced podcasts of *Captain Kremmen,* which, at the time of interview, had gained about 90,000 down-loads and he hints that more 'best bits' from commercial radio archives are likely to be produced for podcasts.

Everett was unique and his performance, even on an average day was highly inventive and creative, meaning it has value even 30 years or so later. The nature of most of commercial radio output – its inconsequential and banal chat, time-limited elements and the general unexceptional nature of the output – means that much of it is unlikely to be of interest or amusement to audiences beyond, at best, a few weeks from the original broadcast. That which is still entertaining in its own right will be edited and the 'best bits' made available for 'listening anytime' as podcasts, rather than, as with Everett's shows on BBC7, complete, new, programmes, designed to be listened to as such.

The BBC7 programmes demonstrate, however, that, in the admittedly exceptional hands of someone like Kenny Everett, such archive material is still of interest and value and that radio's role as a constant but somewhat inconsequential companion to everyday life and routines can still be of inter-est and amusement many decades from now. Such output actually has a nostalgic value for those who were of a particular age at the time of the broadcasts, but it appears they also have value in themselves. What we can call 'everyday radio', may seem ephemeral but it may be that we are under-estimating the importance both at the time of broadcasts and as artefacts of a time and place.

# Notes and references

1. Gilbert, G. (11 December, 2008) 'TV's buried treasure: Classics saved', *Independent.co.uk*, available online at: http://www.independent.co.uk/arts-entertainment/tv/features/tvs-buried-treasure-classics-saved-1061357.htm.

2. Plunkett, J. (29 August, 2010) 'Doctor Who promises 'game-changing cliffhanger' as series split into two', *Guardian.co.uk*, available online at: http://www.guardian.co.uk/media/2010/aug/29/doctor-who-cliffhanger-series-split.

3. McKibben, B. (11 November, 2010) 'All Programs Considered', *New York Review of Books*, available online at: http://www.nybooks.com/articles/archives/2010/nov/11/all-programs-considered/?pagination=false.

4. Rudin, R. (2007) 'Revisiting the Pirates', *Media History*, vol. 13, nos. 2/3, pp. 235–53.

5. See further details on the Internet Movie Data Base (IMDB) at: http://www.imdb.com/title/tt1131729/.

6. BBC Radio 4 (21 July, 2010) *Do Pirates Rule The Air-Waves?*.

7. *Ibid.*

8. Edge, S. (18 March, 2010) 'Kenny Everett: Unhappy Life of the King of Outrage', *Express.co.uk*, available online at: http://www.independent.co.uk/arts-entertainment/tv/features/tvs-buried-treasure-classics-saved-1061357.html.

9. Information from BBC Press Office.

10. In fact, for a time the FM service reverted to the original name 'Capital Radio' – rather than 'Capital FM' – but then re-branded itself 'Capital 95.8', then '95.8 Capital FM'. It is true that, in the commercially crucial area of precise on-air branding, 'Capital Radio' no longer exists in the UK. See http://www.capitalradio.co.uk/.

11. A further transmission of one series of the programmes took place over January/February 2008.

# Local and Global

9

This chapter considers the challenges to established and newer broadcasters created by the spread of satellite and internet technologies, which allow viewers and listeners to consume and participate in broadcasting from many different parts of the globe. In particular it will discuss:

■ How community radio can be both local and global in content and appeal.
■ Case studies of both the BBC World Service (radio) and Al Jazeera.
■ How journalists have to consider that their work can now be viewed by the countries on which they are reporting.
■ How trainers from advanced democracies 'transmit' their cultural and political values with broadcasters in newly democratised states.
■ How and why US audiences engaged with content from UK radio stations after the London suicide bomb attacks in July 2005.

## Community radio – very local, or global?

In comparison with most of the rest of western Europe, the USA, Canada, Australia, New Zealand and many other countries, the UK was extremely late in developing a third tier (neither the BBC nor commercial) of not-for-profit community radio stations. The first full-time, fully licensed community radio stations came on air in 2005. This case study considers Siren FM, which began broadcasting in mid-2007 and at that time was the first such station in England to be run by, and be contained within, the premises of a university – the University of Lincoln. The station therefore has a triple function, being a training facility for university students, particularly those on its journalism courses, reflecting and promoting the university to the local area, as well as performing the traditional community function of 'radio *by* the community *for* the community'.

As with most community stations in Britain and elsewhere, there is a small core of full-time paid managers but the rest of the production and broadcasting staff are volunteers who, at most, receive expenses for their contributions. Around 60 people in a week are involved in the programmes, and the volunteer data base is up to 100.

Moreover, as Station Manager Andrew David argues (personal interview, January 2008), the size of the audience – so crucial to commercial and even BBC stations – is relatively unimportant. In fact, the distinction between broadcaster and listener is deliberately blurred – the listener might well be a broadcaster, too, and there is less interest in audience ratings as a 'be all and end all' of success for the output: serving a few listeners well is more important than entertaining or informing a mass audience. For David, these factors are all part of the same philosophy:

We say 'If you've got an idea why not come and make that idea a reality? Be developed and trained up in the active rather than the passive role.' So I see my listener as someone who will come in and make a radio programme – every listener is a source of programme making not programme fodder.

What I want to get away from is our obsessive interest in how many listeners we have. If I have a programme about allotments done by allotments holders, there might be 35 allotment holders who are listening and there might only be 35 allotment holders in Lincoln, in which case I have a 100 per cent audience. Alternatively, I might have a general interest programme perhaps looking at an aspect of life or history which might have a broader interest of two, three or four thousand. We might only have a microscopic audience but we're still doing a good job.

When the station is not originating local content it re-broadcasts the English language service of World Radio Network (WRN). Here, international issues and debates are aired and so the programme schedule for the community station can switch quite dramatically between very local affairs, concerns and interests, to global issues. Station Manager, Andrew David, believes that these very different approaches in fact work extremely well on a community station:

WRN made us distinctly different. We wanted something that would make a mark on the programming and be a bit different – an hour-long programme around the world in English. We're not afraid to have all-speech programmes, we don't have to have three-and-a-half-minute records and have someone chatting inanely between them. We have programmes where people might think 'well I've learned something there!'

A key aspect for many community radio stations, including Siren FM, is serving local ethnic minorities and those whose first language is not English. Up until around the time Siren FM came on air, Lincoln had not been known for containing any significant numbers of such groups, but the expansion of the European Union to include the mostly former communist states in the east of the continent, has led to a significant influx of people from those states, especially from Poland, who have the right to live and work in any state within the EU.

Consequently, even in a hitherto decidedly non-cosmopolitan city like Lincoln, it is not too much of an exaggeration to say that citizens from across the world are settling there and adapting their lives to very different society, whilst also trying to preserve what they regard as the essential aspects of their own cultures and religions. Community radio can clearly help to ease this transition and can promote multiculturalism and diversity as well as integration with the host, or established community.

## Importance of radio as an international broadcaster: the BBC World Service

The BBC's World Service was both different but also similar to the rest of the Corporation for the first eighty years or so of its life. Similar, because it followed – even exemplified – core BBC values such as editorial independence from government and following 'due impartiality' principles when covering issues and areas of conflict. It was different, because it was financed by a grant-in-aid from the UK Foreign and Commonwealth Office. As such, it can be viewed as an example of 'soft power' – a service which promoted, in the broad sense, the ideals and principles of British society, but although funded by government was independent of it. In the 20th century, it established an enviable reputation for its calm, authoritative and impartial reporting and continues to provide an independent and reliable source of news and current affairs, as well as an important channel for the communication of British perspectives, culture and politics.

So, as the World Service was trusted and respected, so, it was thought, would be the British government. Countless thousands of people who, through political upheaval, social unrest or natural disasters, have found themselves in frightening, life-threatening situations, have relied on the BBC World Service to tell them what is going on.

Furthermore, it is highly regarded for its editorial and production excellence and the high standard and overall quality of radio techniques. As such, it is often regarded as a benchmark of quality, public service radio, which many other broadcasters try to emulate and, indeed, many broadcasters re-broadcast its programmes, especially the major strands of news and current affairs.[1] The BBC World Service will broadcast Foreign Office advice to UK nationals caught in foreign disasters and has occasionally acceded to requests from the Foreign Office to broadcast or *not* to broadcast certain programmes or items.[2]

The World Service also contains a rich mix of programmes, including drama, and a wide variety of music, science and culture. John Tusa was the service's Managing Director from 1986 to 1992 and, writing at around the time of the 75th anniversary in 2007, characterizes its *modus operandi* and worth as follows:[3]

> The service reaches a weekly audience of 183 million ... and is available on FM radio in 75% of the world's capital cities ... British listeners know that the sense of independence from government, the liberal internationalism, the social conscience, the awareness of the big world remain major national characteristics and of their provision by the World Service defines the nation ... no other government in the world funds an international broadcaster and then insists that it broadcasts independently.

The independence of the World Service infuriated Iranian leaders in 2009, who singled the service out for condemnation and accused it of fomenting violent opposition to the much-disputed Presidential election of that year. The UK government tried to explain – seemingly in vain – that it could not control the output of the BBC even if it wished to. The importance of radio when the very legitimacy – and survival – of a regime is in question has been demonstrated time and time again in the 21st century. Governments can – and often do – attempt to block or 'jam' satellite TV and internet connections but preventing radio signals, especially over the old technology of short-wave broadcasting, is extremely hard.

In October 2010, after a round of intensive negotiations between the Corporation and the then still-new coalition government over the latter's Comprehensive Spending Review, it was agreed that, from 2014, the World Service should be funded from the domestic licence fee. This raises significant questions over the position of the Service. How much freedom would the BBC now have on the scope and nature of the World Service; and how would it fare when in competition for funding with the Corporation's other commitments, when, not least because of having to fund the Service itself, it would have a significantly reduced income?

The network that is branded the BBC World Service has, since the introduction of digital technologies, been made available to British audiences and can be heard on the internet, as an audio channel on Sky television and Freeview digital terrestrial television, and on the national BBC's national DAB multiplex. The main appeal to British audiences – in 2010 the station had the largest audience of all the those available on its digital domestic offerings – is likely to be mainly be the rather old-fashioned but much praised news bulletins which, naturally, have much more of an international flavour than those produced by the domestic networks.

The BBC World Service also have to negotiate with very different demands and perspectives, perhaps particularly in Africa. Half of the World Service's audience is in that continent and so the BBC in fact broadcasts to more Africans in a typical week than it does to Britons.

The Hausa language service to Nigeria, commemorating its 50th anniversary in 2007, is a good example of the changing approach by the BBC in its external broadcasting. Until the 1990s the service was run by Europeans but, from 2005, was led by Jamilah Tangaza. The BBC followed Tangaza back to her home village for a documentary to mark the Service's 75th anniversary. Her family were surprised – but certainly proud – that she had gained such an eminent position. To her 86-year-old father, it was equivalent to becoming a head of state. And whilst the African services still employ a significant number of white British journalists and presenters it has also sought to recruit some home-grown talent. One of the key figures, highlighted in the same programme, is Ghanaian journalist and presenter Komla Dumor, who was recruited to bring more personality and indeed informality to the morning show Network Africa. Although Africa is a highly complex and divergent continent in terms of its people, languages, politics, economics, religion and geography, Dumor said this English-language programme seems to break down what might appear insurmountable obstacles for a common engagement on a single programme:

> You have people having what I call this pan-African conversation, so we can be focusing on leading on an issue from Somalia but we're receiving contributions from Liberia or Nigeria ... that's what really engages me, the fact that what we're doing is having a conversation with 25 million people across the continent.[4]

The BBC, having brought people from the countries to which it broadcasts over to London to talk back to those countries, began as it were to reverse the process: to take the programmes back to the countries. However, its independent line – often critical of those countries – is of course often unwelcome. In Nigeria, for example, having established a network of FM transmitters, it found itself thrown off the domestic transmitters, so it is in the peculiar position of sending the transmissions to London via satellite, then over to Ascension Island, which then broadcasts to countries such as Nigeria on shortwave. Fortunately, Chinese-made SW sets can be obtained for the equivalent of £1. The morning Hausa programme comes 'live' via this circuitous route from studios in the Nigerian capital, Abuja. Jamilah Tangaza says this 'closer to the audience' policy is vital if the service is to maintain, or even build, its audience and refuses to be intimidated by the attitude of the Nigerian government to these broadcasting 'squatters' and is not afraid to tackle head-on some of the most controversial areas of Nigerian life:

> We, the BBC, need to set the agenda. There's no point in saying: 'well I am not going to talk about poverty, I am not going to talk about how

badly the regime is administering people's lives because it might upset the government.' You don't do that … We heard about how a group in northern Nigeria went to sit outside the offices of local government chairman. They said they'd heard on the Hausa service of the BBC that the federal government of Nigeria had released a certain amount of money over the last six years and this [money] is what we got as a local government. We want to know what you have been doing with that amount of money.

One of the key questions, however, that broadcasters, in what are broadly called developing countries, are asking is how critical they should be of those in authority and supportive of those who are seeking to make a difference. There is a great dilemma in whether to apply what are perhaps arrogantly considered as the normal, rigorous standards of the free and independent journalism in liberal democracies to very different situations, particularly when the economy might be highly fragile and tensions between groups of different ethnicities and religions may be in danger of exploding. In the former European colonies in Africa there is perhaps an even greater sense that broadcasters should not too readily and too robustly undermine the post-colonial governments even if – perhaps especially if – they have not comported themselves in a way that would be normal and acceptable in western governments. This dilemma and conflicts of approach were witnessed by the team making the documentary on the BBC external services when it showed the reporting and general coverage of the 50th anniversary of Ghana's independence from Britain. The presenter, Komla Dumor, hosted a marathon series of outside broadcasts (plagued by technical problems with the uplink from the satellite dish) for *Network Africa*. He cut off the full, qualified answer of one of the contributors, who had been asked whether he was optimistic about the country's future. 'Yes I am', he began to reply. Dumor interjected, wrapping up that part of the day's output: '"Yes I am"! That's enough, at least for this edition. Yes I am. Yes we all are!'

As the voice-over commentary acknowledged, the BBC's values of balance and impartiality are at risk with such broadcasts and indeed with such broadcast*ers*, who see their role not merely to facilitate discussion on important issues but to take a role to positively develop the countries of Africa. As Dumor put it in the programme they were:

> giving African listeners a platform to express themselves and to debate issues. I think we're contributing in a very positive way.

## Some other international radio broadcasters

A highly important broadcaster – if only in terms of its audience size – which has both internal and external services, is All India Radio – or *Akashwani* (allIndiaradio.org) – which reaches 98 per cent of the country's approximate 1.1 billion population, broadcasting in 24 languages in both its internal and external services, plus 146 dialects for its internal listeners.[5]

Some international radio services, such as the USA's *Voice of America*, which claims a worldwide audience of 115 million (www.voa.com), and Germany's *Deutsche Welle* (www.dw-world.de), have few qualms about being regarded as the 'official voices' for their respective governments. Others, such as *Radio Free Europe* and *Radio Liberty* (www.rferel.org) whose origins are in the Cold War and was initially funded by the Central Intelligence Agency (CIA) and broadcast pro-US Western Europe propaganda to countries behind the 'Iron Curtain', now promote themselves as independent and impartial reporters and commentators on international news.

Attempts to establish satellite radio as a means of educating and entertaining those in developing countries (especially the fast-developing new middle-classes in Africa and Asia) through the World Space company ran into financial difficulties in the latter part of the first decade of the twenty-first century. But it is unlikely to be the last attempt at reaching mass audiences in the countries with the fastest-growing populations.

Finally, in this necessarily brief account of international radio broadcasting, the significant presence of Evangelical Christian services should be noted which, outside the USA, are often unable to acquire analogue licences but which use such methods as audio channels on international TV broadcasters such as Sky and the internet.

Indeed, all of these international broadcasters clearly regard the internet as a vital – and increasingly perhaps even the most important tool – for distributing their content and in establishing a loyal relationship with their audiences.

## Al Jazeera and its challenge to 'western' journalistic narratives and state propaganda in the Middle East

It was an American-based cable channel, the Cable News Network (CNN), based not in the usual centre of media power in the USA but in Atlanta, Georgia, and founded by a somewhat unusual media mogul, Ted Turner, that led the way in international rolling news TV channels. CNN came to huge international attention during the (first) Gulf War in early 1991, ostensibly fought to free Kuwait after that country was invaded by Iraq. The network's Peter Arendt stood on the roof of his hotel and provided dramatic, 'live', commentary for the pictures of US missiles exploding in Baghdad in the opening hours of the salvo (see Chapter 5). For the relatively swift and triumphant ground operation, the military ensured that journalists were 'embedded' with the US-led Coalition forces troops, so that a common bond would be formed.

By the mid-1990s it was clear that the new satellite and multi-channel TV technologies were in danger of being colonised by the USA and other western countries, providing an 'echo chamber' of western values and interests.

Furthermore, most countries in the Middle East region had highly censored broadcast TV outlets, so there was the highly unsatisfactory situation that most viewers in such countries were either seeing a foreign and often hostile perspective to the region, whilst their domestic services were intent on shoring up often corrupt and brutal regimes, headed by ruling elites, subject themselves to little democratic accountability.

Just as CNN had come to prominence in the first Gulf War in 1991, so it was that Al Jazeera first became known in many western countries following the terrorism attacks in the USA on 11 September, 2001 ('9/11'). It became the only channel to cover the war 'live' from Afghanistan, which was invaded by US-led forces a few weeks later. The network (it has a number of channels, including one for children) began in Doha, the capital of Qatar, in 1996, funded by a loan from the Emir of Qatar. The channel has always maintained that its 'arm's-length' relationship with its sponsoring government guarantees its editorial independence. Its English-language service was launched in November 2006 and has broadcast centres in Doha (next to the original channel's HQ), from which it broadcasts 12 hours a day, plus four hours from each of its other centres in London, Kuala Lumpur and Washington, DC. It is available around the world via a mixture of free-to-air terrestrial (it began broadcasting on the UK's DTT service Freeview in July 2010, making it freely available to more than 80 per cent of UK homes), subscription services, satellite and cable and is also available via the web (it had launched an English language website in 2003). Its news release on this development[6] promoted the diversity and fearlessness of its reporting and its different news perspectives; that the service now reached 200 million homes worldwide and that the addition of Freeview was 'a significant step forward'. It also stressed the well-known and respected broadcasters and journalists now working for it, including Sir David Frost (who hosted the service's programme on the night of the 2010 UK general election). Sir David certainly had no doubts about the significance of the channel when he joined it in 2005:[7]

> This is a great adventure – the first and perhaps the only brand-new international TV news network for the 21st Century. Most of the television I have done over the years has been aimed at British and American audiences. This time, while our target is still Britain and America, the excitement is that it is also the 6 billion other inhabitants of the globe. As someone said, a new show for a new channel for the new century.

The service has had mixed press in western countries. Naturally, a network that challenges the consensus of a western-dominated perspective is bound to face attacks on its credibility, motives and independence. There was outrage when the channel broadcast videos of western hostages pleading for their lives and for help from western leaders such as Tony Blair, even though edited versions of these were shown on the BBC and other major broadcasters in the west, and there were claims the channel had shown beheadings of hostages.

This was untrue, but became an established 'fact', which seems to stem from a suggestion made by the then US Defense Secretary, Donald Rumsfeld.[8] These claims appear to have caused problems for the network in gaining public support for wide access in North America, but it received approval in late 2009 from the Canadian broadcasting regulator to broadcast via satellite in that country and began transmissions in May 2010.[9]

Perhaps the most significant impact the network had was in the coverage of the conflict in the Gaza Strip at the beginning of 2009. The Israeli invasion of the disputed territory led not only to many deaths and injuries amongst the civilian population but a huge humanitarian crisis. Western broadcast journalists provided – to say the least – only partial coverage, relying on Israeli support and 'minders' who, naturally steered the camera crews to the less traumatic scenes. Al Jazeera, however, was in the thick of it and made its footage available to other networks in a Creative Commons licence.[10] It would be an easy assumption that Al Jazeera was pumping out pro-Palestinian propaganda. But in fact, amongst the many governments and authorities that have banned and censored the network, is the Palestinian Authority, which barred it from operating in its territory in the West Bank in July 2009, following allegations the station made against President Mahmoud Abbas.[11]

## Other world views

Somalian-born Rageh Omaar became one of the best-known BBC correspondents and acquired the soubriquet of the 'Scud Stud' during his reporting of the Iraq invasion of 2003. In 2006 he joined Al Jazeera's English service. At that year's Edinburgh International Television Festival he outlined his view that reporting the world through the culture and politics of 'the west' was no longer sufficient and that new media technologies had opened up new possibilities and challenges for organisations such as the BBC. Omaar remarked that, although the new technologies and air travel had, at one level, made the world seem smaller, paradoxically we were also now aware of how different are the cultures, aspirations and ways of seeing the world. Omaar's perspectives and experiences as a journalist are especially significant because, unlike most western correspondents, he does not simply go and report about people and places that are – in every sense – foreign, but has personal relationships and experiences of many of the places from which he reports.[12]

> I have relatives and friends who live in a lot of the countries to which I've been sent ... So when I've been to Somalia it wasn't just to a war-ravaged chaotic, anarchic country it's also where my parents currently live ... I think that everybody now owns the news and they have done so for some time but the changes in technology have shattered that completely ... People that we used to think of as subjects in the Islamic world are now viewers ... previously when we did interviews with rebel

leaders or political spokesman and they asked us if we're going to report them accurately and we'd say: 'oh yes, I'll report everything you say'. Now those people can watch us and see it and it's a bit like that moment in *The Wizard of Oz* where the wizard pulled the curtain back and people can see what the western media or the news media or even individual journalists how they are reporting the news, what they're saying about their society and their lives.

The new technologies therefore can open up wider perspectives and indeed compel western broadcasters who have become accustomed, and to some extent are required, to report to and from overseas countries using a uniform and limited world view to re-think their approach. But the stated – although often contested – approaches of rigorous, independent journalism, associated with liberal democracies and which developed from the principles of the Enlightenment of rational enquiry and debate and questioning authority, have continued to exert a strong influence and be much admired, in particular by emerging democracies in Eastern Europe. Roy Saatchi is a former BBC editor and manager who, since early retirement from the Corporation, has helped a number of former state broadcasters which had, until the 1990s, been used as mouthpieces and propagandists for the state, to develop into public service broadcasters along the lines of the BBC. To do so, Saatchi realised that a change of culture was required (personal interview, February 2008):

> You have countries that have the years and years of culture of being in a communist regime. You can't change the culture of a society overnight. They're the same organisations – they may have changed the managing director but the managing director may still be allied to the political party in charge. The history has always been that they are state owned … They have their fixation of reporting every single movement that happens in politics and don't actually report what is happening in the country. Instead of saying 'well let's use our editorial values here and is a political story really the most important story of the day, they say "no no, we have to lead on politics".'

For Rageh Omaar, the 'problem' has been metaphorically viewing the world through a narrow, western-made lens. For Saatchi, the 'lens' in Kosovo or Serbia was very narrow and news was reported only from the perspective of each broadcaster's country. Saatchi believes that the culture of rigorous enquiry and independent, objective journalism, is crucial in such countries:

> They need it there more than anywhere else. If you take the example of Serbia, what I find incredibly frustrating and the same would be true of Kosovo and I have worked in both – if you are in Kosovo you'll get the view from Kosovo. You very rarely get the news from Belgrade. If you are in Belgrade in Serbia, you'll get the views of what the Serbian politicians

are saying, but you very rarely get the view of what the Kosovans are saying.

Saatchi's opinion, formed by his experiences in south-eastern Europe, are in some respects similar to Omaar's views, formed by the latter's experiences in Africa and the Middle East: the needs and demands of the audience are driving changes and are compelling broadcasters to provide a wider and (for the power elites) more challenging form of journalism. Saatchi believes that the attitudes of the former communists will not survive far into the 21st century, although the broadcasters are lagging behind popular tastes and demands.

## Censorship of news – and countries' portrayal in fiction

The censorship and suppression of news coverage by authoritarian countries of material from liberal democracies such as the UK continued to be a feature of the 21st century, despite the promise that satellite TV and the internet would make such attempts futile. In 2009, the Iranian government was especially determined to suppress the BBC's Persian language TV channel, which went on air that year.[13] There have been similar examples of censorship in China. At the beginning of that year, 'live' coverage of President Obama's inauguration speech, broadcast 'live' – with a simultaneous translation – on the country's main broadcaster, China Central Television, was suddenly cut when the President talked about facing down Communism.

The relationship between the Chinese government and the BBC had been tense for some time – the Corporation's Chinese language service had long been jammed – and became particularly strained in 2009 when the BBC's much-respected journalist Kate Adie had made a documentary undercover (using a tourist visa after being refused entry as a journalist) on the 20th anniversary of the pro-democracy protests in Tiananmen Square.

But, more bizarrely, the Chinese took exception to the fictional portrayal of its spies in the BBC espionage thriller drama *Spooks*.[14] The issue was raised in November 2010 during a visit by the UK's new Prime Minister, David Cameron, who was on an official visit to the country, mainly to discuss trade. The Beijing rulers had apparently been infuriated by the timing of the episode, seemingly unable to comprehend that the UK government would have no knowledge of its placing in the schedules, and if they had could not believe they would not have the power to remove it. Nor were the Chinese mollified by the fact that Russia and other nations, including the USA, had fared far worse in the show's portrayal of their nationals and had not made any protests or, apparently, been offended. The programme is, after all, fiction. Nevertheless, staff at the Corporation's commercial arm, BBC Worldwide, were evidently resigned to the fact that their hopes of increasing sales to China had been compromised.

The final main section of this chapter considers the impact of the then still relatively new and novel ability for those in the USA to 'listen in' to coverage by two of the London local stations, BBC London and the commercial news/talk station, LBC after an especially horrific incident.

## International appeal of coverage by local radio stations in London to events of '7/7'

The particular editorial context for 7 July, 2005 was that the previous day had seen the remarkable and, to many, unexpected announcement, that London would host the 2012 summer Olympic Games. Many editorial staff on the two stations were either still *en route* back to London, were involved in special outside broadcasts and reporting from the site in the east of London which is to be used for the Games, or were simply exhausted and perhaps even slightly hung-over from the previous day's events. Also occurring in Britain on 7 July was the G8 summit at Gleneagles in Scotland, which meant that the most powerful men in the world – including the president of the United States – were on British soil. Fifty-two people – not including the four suicide bombers – were killed in four explosions; three on the London underground (subway) and one on the top of a London double-decker bus.

Naturally, the local speech-based stations in London were reflecting on the Olympics decision and the often ambivalent, if not to say hostile, reaction from some Londoners to the thought of staging the Games.

Initial reporting of the attacks was confused and sometimes contradictory. The first reports and confirmation from official sources was that there had been first one and then a number of explosions on the London underground caused by a 'power surge'. Even though there was scepticism from many journalists, and indeed the public, the BBC in particular was keen not to cause panic – or indeed be caught providing false and misleading information – that these explosions were malicious acts.

Once the explosion on the double-decker bus in Upper Woburn Place was confirmed, however, the 'power surge' theory had no credence and the story took on a new and more frightening context. As with '9/11' there was the unknown and truly terrifying question: Were there more? If so, where, and of what type?

At the time of interview (February 2006) David Robey was Managing Editor of BBC London and Jonathan Richards Editorial Director of the London commercial speech station LBC. Robey said that overseas' listeners had previously contributed a significant number of emails, and so on:

We get a lot of anecdotal feedback from around the world to our online listening ... especially sport. In the Iraq war we had Muslims and Iraqis giving their perspective – you were getting the other side and sometimes both the other sides, we had Kurds living in London. Because of the multi-cultural mix of London we had a slice of worldwide life. We also had Americans living in London who were giving an alternative view, saying 'we're not all gung ho' and giving a different point of view. Calls saying 'please don't think all Americans think this is right'. So what was happening was Americans were calling saying 'don't think we're all supporting the war'. With Iraq and 9/11 and, most significantly 7/7, the days and weeks afterwards it was overwhelmingly the dominant topic so working on different aspects of that was the dominant thing ... so part of it was asking people around the world what they thought.

For LBC, too, Richards says the reaction from the USA was significant:

> We do have an overseas following ... we got a significant amount by the early evening of the 7th we noticed a lot of email traffic had come in as America was waking up, and all across the United States, not just New York ... more of the 'brothers in arms' ... more than our UK audience ... most of the comment was coming overseas ... I would say 100% was 'we're thinking of you' sort of thing. So we wrote several of them out and did a 'voicer' [voice report] on it and put aside part of the programme to mark that we had received all these emails. It just happened ... mainly Americans, not many ex-pats, although we do have ex-pats who listen. A lot commenting even in that early stage and reacting how well we had reacted ... we had some saying 'we can't believe how calm you've been and how you've gone about your lives even in this early stage'.

For the managers of both the London stations, the cultural, economic and familial connections between New York and London are especially strong and produced a particularly strong emotional response on '7/7'. David Robey describes the feelings of solidarity produced at that time as similar to those between members of a family when one has been involved in a trauma or death:

> You have this hugely strong relationship between New York and London ... a lot of the feedback was the brotherly–sisterly relationship ... even closer than some of the cities in their own country. A number said: 'We had 9/11 and you had 7/7.' We talked to lots of New Yorkers both here in London and New York. On the anniversary of 9/11 we sent one of our programmes out there and he had a simulcast with one of the New York talk stations.

Jonathan Richards agrees: 'A few weeks afterwards we linked up with New York. We do think of New York as our sister city.'

Both LBC and BBC London had been streaming their respective outputs for over five years (LBC began streaming well ahead of BBC London, which itself was ahead of the rest of the BBC local radio chain) by the time of the bombings and have significant degrees of listening via this method. This increased dramatically in July 2005, as can be seen in Table 9.1.

**Table 9.1**   Increase in 'hits' in response to '7/7' bombings

|                            | 'Hits' in July 2005 | 'Normal' numbers (2005) |
| -------------------------- | ------------------- | ----------------------- |
| BBC London – streaming     | 250,000 +           | 15,000                  |
| LBC – combined             | 165,000             | 100,000                 |

As well as the streaming of their respective outputs, both LBC 97.3 and BBC London provide 'time-shifted' listening to their key programmes. On the BBC this, in the relevant period, was provided through their 'Listen Again' facility which is free of charge. LBC began a podcasting service in January 2006 and, according to the station's Jonathan Richards is a 'significant revenue stream'.

For both the BBC and commercial stations there are debates over the legitimacy of expenditure and staff time on the streaming of output for local services. In the BBC's case there is a requirement and expectation that they will use all available means to make programmes available for the widest possible audience of licence-fee payers, and in the way in which their audiences may wish to access the output. However, there are certainly issues within and outside the BBC over the spending of licence-payers' money providing services which are equally available to non-licence-fee payers – i.e. those resident outside the UK. The BBC was required to separate its spending on BBC World – which is a commercial venture and is paid for by its subscribing partners, mainly through their respective commercial revenues – from its domestic television news output. As noted above, at the time of this incident the BBC radio external services – including the World Service – were funded separately, through a Foreign Office grant-in-aid. However, both BBC World television and the radio World Service use correspondents who provide the same or similar reports and 'packages' for domestic output – so there is, inevitably, a 'blurring' of costs and revenue. BBC London is funded out of the general licence fee, so it is certainly arguable that any licence-fee payer in the UK should have access to its output.

So far as LBC is concerned there are both commercial and editorial advantages in having 'out of area listening'. The commercial revenues mainly come through the podcasting and through advertising links on its website, but most of its advertising revenue derives from its cost-per-thousand commercial rates based on its RAJAR figures for London.

There can be no doubt that BBC London had a significant advantage in one major respect over its local, commercial rival: it *is* part of the BBC. However, the BBC branding is not necessarily an unqualified asset. There are also negative attitudes to the BBC held by some Americans, or at least a belief that the BBC is unlike the familiar commercial news/talk services in the USA and this can be a drawback so far as some US listeners are concerned. Jonathan Richards believes that the bulk of their American listeners on '7/7' were already familiar and comfortable with the LBC brand.

It is clear from this research that for most of the time the 'outside' or 'unintended' audiences to these services is of, at most, marginal interest and concern to editorial figures and broadcasters. However, when a major and horrific event or series of events such as '7/7' occurs, after the initial reporting and commentary, the views and interests of a global audience become more relevant and contributes to the bonds between peoples in different nations. It is also clear that many New Yorkers and Londoners feel a special affinity, caused by a combination of blood-ties, common commercial and employment interests and by mutual identification as being citizens of major world cities. The fact that both have now suffered from internationally inspired terrorism has further strengthened these feelings of mutual identification.

For LBC, mutual identification of a different and more recent kind was relevant. Intriguingly, in this case the identification with the station by Americans was due to the fact that it sounded *more* like US stations than is the case with most UK radio; this is especially true for Americans who visited, lived and worked in London in the 1970s and early to mid 1980s, before UK commercial radio was de-regulated. As LBC was consciously patterned on news services such as New York's WINS this identification is hardly surprising. Of course, the fact that the local London stations can openly 'boast' of listeners in such glamorous locations as New York adds to their credibility and 'coolness' to their image and appeals to their core audience. The rapid growth of broadband and general internet usage is bound to increase this two-way traffic and relationship. Only the copyright bodies, it seems, can thwart this growing phenomenon of international audiences to 'local' output.

## Notes and references

1. Crook, T. (1998) *International Radio Journalism – History, Theory and Practice*, London: Routledge, p.15.
2. Walker, A. (2004) 'British Broadcasting Corporation: BBC World Service', in: Sterling, C. (ed.) *Encyclopedia of Radio*, vol.1: 222–7, New York: Fitzroy Dearborn.
3. Tusa, T. (16 December, 2007) 'This is London, still calling', *Sunday Telegraph*, p.23.
4. BBC Four (10 December, 2007) *London Calling: Inside the BBC World Service. Part 3: Changing Faces.*
5. Pendakur, M. (2004) 'All India Radio', in: Sterling, C. (ed.) *Encyclopedia of Radio*, vol.1: 35–7, New York: Fitzroy Dearborn.
6. Al Jazeera (30 June, 2010) 'AJE launches on Freeview', *Alajazeera.Net*, available online at: http://english.aljazeera.net/watchaje/20107194036201514.html.
7. AME info (8 October, 2005) 'Media legend Sir David Frost joins Al Jazeera International', AMEinfo.com, available online at: http://www.ameinfo.com/69504.html.
8. Mason, R. (23 March, 2009) 'Al Jazeera English focused on its American dream', *Telegraph.co.uk*, available online at: http://www.telegraph.co.uk/finance/

newsbysector/mediatechnologyandtelecoms/5039921/Al-Jazeera-English-focused-on-its-American-dream.html.

9. CP 24 –Toronto's Breaking News (4 May, 2010) 'Al Jazeera English begins broadcasting in Canada', available online at: http://www.cp24.com/servlet/an/local/CTVNews/20100504/100504_al_jazeera/20100504/?hub=CP24Home.

10. Aljazeera.net. (13 January, 2009) 'Al Jazeera Announces Launch of Free Footage under Creative Commons License', available online at: http://cc.aljazeera.net/content/launch-press-release.

11. *Telegraph.co.uk* (16 July, 2009) 'Al-Jazeera banned from West Bank', available online at: http://www.telegraph.co.uk/news/worldnews/middleeast/palestinian authority/5838466/Al-Jazeera-banned-from-West-Bank.html.

12. From notes taken at the time and subsequently checked against video of speech, made available to those registered at the Festival.

13. Public Radio International (24 June, 2009) 'BBC Persian TV battles Iran media censorship'. available online at: http://www.pri.org/world/middle-east/bbc-persian-tv-iran-censorship1449.html.

14. Pidd, H., Sweeney, M. and Branigan, T. (11 November, 2010) 'Taking Spooks seriously: Beijing on the warpath over BBC spy drama', *Guardian co.uk*, available online at: http://www.guardian.co.uk/world/2010/nov/11/bbc-spooks-chinese-government-portrayal.

# International
# Television

10

This chapter considers the impact of transnational and cross-border television, in terms both of production and output and the cultural impact of the programmes on audiences. In particular, it discusses:

■ The 'translation' of individual programmes from their original, domestic market to other countries, especially between the UK and the USA.
■ The significance of television formats and their impact in different cultures, including China with its adaptation of Reality TV programmes.
■ How the theory of 'cultural proximity' helps explain why some programmes and formats 'work' better in some countries than others.
■ How the cultures and issues in the developing world are represented to developed countries through television.
■ How those whose family origins are in the developed world relate to programming from their 'original' countries in their adopted homeland.

## Programmes and formats

Four main types of international television production and output will be discussed in this chapter. In order of importance to the discussion these are:

1. Programmes made primarily for the domestic market but which are sold for re-broadcasting overseas (e.g. *Doctor Who*).
2. Programme formats, where different versions of the programmes are produced in different countries. These are most likely to be Reality TV or quiz shows (e.g. *Who Wants to be a Millionaire?*).

3.  Programmes which follow the same broad themes or ideas, but are adapted and re-shot to reflect local cultures and styles (e.g. *The Office*).
4.  Programmes which are co-produced between broadcasters in two or more countries. This is most apparent with highly expensive drama and wildlife productions (e.g. *Planet Earth*) and are usually between broadcasters with similar values, such as the UK's BBC and USA's PBS network.
5.  Programmes which, due to their means of transmission, especially satellite, are expected – or even intended – to be simultaneously viewed over several countries, usually in the same region. This chapter though will not concern itself primarily with the effects of new technologies on viewing over national boundaries as this is further discussed in other chapters.

As with all attempts at categorisation, however, some examples contain a mixture of two or more categories; for example, the BBC's motoring magazine show *Top Gear* (also revived and renewed in the 21st century in a manner that made it almost unrecognisable from its incarnations from the 1970s to 1990s) whilst sold to 42 countries in its originally produced form, has versions produced in Australia and the USA. *The Office* only became known to mainstream American audiences when NBC made its own version; the original, British production was shown on BBC America, but this service has relatively small audiences, which made the programme's awards – beating such major US network hits as *Sex and the City* and *Will and Grace* – even more impressive.

## A two-way flow?

Whilst much is made of America's claimed 'cultural imperialism' – exporting its television programmes and movies and the lifestyles and attitudes supposedly contained in them –British television, from its early days, had done something to reverse the flow. *The Adventures of Robin Hood*, (from 1955) from Britain's ATV which, with its feature-film technical and production standards, was one of the first huge hits of the new network and, most significantly, was sold to the USA when it was widely syndicated – the first episode being seen in the USA just the day after its UK debut. Ironically, some of the writers on this series had fled from America to Britain having been named as potential subversives by the House Un-American Activities Committee in the 'witch-hunt' against Communists. Other action adventure film series, both live-action and puppet animation series, starting with *Fireball XL5* and *Supercar* followed and also found an international market, along with other filmed series, notably *Danger Man* and *The Saint*. ATV's Lew Grade even combined puppetry with variety in the much later, UK-made, *Muppet Show*, which featured puppet characters that had become famous in the USA through the Children's Television Workshop's *Sesame Street*.

The BBC's *Steptoe and Son* (from 1964) which, with its pathos, realism and often bleak set-up, re-defined the sitcom genre, was just one of many programmes which were taken up by a US network. *Sanford and Son* used many of the same plot-lines and even dialogue as the British original, albeit necessarily changing the locations and adapting it, to make it credible to American audiences. Chapter 1 discussed how a similar transposition happened with another ground-breaking BBC sitcom of the 1970s and 1980s, *Till Death Us Do Part*,[1] which confronted many of the social, political and generational issues of a society in transition, and translated into CBS's *All In the Family*. At the other end of the realism scale is the TV show which became the only British-produced drama to be shown on peak-time US network television. *The Avengers*, from ABC Television, began as a fairly routine and studio-based police drama but by 1964 developed into a slick glamorous fantasy, with feature-film production values in which two upper-middle-class characters, John Steed and Emma Peel, battled against fantastic conspiracies, lurking behind apparently respectable if eccentric facades of archetypal British characters and locations. So popular was it in the USA that the fifth season, to be shown from autumn 1965, was made in colour for the American market, several years before Britain was to have its own colour TV service. In the 20th century, the BBC's major successes in the USA had tended to be its costume dramas, often based on novels such as *The Forsyte Saga* (1967).

Moreover, this trend accelerated in the first decade of the 21st century. Not only were UK programmes and formats succeeding in the toughest, most competitive TV market in the world, but British actors, performers and directors were also finding favour amongst both audiences and executives. For example, the hitherto very British-sounding actor Hugh Laurie, who had attended both Britain's top public, that is to say, *private* school[2] (Eton) and university (Cambridge) and become known for playing the distinctly upper-class Englishman in TV adaptations of P.G. Wodehouse novels, found great success as the brilliant if cranky surgeon, replete with an authentic 'American' accent, in Fox Television's hit drama *House*. In 2004, Ricky Gervais became the first British actor to win a TV comedy acting award at the prestigious Golden Globes for *The Office*, which he created with fellow Brit, Stephen Merchant.[3] In his acceptance speech, Gervais first thanked what he called the 'Hollywood Foreign Press' by waspishly pointing out: 'I'm not from these parts ... I'm from a little place called England. We used to run the world before you.'[4]

## Time travelling and cultural combinations

In July 2008, internet forums and discussion boards in the UK and USA were buzzing with speculation and excitement about the final episode of the fourth series of the 'revived' BBC sci-fi classic *Doctor Who*. The show had become part of British culture and for many years a regular feature of Saturday-night family viewing. It somewhat limped off the screen in 1989, following various and unsympathetic schedule changes and its low-tech charm unable to counter the demands and expectations of audiences used to much higher production values in the genre on both TV and movies. Its revival in 2005, with longer episodes, new scriptwriters, headed by Russell T. Davies, who had loved the show as a boy and had made his name with ground-breaking adult dramas such as *Queer As Folk*, proved to be a big ratings and critical success. Much bigger budgets (even allowing for inflation) and computer-generated images (CGI) took the show to a new level, whilst some of the iconic foes from the 1960s and 1970s, such as the Cybermen and, most famous of all, the Daleks, were cleverly reintroduced. These had terrified several generations of Britons and one of which was to be found in the foyer of the BBC's television headquarters in west London – thus reinforcing the idea that these creations were an integral part of the BBC's history. The revived show quickly established itself as 'water cooler TV'. The penultimate episode of series four provided more than the usual cliff-hanger ending: not only were the Doctor and his companions in peril but it seemed as if – quite unexpectedly – the Doctor himself had been killed and was about to regenerate. But it was known that there would be a full new series in 2009 – even though David Tennant, the actor playing the Doctor, was unavailable due to a 'gap year' in order to play Hamlet on stage (discussed in Chapter 3).

The internet had enabled American fans to find out the latest twists and turns of the plots and they were by that stage only a couple of weeks behind the British viewers, thanks to its showing on the Sci-Fi Channel. Needless to say, various scenes from the series had been posted up on internet sites such as YouTube. It was testament to the cast and crew that, in a period in which various supposedly secret files had been 'mislaid' by the UK government, the storyline of the final episode was kept a complete secret until its transmission. It is also testament to the creativity of the team and its high production values that a programme that had been seen as quintessentially British, had (rather like the good Doctor himself) regenerated into a show of wide international appeal. Whilst many of the plot lines involved Britain, past or present (including an extraordinarily high number set in Wales, reflecting the fact that the show was produced in the Welsh capital), the enduring, if not endearing, themes of the show are certainly international, even if the genre of sci-fi arguably contains cultural specifics. In any event, the international sphere of cyberspace meant that the citizens of many countries were caught up in the speculation as to the plot turns of the series.

The success of the revived *Doctor Who*, however was part of a golden period of British TV exports in both programmes and formats, with the country seemingly catching up (and, in the case of formats, overtaking) the previous dominance of the USA in the international TV market.

A discernable pattern is that when Britain was portrayed in a historic context, the original programmes were exported; when they were portrayals of contemporary society, they were adapted for the domestic market, at least in the USA. There was a strong appetite, though, for such UK stalwarts as the 'soap' *Coronation Street* amongst the many ex-pat British in Canada and New

Zealand. Britain seemed more than ready to watch contemporary 'soaps' set in Australia, with its very different climate and enviable scenes of characters walking around in shorts and sandals (as well as the opportunities these provided for the exposure of flesh of the mostly highly telegenic actors). The plot-lines of *Neighbours* and *Home and Away* may have borne some resemblance to those in British 'soaps' but the locales and lifestyles provided a fantasy, even erotic, element, not so apparent in *Brookside* (which was set on a new housing estate on the outskirts of Liverpool), or *Emmerdale* (set in a village in northern England).

## How much broadcasting of non-domestic output is there?

There is a wide variation between nations in the amount of broadcasting from other nations. As might be expected, the USA, as it exports so much of its programme output, conversely, has the least amount of 'foreign' produced programmes. Canada, due both to its proximity to the USA and, in terms of its population, being a much smaller country, has a much higher percentage of imports. Geographical distance, however, may not be as important as historic, cultural and blood-ties between nations, as can be seen by the high percentage of imported programmes shown in Australia (mainly from the UK and USA).

The Australian Companies Institute (Ausbuy) – which encourages Australians to buy products and services owned and made in the country – produced this comparative table (Table 10.1): the right-hand column shows the comparative economic performance rankings of the relevant countries, as determined by their Gross Domestic Product (purchasing power parity).

The contrast between Canada – with three-quarters of its output home produced – and Australia, with less than a quarter, is stark and certainly cannot

**Table 10.1**   Locally produced TV on mainstream channels

| Country | Amount of 'homegrown' TV (%) | Economic output – world ranking | Population size – world ranking | Geographic size – world ranking |
|---|---|---|---|---|
| USA | 96 | 1 | 3 | 3 |
| UK | 91 | 6 | 22 | 78 |
| Germany | 91 | 5 | 14 | 62 |
| Italy | 83 | 10 | 23 | 70 |
| Canada | 75 | 13 | 36 | 2 |
| Spain | 68 | 11 | 28 | 51 |
| France | 67 | 8 | 19 | 48 |
| Australia | 24 | 17 | 53 | 6 |

*Sources*: Ausbuy (2007) *Media Policy*, available online at http://www.ausbuy.comau/policies/media-policy: CIA (2008) *The World Factbook*, available online at https://www.cia.gov/library/publications/the-world-factbook/rankorder/2001rank.html.

be explained by Canada's 50 per cent greater population (approximately 33 million, compared with Australia's 20 million).[5] However, as can be seen in Table 10.1, not only is Australia near the bottom of the world's economic performers, unlike Canada (or the USA, UK, Germany, Italy and France), Australia is not a member of the G8 leading industrialised countries.

We might expect that large countries such as Australia and Canada would find that their own programmes – reflecting a far-flung but shared culture – might provide particular appeal to the domestic audiences and, indeed, that is true in North America but dramatically less so in Australia. On the other hand, Australians, being so far from the country of origin of most of the settlers, may find there is more value and interest in output that reflects that country and its culture on the other side of the world; such large countries might also find that radio is much better at binding together far-flung communities.

However, something other than geography, population size and economic output and cultural proximity must be at work here, as the latter surely equally applies to Canada as it does to Australia. The juxtaposition of Canada with its much more powerful neighbour to the south, seems to have produced an *inverted* factor of 'cultural proximity': it is keen to stress its *distinctiveness* from the USA. This, unsurprisingly, is most pronounced in the province of Quebec, where French, not English, is the official first language, and which self-consciously links to a European, not American, culture. But the other parts of that vast country – second only to the Russian Federation in its geographical size – also seem proud to proclaim their European connections and influences: in its constitutional, UK-based monarchy, its UK-modelled Parliament and, not least, in broadcasting. Its CBC was self-consciously modelled on the BBC and, like the BBC, offers national, local and regional output on both radio and television – there is no equivalent in the USA. Canada even adopted a European digital radio technology – the Eureka 147 digital audio broadcasting system, rather than the In Band On Channel (IBOC) convention (later HD Radio), which, as noted in Chapter 2, was developed in the USA at around the same time. Both the style and content of Canadian broadcasting has elements of both the UK public-service model and the US free enterprise/market-driven models. Furthermore, until the streaming of broadcast content via the internet, most Canadians could watch and listen to US TV and radio services (80 per cent of Canadians live within 200 miles of the border with the USA), any time they wished. It therefore made ratings and economic sense for Canadian broadcasters to produce a high percentage of 'local' content: better be 'first-rate Canadian', than 'second-rate American'. Clearly, other than international radio short-wave broadcasters, Australians had no such opportunities; the only way to watch USA (or indeed UK) output was for it to be broadcast over an Australian station.

That cultural proximity is partly defined in terms of a shared public service broadcasting ethos. Steemers argues that demand for British drama is highest in countries which share Britain's public service ethos in broadcasting but do not have the resources to produce their own drama.[6]

In the USA, Steemers notes, the emphasis at the public broadcasting system (PBS) channel is on 'quality' period drama and literary adaptations for its Masterpiece Theatre strand. Importantly, PBS – which lacks resources to fund its own productions – is an important co-funder of British drama.

Michael Keane and Albert Moran provided an extremely useful comparative study of the representation of local content across eleven countries in Asia and the Pacific regions.[7] They identified three broad cultural continents: east Asia (Japan, South Korea, Taiwan, Hong Kong and the People's Republic of China), south Asia (India, Singapore, Indonesia and the Philippines) and Oceania (Australia and New Zealand). They found that within east Asia, Japan television industries 'play an influential role, circulating content that is "already local", and facilitating adaptation according to taste and cultural values'. In south Asia, television formats (as opposed to programmes, see above) 'absorb and reflect local cultural nuances'. Countries such as India, Singapore and Malaysia have 'greater porousness' to English language programming, in contrast to Japan, Korea, Taiwan and China, which face less competition from English-language programming. Broadly, the greater 'linguistic isolation', the greater the local content production in east Asia. The study found that in south Asia, local producers and broadcasters had little contact with international television production and tended to produce 'copy-cat' and often unlicensed versions of TV formats for the various Hindi, Malay, Chinese and Tamil constituencies. The study confirmed the argument, developed above, that so far as the cultural and economic trade of TV production is concerned, Australia and New Zealand:

> are part of a different 'cultural continent' whose geographical centre is located in the Northern Hemisphere ... the reality seems to be that both these white, settler societies remain firmly within a Western Anglophone region whose centre is the United States, the United Kingdom and Western Europe.

From these examples we can conclude that international success of programmes ('fully formed' programmes without adaptation) in receiving countries (those buying them) is likely to be enhanced where one or more of the following conditions are present:

1. There is cultural or geographical proximity to the originating country (a shared language also being an obvious advantage).
2. There is curiosity or even envy about lifestyles projected by programmes from the originating country.
3. The receiving country is relatively small or poor, and is therefore unable to produce programmes perceived as being high in quality to fill its schedules.
4. The receiving country has a relatively small but wealthy and/or educated elite which is keen to see programmes perceived as being of 'high culture' produced elsewhere.

5.  The receiving country has a common, shared national identity.
6.  The receiving country partly defined itself by distinguishing itself from a neighbouring (usually larger/more powerful) country and wishes to associate more with the country producing the programme.

## The impact of international TV sales

By 2004 the UK was the world's leading exporter of TV formats – a fact that is enormously important to the TV industry and the British government. British governments took an increased interest in the potential for valuable exports in the 1990s, seeing the BBC, in particular, as a potentially lucrative source of foreign earnings – and much more besides. This enthusiasm was shared by the then Leader of the Opposition, Tony Blair, who in 1995 declared to the Labour Party annual conference[8] that Britain had:

> such huge advantages – some of the finest telecommunications companies in the world; world leaders in broadcasting; the world's first language, English. They could put us years ahead in technology and business.

By February 2005 – shortly before Blair was to win a third successive general election victory – his Minister for Trade, Investment and Foreign Affairs was able to gloat in a foreword to a report[9] sponsored by the government and various broadcasters and trade bodies, that television exports in the previous year were worth $1 billion – and this had been an increase of 22 per cent over the previous year. Furthermore, the total number of hours of made-for-TV (that is, excluding movies) programme imports on British TV had reduced by around 16 per cent in 2003 compared with seven years previously – with mainstream broadcasters replacing imports with original local production.

By 2008, the exports of BBC programmes and formats, through the Corporation's commercial arm, BBC Worldwide, had an operating profit of nearly £120 million, up 17 per cent on the previous year; the following year saw profits up by over a third.[10] The company exploited a number of programmes through its Global Brands division, with *Top Gear* being the first programme to benefit from the new approach and being sold to 42 countries. Drama series *Doctor Who* and *Spooks* and a 'superbrand', CBeebies, the pre-school channel on both digital television and radio, had also achieved a global expansion.[11] Indeed, the whole of the BBC could be said to be a brand, with worldwide recognition and appeal, associated with high quality, public service programming – but which, crucially, was also known for strong drama and entertainment series. UK made-for-TV programme exports had increased by nearly 10 per cent over the same period, to more than 8,100 hours. This increase in exported programmes from the UK compared favourably against the slower growth by the USA and Australia, whilst exports from France had fallen. Sales to the USA accounted for some two-thirds of the net growth, with all markets, except Latin America, growing in real terms. Although – due to much more international competition – there had been a decline in the value of these exports, this had been more than compensated by sales of formats (up over 40 per cent), DVDs/videos and merchandising (both up by more than a third) and co-production up by nearly a fifth in the same seven-year period.

The global appeal of the BBC was recognised by YouTube in 2007 when the Corporation became the company's first major partner outside the USA to have its own video-sharing website. Faced with declining political and public support for publicly funded broadcasters and competition and erosion of revenue for commercial organisations, the whole question of brands of programmes and services has become increasingly important in the very survival of broadcasting organisations in the 21st century. Spreading these brands across international cyberspace could be seen as both an offensive and defensive measure.

## Same formats, different cultures

It is a curious experience to switch on a TV set in a hotel room or apartment many thousands of miles from home and see a programme which has all the look and elements that are very familiar but which has a different presenter from the one back home and may well be speaking in a different language. That 'so familiar but so different' experience is engendered by the worldwide adoption of television formats. But what is a format? Legal experts will tell you that there is no copyright (and therefore no commercial value) in an *idea*: many people could, in around 1960 for example, have sent off an idea to Granada Television in the UK about a group of working-class characters, their trials and tribulations, set a round a pub and the back-to-back homes of a northern industrial city. But only one person set out in detail the characters, story-lines and structure in terms of scenes and use of studio and external filming. That level of detail – in *Coronation Street* – once set down on paper could provide a protection for copyright if somebody else tried to produce the same type of programme. In an article on formats and television exports, Des Freedman has noted that the basic premise of *Coronation Street* has been taken up in a 'soap' *Joy Luck Street*, watched by 400 million Chinese people.[12] Furthermore, Freedman points out that Indian viewers watch a Hindi version of the BBC sitcom *Yes Minister*, broadcast on Star. Fitting almost too perfectly with the theory of cultural imperialism, Freedman then cites a quotation in the New York Times from Paul Smith, Managing Director of Celador, the production company that originally devised *Who Wants to be a Millionaire?* (WWM):

> It's a bit like the old days of the British empire. We've got a map of the world in the office coloured in pink where we've placed the show. Most of the world is pink.

The thoroughness of the copying of the format for this show, sold to 106 countries,[13] extends to the most minute and thorough replication of structure, music, lighting, graphics and camera angles. The pleasures, or 'gratifications' of the show – which clearly resonate in very different cultures – include:

1.  Tension over whether contestants will risk the money they have already 'won' with the answer to the next question which could provide a very large prize.
2.  The use of the three 'Lifelines' ('phone a friend'; 'ask the audience' and '50/50') – when to use them; do you trust the friend or audience?
3.  Although some versions – including the UK – have included a chance for members of the watching audience to win relatively small prizes by contacting the show with answers, it is the identification by the viewing audience with the participants, and (obviously best enjoyed in company) with shouting at answers at the television (perhaps competing with others viewing in the same room), that provide the most powerful 'uses and gratifications' of the show.

## The impact on the Chinese population of *Super (Voice) Girl*

This programme is based on *American Idol* – a singing contest for young women – and was launched by a TV station in China's central Hunan Province in 2004, with sponsorship from the Megnui Dairy. The 2005 competition became one of the most-watched programmes ever in China, with the finals drawing an estimated 400 million viewers. The winner drew over three-and-a-half-million votes, and ranked fourth in that year's list by *Forbes* magazine of top Chinese celebrities and was the cover feature of more magazines than any other celebrities in the country. But not everyone was enamoured with the show. Liu Zhogde, the Director of the Science, Education, Culture, Health and Sport Commission and member of the Communist Party's Central Committee (CPPCC) told the *China Times*:[14]

> The audience watches the program under a distorted mentality and in an unhealthy condition. Open the doors and windows to let in fresh air, and flies and mosquitos are bound to come in too. This is nothing to be surprised at; it is completely understandable. The problem lies in how we face these mosquitos and flies. We cannot let our youth be contaminated in the midst of entertainment and laughter.

Such uncompromising views might shock western readers but they are not so different from those of establishment figures and moral guardians (as well as many other citizens) in Britain in the 1920s and 1930s about jazz – described an insidious, alien culture – or by those in the UK and USA to the corruption and collapse of moral values of their respective youth from rock 'n' roll in the late 1950s.

However, *Super Girls'* position as China's top TV show was usurped in 2007 by Shanghai TV's *My Hero*,[15] in which, as Britain's *The Independent* newspaper put it:[16]

> good-looking lads flex their muscles, sing songs, apply hairspray and resolve crunching moral dilemmas ... They also have to answer tricky questions, such as 'Why do you think you are a good man?' or 'What will you do if someone says your girlfriend is not pretty?'

This programme is especially interesting because, like the sexual revolution in the 1960s and 1970s in 'the west', it has helped to re-define masculine identities. As one rapturous viewer, 23-year-old Shen Si, put it: 'I like the way the boys dress, and I find it amazing to see the boys cry when they're moved.' Dragon TV's vice-president Xiang Haiqi had told Chinese radio that the focus was on courage, versatility and a sense of responsibility and that 'it should be about a feeling instead of just singing and dancing'.[17]

Perhaps the critics of the pernicious effects of such shows would be more positive about a Reality TV show – *Win in China* – which aimed to show how people could succeed in business. This, clearly, is based on *The Apprentice* – which was originated at NBC in the USA,[18] with a team of judges headed by property billionaire Donald Trump, and successfully adapted in the UK, with Alan Sugar in Trump's role. However, Wang Lifan, the producer and host of the show, claims that *Win in China* had higher aspirations than *The Apprentice*:[19] 'We want to teach values. Our dream for the show is to enlighten Chinese people and help them realise their own dreams.'

In his article on the show,[20] James Fallows ruminates on the historical and cultural background to the show and its significance at this stage in China's astonishing economic development:

> Reduced to a moral, *Win in China* instructs Chinese people that they have chances never open to their compatriots before – but also that, as one contestant told me at the end of the show, 'The only one I can rely on is myself.'

It is also important to consider the ways in which China is represented to others through 'western'-type television. An example of this was with the CBS TV show *Survivor*. In 2007 the contestants were sent to Jiangxi Province in eastern China. The opening scene was shot in Mi Tuo Temple. As the *National Catholic Reporter* described it:[21]

> a foreign company must first submit a shooting schedule for approval for China's State Administration of Radio, Film and Television. However, if

the production includes scenes featuring the military, religion or other sensitive issues, the agency requires a full script review.

Clearly, then, the authorities are highly sensitive to the way their country is presented in the western media – perhaps especially so for this series, as it was shown less than a year before the Beijing Olympics. But, as in Chapter 6, the question of what is 'truth' raises its head in this foreign locale for *Survivor*, not least by Chinese in the USA, to see how their nation is portrayed. The magazine article[22] reported some of the reaction on a blog compiled by Son Chou at chinabooks.com:

> Chinese from Jiangxi say they didn't recognise the 'traditional welcoming ceremony' as any tradition they ever practiced. They also noted that the wilderness in which the *Survivor* cast camps is in a nature preserve at the cross-roads of several highways and a popular, crowded tourist site.

Overall, the article concluded that *Survivor China*:

> is a fiction created by Western TV and no doubt guided by China's State Administration of Radio, Film and Television. That doesn't – shouldn't come as a surprise, but it does bear keeping in mind.

## How much do 'we' learn about 'them'?

The final area to consider is the representations of countries and the lives and ambitions of their citizens in other very different societies; particularly how the developing world is represented on screens in developed countries. This is a huge topic which can only be introduced in this book, but the International Broadcasting Trust (IBT), an educational charity which campaigns for quality TV coverage of the developing world, published a major report in 2008 called *Screening the World*.[23] Andy Glynne, director of the Trust, noted[24] that, whilst factual coverage of developing countries on UK digital and terrestrial channels had increased by 44 per cent over the previous five years, this was not the 'good news' that it might at first appear to be, with much of the coverage on 'soft topics' such as wildlife and holiday shows. However, the coverage of 'harder topics' on the developing world, which account for only 7 per cent of the UK's factual programming:

> may give us a distorted sense of how people live, leaving us with an impression of war-torn countries, where everyone is starving to death, all governments are corrupt, half the population has Aids and most children are either in full-time employment or have been recruited as soldiers by some armed resistance.[25]

In short, then, the overwhelming picture is of the developing world being both 'the other' and being 'a problem'. Furthermore, the picture presented about the developing world is one reliant on 'the west' (developed/industrialised world) for aid and support, whether that be direct economic/food aid or in aiding a transition to 'western-style' democracy.

The situation is even more complicated – and potentially toxic – by the growing numbers of first and second-generation immigrants to the UK from such countries, especially sub-Saharan Africa. Figures produced in 2005[26] showed that, of those not born in the UK, excluding the Republic of Ireland, and Germany – mostly thought to be children of British Forces and attached civilians serving there at the time of their birth – the greatest number were from India (466,000), Pakistan (320,000) and the Caribbean (255,000). These are substantial numbers and public service broadcasters, in particular, have to be sensitive on the portrayal of the 'home' countries. This is not just a matter of 'doing the right thing' but out of self-interest: there are differences in viewing habits of ethnic minorities (around 10 per cent of the UK population, with almost half living in Greater London) and the likelihood is that such audiences will not view programmes if they feel that broadcasters are not reflecting 'their' cultures and lives. 'They' are likely to bypass the mainstream broadcasters completely and opt to watch satellite channels relaying their 'home' services. Such moves also pose major questions over the desirability – or even feasibility – of an integrated society with shared values, if not customs.

At the heart of this is the complex issue of mixed, or variable, identities. There is undoubtedly a more assertive identity by young British Asians in particular, with the cultures and languages of their ethnic roots. The British newspaper *The Independent* highlighted this phenomenon in a feature[27] which discussed the viewing habits of a particular family, the Mandalias who came to Britain in the early 1970s and live in a small Victorian townhouse in north London. Initially, their only entertainment was a small television set with three channels – BBC1, BBC 2 and ITV. The parents had grown up under British colonial rule in Kenya and spoke English well, although their mother tongue was Gujarati and they spoke Hindi – India's most widely spoken language. British terrestrial TV had helped them learn more about their adopted homeland but they longed to enjoy the Bollywood epics they'd grown up with. In time, these became available via specialist video stores. The thought of these being available on a British TV service seemed unthinkable. Now though – largely thanks to News Corporation's Star TV, owned by Rupert Murdoch, who brought satellite TV to millions of Britons – the Mandalia household reverberates (thanks to 'an enormous flat screen monitor'[28] hung on a living room wall) to Hindi music, movies, 'soaps', quiz shows ('including the highly popular *Kya Aap Paanchvi Paas Se Tez Hain* – a sort of Hindi equivalent of *Are You Smarter than a 10 Year Old?* hosted by India's Brad Pitt, Shah Rukh Khan')[29] and reality TV shows, to the extent they hardly watch the mainstream UK domestic channels.

Star UK's marketing manager, Ajay Ochani, believes that the appeal of such satellite TV to British Asians is that it allows them both to express their pride in the new international status of their original homelands and to reconnect to their ancestral roots:

> 'Clearly this particular phenomenon has been helped by India's economic miracle, but I think it's more than that,' he says. 'There's a reason why British Asians want to reconnect to India and that's because they're proud of its success. And it's not just pride in India, there's a real sense among our viewers that they're proud to be British Asian.'[30]

## Notes and references

1. See page(s) on *Screenonline* at: http://www.screenonline.org.uk/tv/id/465503/.
2. This anachronistic term stems from the historic roots of such schools, which were 'public' because they were open to those who were not necessarily from aristocratic, noble families. In Britain, a 'public school' is one which is outside the state system and which charges fees directly to the pupil's family.
3. BBC News (2004) 'Gervais' surprise at Globes win', available online at: http://news.bbc.co.uk/1/hi/entertainment/3423649.stm.
4. *Ibid.*
5. Both the UK and Germany have approximately 60 million, whereas the USA has around five times these at just over 300 million. All population figures quoted are estimates from the CIA at July 2008.
6. Steemers, J. (2005) 'No longer 'The Best in the World': The Challenge of Exporting British Television Drama', *Media International Australia incorporating Culture and Policy*, no. 115. pp. 33–46.
7. Keane, M. and Moran, A. (2005) '(Re)Presenting Local Content: Program Adaptation In Asia and the Pacific', *Media International Australia incorporating Culture and Policy*, no. 116. pp. 88–99.
8. Cited in Freedman, D. (2003) 'Who Wants to be a Millionaire? The politics of television exports', *Information, Communication & Society*, vol. 6, no.1. pp 24–41.
9. Television Research Partnership (2005) *Rights of Passage – British Television in a Global Market*, available online at: http://forums.rave.ac.uk/jive/servlet/JiveServlet/download/134-2267-5891-676/britishtvinaglobalmarket.pdf.
10. Sweeney, M. (5 July, 2010) 'BBC Worldwide reports record profits', *Guardian.co.uk*, available online at: http://www.guardian.co.uk/media/2010/jul/05/bbc-worldwide-profits.
11. *Ibid.*
12. Freedman (2003) as note 8.
13. *Screen Digest* (12 April, 2005) 'Who Wants to be a Millionaire, Big Brother, Pop Idol, The Weakest Link and Other Programme Formats now Dominate the Global Television Industry', Press Release, available online at: http://www.screendigest.com/reports/gttf05/EBAN-6BFCYH/pressRelease.pdf.
14. Martinsen, J. (26 April, 2006) 'CPPCC: Exterminate the Super Girls', *Danwei.org*, available online at: http://www.danwei.org/trends_and_buzz/cppcc_exterminate_the_super_girls.php.

15. As the article points out, the show's Chinese name is Jia You, Hao Nan Er! which translates literally as 'Add Oil, Good Boy!' – 'add oil' is what people shout at sporting events and it means 'come on'. But producers have opted for the snappier English title *My Hero!*

16. Coonan, C. (2 April, 2007) 'Move over Supergirl, China wants a new hero', *Independent. co.uk,* available online at: http://www.independent.co.uk/news/world/asia/move-over-supergirl-china-wants-a-new-hero-442948.html.

17. *Ibid.*

18. Further details online at: http://www.nbc.com/The_Apprentice_5/.

19. Fallows, J. (April 2007) 'Win in China!', *Atlantic Monthly*, vol. 299, issue 3: 72–8.

20. *Ibid.*

21. Ryan, E. (2 November, 2007) 'Beating the odds on *Survivor'*, *National Catholic Reporter*, 18.

22. *Ibid.*

23. Available online at: http://www.ibt.org.uk/all_documents/research_reports/screening_the_%20world_June2008.pdf#page=1.

24. Glynne, A. (11 June, 2008). 'Hot Topic: TV and the developing world', *Broadcastnow*, available online (subscribers only) at: http://www.broadcastnow.co.uk/opinion_and_blogs/hot_topic/2008/06/hot_topic_tv_and_the_developing_world.html.

25. *Ibid.*

26. BBC News (2005) 'British immigration map revealed.',aailable online at: http://news.bbc.co.uk/1/hi/uk/4218740.stm.

27. Taylor, J. (23 June, 2008) 'The rising star of Asian language programming', *Independent.co.uk*, available online at: http://www.independent.co.uk/news/media/the-rising-star-of-asian-language-programming-852211.html.

28. *Ibid.*

29. *Ibid.*

30. *Ibid.*

# Convergence and Citizens' Journalism

## 11

This chapter considers the nature and significance of technological innovations leading to convergence in broadcasting and how this has enabled the public to interact with journalistic and other output, often breaking down the previous distinctions between broadcasters and audiences. In particular the chapter discusses:

- The nature and types of convergence, both technologically and in the impact of broadcast consumption.
- How convergence has resulted in new types of content and how this has impacted on more traditional forms of production and transmission.
- The significance of convergence in engagement and interaction with younger audiences.
- The particular impact of convergence in the uses by audiences of news output on the BBC and Sky News.
- Whether user generated content in factual areas can be classified as 'journalism'.

## What do we mean by 'convergence'?

Before getting into the detail of how convergence is manifesting itself in broadcasting it will be useful to establish exactly what we mean by convergence in the mass media. It is also necessary to briefly discuss digitisation – the conversion of audio, video and other content into streams of '0's and '1's and the rate and number of these that are transmitted and received determines the quality and to some extent the reliability of the reception. Put simply, you cannot have convergence without digitisation. Digitisation is often both 'platform neutral' and 'content neutral' because once something has been digitised it is capable of being converted or re-versioned in many different ways and in terms of the radio spectrum used for the transmission of digital content, there is not necessarily any particular reason why one piece of radio spectrum is better at one type of content or another. Digitisation allows a variety of different types of content to be converted and accessed on a variety of different devices from a variety of different transmission methods or platforms.

Most obviously though, the concept of convergence in terms of mass communications is when one form of mass media takes on the form and properties of another to the point when it is impossible to distinguish in any meaningful way between the two. This can be – in fact usually does – result in a blurring in both from the type of *reception* (what kind of device is being used to access the content) and *content* (the material being created and received on old and new media).

A simple example of this is when, what are to all intents and purposes, 'radio' services broadcast on audio channels on digital television receivers. Listening to their 'radio' on the television proved surprisingly popular in the UK and ironically, the bit rate broadcast for the radio services transmitted via the Sky satellite and Freeview (terrestrial) platforms was higher and therefore produced better quality audio than that transmitted over the DAB digital radio platform. In fact, the most successful of the BBC's digital only radio offerings, BBC Radio 7 (re-branded as Radio 4 Extra in April 2011), was broadcast only in mono over DAB, whereas it was in stereo on satellite, cable and (terrestrial) Freeview systems. However, despite the fascination and much comment in the broadcasting industry over the phenomenon of 'listening to the radio on the television' listening to radio via the DAB platform, in the UK, greatly exceeds listening to radio services via TV or the internet.

The phenomenon of convergence, therefore, at one basic and important level, is a technical one: attributes we have associated with one form of mass communications being present on another, and there is a general blurring of distinctions between what is 'a radio' and what is 'a television'. The situation is not helped by the fact that we use the nouns 'radio' and 'television', as both to describe the receiving *equipment* and of the *content* of media output. That is why, for example, many broadcasting organisations have changed the names of their departments and personnel to reflect the fact that they are responsible for creating 'audio' or 'video' so that the type of output is no longer necessarily associated with a particular kind of receiver or platform.

Having established what we mean by convergence, the next obvious question is 'does it matter?' Given that there is a whole chapter in this book devoted to the subject and that in fact convergence is discussed at different levels in several other chapters, clearly from the perspective of this book at least, it certainly does! Why I think it is so important is that this is certainly not – unless you are of course employed in particular research and development areas – principally a technical issue. Convergence is important because it affects the way that the relationship between audiences and broadcast output is changing. Convergence may well and indeed must be initiated and to some extent driven by technological developments, but its effects on the whole of the broadcasting culture and the relationship between broadcasters and audiences is the really significant change in the 21st century.

The 'driver' behind this change is, of course, the development of the internet and the world wide web from being a fairly passive and text-based form of communication to one which encompasses all the types of output we had hitherto associated with broadcasting – sound and vision, in short and long form; for viewing and listening at a time, date and place and increasingly on the type of device, that is most convenient and provide the greatest satisfaction for the audience. There are technical, financial and copyright constraints on all of this but the essential principle is that the combination of the digitisation of forms of broadcast content and their distribution via the internet and the world wide web has – as discussed in Chapter 8 – released broadcast content from being 'shackled' to transmissions at a particular time, place and form.

The phenomenal success and demand for mobile phone technology has been of major importance. Far from being a device that merely enables phone calls and text messages to be made and received on the move, a mobile/cell phone has rapidly developed into a multimedia player and consumers are clearly fascinated by the ability to listen to music, and watch all types of audio and video content and most crucially, interact with that content. It is the interactivity which is the final most important concept and development.

## Types of broadcast convergence technologies and usage

These can be broadly classified into four broad categories:

1.  The broadcasters using web-delivered services to make available (usually) material on demand but simultaneously being broadcast over radio/TV services, or already broadcast over 'traditional' TV and radio, although some might 're-versioned' for the web delivery. An example is the BBC's iPlayer. Programmes can be streamed or downloaded and viewed/listened to again for up to 30 days (depending on copyright). After this, the programme is automatically 'wiped' from the computer. A similar version for the radio – the Radioplayer – combining BBC and commercial stations, was launched in late 2010. This also has the intriguing effect of directing audiences to competitors' output.

2.  Those that use a convergence technology – usually the internet/broadband – to deliver broadcast or other content (sometimes edited for copyright or other reasons), specific to the citizen's interests and/or favourite programmes, etc., which can then be played on mobile or static devices at a time and place of their choosing. Examples are podcasts (audio content, sometimes with limited text, pictures and graphics) and vodcasts (audio and video) are usually of weekly or daily programmes which can simply be listened/viewed as a stream on demand, are designed to be downloaded

and automatically 'refreshed' with each new episode using 'really simple syndication' (RSS) and a 'podcatcher' piece of software, such as Apple's iTunes onto a computer and then synchronised ('synched') on to similar software on portable devices such as the iPod.

3.  Those that deliver broadcast-type material over the internet which can then be viewed on a standard TV or other device. An example is internet protocol TV (IPTV). A joint project for the UK's main PSB TV broadcasters, YouView (described as 'Freeview for the internet'), was due to launch in 2012 and using broadband connections to link to TV sets. The aim is for complete and seamless inter-operability between the TV and the computer, so material downloaded via PC can be viewed 'full screen' on the TV set, usually placed elsewhere in the house.

4.  A variety of content usually already broadcast by 'traditional' TV, but which allows an interaction between user and broadcaster and for the user to 'personalise' the content and merge it with other forms of content and social networking spaces using new technology. An example is Hulu, which has done commercial deals to provide content from several US TV networks. Increasingly looking and 'feeling' similar to social networking sites such as YouTube, these sites, which began as the names suggest to offer clips made by subscribers, not broadcasters, are also now increasingly showing content from traditional broadcasters. Perhaps most intriguingly, YouTube allows the audience to be creative and to manipulate and 'mash-up' content, often mixed with music tracks, to create a new audio-visual artefact. The 'comments' section then allows others to assess critically (often in scathing and obscene terms) the efforts by others. Sometimes whole strings of videos are created in new 'channels.' Again, however, there are often copyright issues here; the broadcasters, naturally, do not wish others to use their content for their own reasons and copyright laws in fact are designed in part to prevent such re-versioning.

The above four types seem certain to be major parts of the development of broadcasting in the 21st century. An additional category, mobile TV, where content is streamed on mobile/cell phones, has been successful in some parts of the world, notably South Korea, but has been much less so in other countries such as the UK.

## Web 2.0 and the two-way flow

It is indisputable that what has come to be known as Web 2.0 – the evolution of the internet, which started by giving access to pages, plus hypertext links, first to text, then to audio and video, to an interactive medium whereby the user contributes to the content – is transforming broadcasting and indeed challenging the whole meaning of 'broadcasting' and blurring the boundaries between what we may call old and new media. Anthony Lilley, chief executive of British independent TV producer Magic Lantern, helped explain to the Royal Television Society the equation which explains the difference between TV (as we knew it in the 20th century and the early years of the 21st) and Web 2.0.[1]

He attributed the traditional one-way operation of networks from broadcaster to many receivers to NBC founder David Sarnoff, which applied first to radio and then with television. A hypothetical Sarnoff network with 20 viewers can be said to have a score of 20 points. The second type of network, named after Bob Metcalfe one of the inventors of the internet, allows each of its users to call each other one-to-one. Because everybody can call one another, the total possible number of calls and therefore the score of the network is 20 squared or 400. It is therefore potentially much more powerful than the communication of ideas than a Sarnoff network and there is a third type of networking that is morphing with the first two – social networking. Lilley explains that this allows the individual to belong to and connect with a number of groups which then overlap with groups identified by others.[2]

It is, therefore, the personalisation and 'virtual social networking' aspects of the converged technologies that perhaps provide the most interesting and radical development in internet technologies converging with broadcasting.

Not only are broadcasters using their main news sites for inclusion of material by citizens (see below) but they are creating new, specific sites which are not directly connected with their main broadcast services. Key to this is the personalisation of such sites: citizens being able to define and set up particular types of material to meet their particular interests and needs. The whole of broadcasting, which developed from a 'one to many' approach is shifting to a much more intimate relationship.

## Radio and convergence

Listening to radio via the internet, mobile (cell) phones, time-shifted listening via 'Listen Again' and podcasts shows increasing use during the first decade of the 21st century. Research by RAJAR in 2010[3] showed that nearly a third of adults claimed to have ever listened to the radio via the internet and a quarter had time-shifted their listening using 'Listen Again' services. Fifteen per cent of the adult population had downloaded a podcast, with almost half doing so at least once a week. A typical podcast user subscribed to just under five podcasts but only 25 per cent found the time to listen to all of these; causing a further problem, as discussed in Chapter 2, in measuring the actual audience for any particular programme. The survey – the sixth of its kind – confirmed that comedy and music remained the two favourite genres. Encouragingly for the radio broadcasters, 36 per cent said they listened to programmes to which they did not listen previously – and this had risen four per cent in just six months. Perhaps unexpectedly though, less than half listened to podcasts in the car or on public transport, whilst more than three-quarters listened at home. A previous survey[4] showed that the demographic for podcast listening is even more pronounced than that for the iPlayer – 65 per cent were men and 54 per centof all users were in the 15–34 age group. Radio listening in the UK is slightly higher amongst males and more popular in the older age groups but there may be good news for broadcasters in that the increasing use of podcasting may help balance the ageing profile of 'live' listening. Even better news – for commercial broadcasters – was that 50 per cent of respondents said they would be interested in downloading podcasts containing advertising; provided those podcasts were free. This dropped to a third of users if the podcasts containing commercials also had to be paid for. This suggests an understanding that advertising has to be tolerated because it helps to pay for content that would otherwise have to be paid for directly, but there is resistance to both directly paying for content and then *also* being subjected to advertising messages.

As might be expected and in line with the Middletown Media Studies research discussed in Chapter 2, listening to the radio via the internet is very much a complementary activity. A study of the figures by Adam Bowie of Absolute Radio[5] showed that only a couple of per cent of those who ever listen to the radio via the internet did nothing else; around a quarter were using the computer for activities such as shopping and playing computer games – which must take up a fair amount of mental concentration – and nearly 80 per cent were simultaneously checking their emails.

There have also been a number of experiments of actually putting video in radio programmes, for example by putting a camera in the studio, directly on television. Indeed, BBC television's earliest experiments in breakfast television in the 1970s used this technique. In 2007 the BBC radio network 5 Live linked up with television's *Newsnight* for phone-in programmes, and, during the campaign period for the Labour party leadership in the summer of 2010, a 'live' debate on BBC Radio 5 Live with the five contenders and an audience was also videoed and broadcast later on the BBC's Parliamentary channel. These were 'one offs' but the radio-turned-TV became an established feature of daily output by 2010. The early static webcam shots, refreshed perhaps every 30 seconds, had by then been replaced on many stations by continuous, high quality and in some cases, multi-camera video feeds of the radio programmes. This was particularly notable in the UK in the Corporation's top-rated daily current affairs programme, *Today*, and on the national commercial rock/pop station Absolute Radio, which also took to posting videos of inter-views on its website. In many ways though, watching such output on the web is akin to being a voyeur. The material and activity was not primarily intended or produced for a viewing audience and there are no concessions from the presenters or producers to such an audience. It is merely 'added value' but of some additional interest to those who either study the media or are interested in body language and an aspects of the physical and psychological interplay between the presenters and the studio guests.

The BBC made further use of its 'red button' (on remote controls) facility on digital channels by making available the (admittedly more obviously visual content) of the Terry Wogan's Sunday show on BBC Radio 2, which contained a 'live' audience and music performances. Some of the chat and the playing in of records were cut, but the 'live' show was edited so smoothly that, aside from the sight of Wogan and guests wearing radio studio-type headphones it could be viewed as a TV show. Evidently the public think so, as, according to Wogan's blog,[6] the second run of the show (from May 2010) attracted over one million red-button viewers. The first comment on that blog provided a perceptive analysis of this converged, multi-platform world:

> Hey Tel!
> It was good listening to you on your weekend show, although it really felt like television on the radio and I'm sure when you were 'doing it' on the telly, they said it was like doing radio on the telly.
> It just goes to show what goes around, comes around ... again and again and again.

## Platform-neutral content

For the BBC, concerned about the declining appeal of traditional broadcasting output to younger people, the success of its digital youth-orientated network, BBC Three, was crucial. The relative expense of operating this channel compared with its relatively low audience figures have led many, both within and outside the BBC, to question whether the Corporation's investment was wise or prudent. It is also true that when the audience did come to the channel it was in general for repeats of programmes that had already been broadcast on one or more of the BBC's other TV channels. The start of 2008, however, saw what was perhaps a 'tipping point' in the BBC's, and by implication the wider broadcasting world's, treatment of television: the Corporation announced that from now on the network would be 'platform neutral', that is to say it did not matter whether programmes were originally created as traditional television offerings or for the internet and those who were pitching for commissions on the network were obliged to take into consideration the distribution of the output across all relevant platforms.

The other significant UK public service network targeted at young people is Channel 4's E4. This, too, has largely featured repeats of programmes already broadcast on Channel 4 or extra content from such programmes as *Big Brother*. But in 2008 the most significant of its original commissions was the drama *Skins*, featuring teenagers at a sixth form college in Bristol. Not only were episodes available for downloading through Channel 4's 4oD site, but the first three first episodes of the much anticipated second series, which began in February 2008, were available for downloading 24 hours before it was screened on E4.

The first series, transmitted in 2007, drew the channel's biggest ever audience and can be considered both a popular and critical success, with reviewers, even in the normally staid *Daily Telegraph*, praising its narrative strengths and general success as a television drama. This is despite the fact that most of the narrative involves the teenagers engaging in a somewhat idealistic lifestyle, involving sex (heterosexual and homosexual/bisexual, and a relationship – between a tutor and pupil), drinking alcohol to excess – with the usual results – and illegal drugs. There are several noteworthy aspects of the production, not least the fact that the actors are, for once, actually the age of the characters which they are playing – TV drama producers normally employing actors in their 20s who look some years younger. More than that, the writers are nearly all in their late teens or early 20s and the creators are a father-and-son team and although some parental conflict is shown, in general there is sympathy and empathy between the generations. Although a number of newspaper and magazine articles featured parents stating how appalled they were at some of the behaviour demonstrated, there was a consensus that the drama was a realistic portrayal of middle-class teenagers in Britain and there was great admiration for the stylistic and production devices in the writing and direction, as well as the truthfulness of the acting performances. Life certainly imitated art when one episode featured a smashing up of a home by the teenagers when the parental owners were away, and this was replicated in a notorious *Skins* party in 'real life', with invitations sent out using social networking sites.

Digital, multi-channel television, combined with Web 2.0 and social networking, therefore, have made at least one television programme a success with an audience that has been elusive to many channel controllers. But youth is not the only 'problem area' for broadcasters. As noted in Chapter 1, significant sections of the potential audience have felt, and continued to feel, underserved or even ignored by mainstream broadcasters.

One of Britain's most respected black performers is Lenny Henry. He first came to national attention in the mid-1970s as something of a novelty act – an African–Caribbean impressionist who 'did' well-known white performers and personalities (as well as Trevor McDonald, for sometime the only non-white major newscaster). In an interview with the *Media Guardian* Henry opined that if there wasn't a 'fundamental change' the BBC, ITV and Channel 4 were in danger of losing an entire generation of viewers and sealing their own demise.[7] To Henry, African–Caribbean and Asian culture is in fact youth culture and unless the broadcasters engage with it they would lose audiences across all ethnic groups. He believes that broadcasters are complacent and need to make more effort to engage with all young people, who are fully media literate and are often making media themselves.

The connection between traditional broadcast TV and the new video-sharing websites took a major step forward in the UK in 2009, when Channel 4 did a deal with YouTube to make much of their content available on the site. Most media commentators agreed this was a recognition of the inevitable: so much material was finding its way to the site, with the broadcasters receiving no payment, that it made sense to legitimise this activity, so at least some revenue would be gained.

Another significant development has been 'webisodes' – short versions of TV programmes, perhaps one or two compressed scenes, often used as promotional devices for the broadcast TV shows, but which nevertheless added a further 'immersive' element to the relationship between audience and programme content. A further use to which broadcasters have put the web is by trialling content. In the summer of 2010, STV the UK contractor for the main commercial network, ITV, in Scotland, announced that its digital and on-air teams had joined forces to trial comedy-sketch shows to help it decide which show – its first for 20 years – should be commissioned. Web viewers voted for their favourite sketches.

Competition is an important spur to developing interactive elements and strengthening the relationship between broadcaster and audience. The soccer World Cup in 2010 had Britain's two original, and still leading, TV broadcasters in competition for audiences for the games – the group stages being divided between them but the knock-out games saw them in direct competition. Traditionally, when in competition, the BBC has been the clear winner, as indeed this proved in 2010. But before the competition started, *Broadcast* magazine described the elaborate interactive elements that would be provided by ITV – some of which, being a commercial broadcaster, were also designed to produce additional advertising revenues, including podcasts, apps (applications) for mobile phones, and a 'red button' facility, providing extra comment and interviews.[8]

We can see, therefore, that the convergent, multi-platform aspects produce both additional and interactive content via the traditional TV broadcast but are also designed to be accessed on a range of mobile and web-based devices.

## New media, new content

A major type of new media content meeting the old is in content that looks a lot like traditional television but is in fact created specifically for the web. An example of this is from Endemol, which produced *Big Brother. The Gap Year* followed six users of the social networking site Bebo as they travel the world competing, or at least interacting, with other social networkers. It was the third original content commission from Bebo within six months. By the end of 2007 the site had 10.7 million regular users in the UK alone and had a young audience of 15 to 24-year-olds who are light consumers of traditional media.[9] Each 'programme' can be viewed via its own profile page on the social network site and some, such as the previous social interactive drama, *Kate Modern* on MySpace and YouTube. Each episode of *Kate Modern* cost just £6,000 – a fraction of a conventional TV drama – and over 25 million users watched each of the daily for many episodes. Joanna Shields, Bebo's International President, said the dramas could migrate to a traditional TV outlet, but the strength of using social networking sites is the personalisation and interaction that turns the passive viewer into an active participant in the unfolding content:

The strength of Bebo is that it offers instant feedback from a built-in forum of interested and committed users eager not just to consume content but to actively get involved, so we can satisfy the level of involvement young audiences now expect.[10]

Advertisers certainly appreciate the specific targeting of their messages and avoiding the larger wastage that occurs in the traditional broadcasting mass audience model. Advertising on the internet exceeded that of radio in the UK in 2006 and ITV in 2007: some of the biggest spenders on commercial TV have been seduced by the new media – the detergent manufacturers Procter & Gamble and mobile phone company Orange paid up to £250,000 to have their names integrated into the *Kate Modern* story-line.

Services such as Hulu, and indeed all media using the internet, have a distinct advantage over broadcast advertising because each computer has its unique internet protocol (IP) address which can be detected by the provider of the material and 'cookies' can be integrated into the software used to view or listen to the material, providing detailed information about the usage on each computer.

Tony Orsten, who worked on the Joost web-video service, believes that this factor will be hugely significant in driving advertisers – who above almost everything else crave to know the most detailed possible information about consumers – to these new forms of television and that in itself will cause a fundamental change in the way that content is created and distributed:

> Clearly if you watch lots of news and documentary programmes the chances are you are a certain kind of person. If you just watch hip-hop music and comedy clips you are a different sort of person, so the software is able to determine very accurately the sort of person you are and therefore be able to tell the advertisers through the software what sort of products the user might wish to have. (Personal interview, January 2008)

## Convergence and news production

The convergence of what used to be at least three different types of creation and output – radio, television and online – is feverishly debated amongst and within news organisations. The BBC, faced with a less than hoped-for increase in its licence fee, made a virtue out of necessity by announcing, in October 2007, that it would be, physically and editorially, bringing together what were separate strands and processes of its production. No longer would there be separate teams in the main BBC newsroom, at any rate from the different media covering the same story. This seems to make sense and undoubtedly there had been duplication and waste. But many who had worked exclusively in one of the media – perhaps especially radio – and indeed many listeners and viewers, worried that this amalgamation of processes and output would result in a kind of media porridge: a bland and homogeneous mix of storytelling that eradicates the different strengths and attractions of each medium. If every report or indeed whole programme had to be capable of working on different platforms the subtleties and nuances of each would be lost.

Furthermore, the audience's ability to 'pick 'n' mix' their news consumption worries some broadcasters, who fear that it will lead to the trivialisation of news and current affairs and that many people will miss out on more demanding, and arguably more important, news. The BBC's political editor, Nick Robinson, who cannot be regarded in any way opposed to, or reluctant to use, new digital technologies in his craft having been one of the first of the Corporation's bloggers, is aware that personalisation could lead to viewers' disengagement as they self-selected an ever narrower news agenda.[11] The BBC's Pete Clifton (at the time of interview – September 2007 – Head of Multimedia Development, BBC News) however, is less concerned about this and in any case regards this as now an unstoppable tide:

> The audience for the traditional [news] bulletins will slowly decline, particularly in digital homes, so clearly a central part of our approach is to invest in the website and mobiles to keep the audience up, so when that [the TV audience] declines we need to build our [online] audience. I don't think that as people move more to our platform to consume their news from the BBC means [it becomes] much lighter in tone. The front page will have to offer a broad cross-section of the darker and the light, audio and video and giving people more of an insight into what people are looking at that time.

But Pete Clifton believes that the Corporation will continue to have and to utilise the distinct craft skills of different media for key parts of the output for the foreseeable future and that bringing together skilled people and new approaches will produce benefits for both the journalist and the citizen:

> There will still be craft people who are expert in their particular platform. So the website won't simply be handing itself on to whoever is on the rota that day. There will still be web specialists but what it may mean is that when we send one of our web reporters out on a story they may do something for radio or television as well. It won't mean a rapid dilution of skills, online or around TV and radio. Over time people do work across platforms. If you send someone out to do everything they'll do everything really badly ... our intention is to raise the profile of video by embedding it into the site but in doing so we will need to ensure it is high quality and worth its prominent position on the page.

The distinction between professional and amateur footage has narrowed considerably in the 21st century and seems likely to disappear to the point where most viewers will find it hard to detect material that has been produced on equipment costing thousands of pounds and that which can be bought for less than a hundred, provided there is some skill in the shooting and editing of the video. Furthermore, broadcasters increasingly take footage that had originally been created for the web and incorporated it into all kinds of news and current affairs programmes. Thus, by 2010 both *form* and *content* were merging to the point where discussions about *how* content was produced and where it was first made available seemed increasingly irrelevant.

## The role of the citizen in news coverage

Citizens have always contributed to the processes of even the most professional of journalistic operations. Amateur photographers have often been present at what transpired to be dramatic and newsworthy events and eyewitness accounts, although usually framed and circumscribed by the 'gatekeepers' of established journalism and become an important feature of most broadcast news operations. John Ryley, Executive Editor of Sky News, in an interview with the author in September 2007, points out that there is even a 'pre-history' of what is now called 'citizen journalism', or user-generated content (UGC) journalism:

> Descriptions of battles taking place in the classical world are UGC and from the First World War, of infantrymen in the trenches in France is UGC, but now with technology is changing the scale of it. The speed and the big difference is that it's a picture ... the power of a picture cannot be over-estimated. So on the days of the [terrorist] attacks on Glasgow airport [in 2007] we were very lucky editorially; a holidaymaker at the airport filmed what was happening on their mobile [cell phone]. Within a minute they'd sent it to Sky News and within two minutes we had it on the air. That couldn't have happened when I started in journalism 25 years ago; it wouldn't have happened five years ago and it probably wouldn't have happened three years ago ... three years ago somebody might have taken some pictures and might have emailed it, possibly. The speed of delivery has made all the difference.

Viewers and listeners have also been important to broadcast journalists in 'tipping off' about news stories and newsrooms often hear about fires, road accidents and even murders first from members of the public, with some stations offering a small tip-off fee for such information. There is always the danger of malicious or hoax calls, or the member of the public simply being mistaken in what they believe to have seen or heard, so news organisations almost always wait for confirmation from official sources or their own journalists or those of rival news organisations (clearly more risky). So the question of veracity is crucial and, as this chapter will discuss, an even more crucial element in the almost instantaneous supply of images from supposed news events.

For John Ryley there is clearly a generational difference in attitudes towards such content:

> There's an age difference: people over [about] 40 think that it is important that what you are putting on air is accurate. Younger generations are not so bothered, they have a different 'take'. They want to see it and make the judgement themselves and the whole web revolution and UGC and the changes in technologies have empowered people and it's quite patronizing of me to say 'I am the editor in chief of Sky News and we will decide whether people will see this picture: we will decide whether it's an image of the tsunami.' People out there are saying 'well show us and we will decide'. Younger people want that information first and they'll decide and compare and contrast it with other bits of information when they come to their decisions, whereas the older generation, who are used to terrestrial radio and television bulletins, just have a different take on what news is.

Simon Waldman, at the time of interview in September 2007 the Morning News Editor of BBC News 24 (later re-named BBC News Channel), says the BBC has always attempted to obtain pictures from members of the public who may have captured a major news event:

> Twenty years ago we would get tip-offs from freelancers and occasionally members of the public [but] they were treated with a greater degree of caution than was warranted: 'oh we'd better check this out, it's only a viewer!' It was very much 'we are the broadcaster …' but now we realize that, particularly in terms of television and the explosion in the number of mobile phone cameras, means you can expect to get images of an incident so much more quickly than you could ever expect to get a camera crew there. In television news whenever there has been a major incident we have always dispatched a producer to knock on doors to ask if they had a film or video camera running. Now you don't have to knock on the door … They can send it directly in and that's what's changed and that's what's caused the explosion in the amount of material we get. There's an immediacy about an audience's photo that really is electrifying, it's fantastic.

But what constitutes citizen journalism and why are leading news organisations, including the BBC, reluctant to use the term, preferring instead user generated content? This makes it necessary to define what we mean by 'journalism' and, indeed, what constitutes a 'journalist'. Journalism is normally defined as not simply the transmission by some means of an event. To qualify as journalism there must be elements of editing, selection and placing the event into context; by these methods the event becomes a 'story'. Stories are so-called because they require a narrative of some kind, which the transmission of an event does not – it just happens, or 'is'. Most journalists will also define their work as the assessment of often competing and contradictory pieces of information, which again is not required in the merely relaying of an event.

Liberal democracies have often been reluctant to restrict and demarcate journalists, as to do so would require the state in some form to organise or oversee the bodies and training requirements for journalists and decide who can practise as one.

The 'tipping point' in the UK for citizens journalism or UGC was undoubtedly 7 July, 2005 – for short-hand '7/7' – when, as noted in Chapter 8, for the first time in western Europe, suicide bombers went into operation.

Simon Waldman readily concedes that the BBC newsroom, a few miles from the blasts, was 'overwhelmed' with the response from the public and simply could not cope with the quantity and significance of the material that was coming in.

> There were quite literally thousands of still images sent to us, hundreds of clips of video and text messages, email messages on blogs and so on. Suddenly there was a completely new source of information available to us and that was the audience. They were ahead of official sources and it was quite clear from our own eye-witness accounts that we were dealing with a major terrorist incident.
>
> The iconic images that I remember from July 7th was the mobile phone video from the guy in the tube train; he holds his watch up to the camera such that we know when the bomb had gone off which was a few minutes before the police said the bomb had gone off and it changed the narrative of the story quite considerably ... Where we went wrong on News 24 was not being able to cope with the amount of stuff that was coming ... We have changed our systems since so that we can deal with it better.

Pete Clifton says that it is a matter of adjusting to the new realities and the opportunities afforded by the converged world and a new relationship between broadcasters and the audiences – the citizens – is required:

> What we're doing day in and day out is tapping in to what our audience knows about subjects and they just have a range of much easier ways of connecting with us and sending us information. In being seen to be open to that and using it well and intelligently as part of our journalism I think we in turn do change the nature of the relationship with the audience. I hope it's one where we build a stronger relationship and one built around even more trust and people can engage with our brand and use it intelligently.

The rapid lowering of entry costs to the broadcast media and the ability for pretty well anyone with a broadband connection to get their material out over the internet has led to the democratisation of the media and reduced the power of the 'gatekeepers'. However, it is of course one thing to publish material over the internet and quite another for significant numbers of people to view or listen to it. Established and generally respected organisations such as the BBC believe that they become even more important; islands of reliable and impartial coverage in the vast seas of unreliable and biased swathes of commentary and speculation. By 2007, the BBC's main news site was receiving an impressive 14 million 'hits' in an average week, with 5.2 million of these being unique users. Fifty per cent of these were from outside the UK, which certainly seems to demonstrate beyond doubt that the BBC's international reputation is highly significant in the 21st century. Furthermore, almost 10 per cent of those who access the news portal also click on audio or video streams.[12]

## Comment is free but how 'real' and 'nasty' should we let it be?

Chapter 7 discussed the persistent claims of the BBC (in particular) having a liberal–left bias and that the 'true' feelings of much of the population was never, or rarely, given due consideration. One of the aspects of convergence which has tilted the balance very much in favour of revealing popular opinion are the 'Your Comment' type sections on the websites, which are also sometimes generated in part and followed up in the on-air coverage. When those comments turn into vitriol against a racial group, religion, or otherwise potentially vulnerable section of society, then there is a real problem for an organization like the BBC.

This dilemma came into sharp relief in the comments posted on the BBC's *Have Your Say* comment section on its news website in reaction to the apparent assassination of Pakistan's opposition leader Benazir Bhutto at the end of 2007. About 10 days later, Peter Horrocks, rejoicing in his new title of Head of the BBC's Multimedia Newsroom, made a keynote speech at a conference at Leeds University,[13] which I also attended. He began his remarks by noting that the political 'centre ground' in the hall – with most attending either from academe or from broadcast news organisations – was probably more liberal-minded than many of the contributors to the BBC's website and that that the comments posted might appal the attendees: at any event, some of the comments, attacking Islam in a most virulent way, had posed a major dilemma for the BBC.

There are other ways the audience – or at least part of it – are influencing what is covered by the news channels. Both the BBC and Sky run regular programmes which show the most 'clicked on' news items of the day, which can range from major international stories, to the sort of amusing 'home video' type story that you might find on YouTube. But the power of the user is even more profound than that. Both Sky and BBC newsrooms monitor the numbers of 'hits' for each story. John Ryley says that this is, to some extent, bound to affect editorial decisions and helps keep the news teams 'grounded' as to what is actually interesting the public – rather than always being led by the traditional notions of what constitutes an important story. It seems that changing public attitudes are not otherwise necessarily picked up on by professional journalists:

> We have screens up, which show us which stories people going on line are interested in. They have green and red, green for going up, red going down. It doesn't for one moment decide our running orders but it informs our view of stories. At the moment we look at the big monitors … I think gradually as time goes on people will say 'Why are we doing these stories when there is no interest in them?' It will make a difference not to the significant stories but the ones lower down [the running order].

There is a problem here – by no means new to the 21st century – of determining the representativeness of views expressed to broadcasters by the public. In the past (and to some extent also the present) it was a question of the representativeness of, say, one letter or a few 'phone calls. Reaction was always from a small proportion of the audience, so how well did they represent the audience's views? Did one person who took the trouble to write in perhaps represent a thousand who thought similarly?

Finally, in a theme that has cropped up over and over again in this book, for all the undoubted importance of citizen journalism/user generated content, bloggers, podcasters, web 'hits' and all the rest of it, the interviewees for this book were clear that this does not mean that the long-established patterns of either news production or of viewing will disappear and that this is not a 'zero sum' game: it does not mean that a rise in one aspect, or one outlet, of TV news journalism, will mean that the rest will come to a shuddering halt. John Ryley believes there is need for adaptation and to embrace the new media but the 'death of TV' is some way off:

> People used to write off newspapers when television came along and people have started to write off television because of online. The different mediums evolve and survive. To quote Darwin, it's not the cleverest and the strongest that survive, it's the most adaptable to change. Sky News will adapt and evolve and change. Five years ago we were a TV news channel, now we are a TV news channel, we are a non-stop online site and we are a radio service. The emphasis has shifted a little bit but I think it would be wrong to say the television service will be eclipsed.

## Notes and references

1. Lilley, A. (1 October, 2007) 'Why web 2.0 adds up to a revolution for our industry'. *Media Guardian*, available online at: http://www.guardian.co.uk/media/2007/oct/01/mondaymediasection.digitamedia.
2. *Ibid.*
3. RAJAR (14 July, 2010) 'News Release – RAJAR Publishes Findings of MIDAS 6', available online at: http://www.rajar.co.uk/docs/news/MIDAS6_news_release.pdf.
4. RAJAR (2009) 'News Release – RAJAR Publishes Findings of MIDAS 5', available online at: http://www.rajar.co.uk/docs/news/MIDAS5_news_release.pdf.
5. As 2
6. Wogan, T. (14 May, 2010) 'Wogan's Blog – Cruisin …' TerryWogan.Com, available online at: http://www.terrywogan.com/terrys-blog/73/cruisin.
7. Gibson, O. (11 February, 2008) 'Where are all the black new faces?' *Media Guardian*, p.5.
8. Kanter, J. (27 May, 2010) 'ITV reveals World Cup strategy', *Broadcastnow*, available online (subscription only) at: http://www.broadcastnow.co.uk/news/broadcasters/itv-reveals-world-cup-strategy/5014446.article.
9. Carter, M. (2007) 'Online drama proves a lucrative hit', *Media Guardian*, 12 November: p. 7.
10. *Ibid.*
11. Gibson, O. (5 November, 2007) 'The News at ten', *Media Guardian*, p.2.
12. Figures from interview with Pete Clifton.
13. *Value of Citizen Journalism*, speech made on 7 January, 2008 at conference 'Broadcast Journalism and the Active Citizen', Institute of Communications Studies, University of Leeds. Speech and comments posted by Peter Horrocks on same date on his editor's blog. Available online at: http://www.bbc.co.uk/blogs/theeditors/2008/01/value_of_citizen_journalism.html.

# The Power and Effects of Broadcasting

12

This final chapter uses a number of case studies to consider the impact of broadcasting in the 21st century and how this has been affected by the use of social media. In particular it discusses:

■ Responses to the broadcast coverage of two separate cases of mass murder in England and whether broadcasting encourages 'copycat' killings.
■ The impact of the first TV leaders' debates in a UK general election and the potential long-term consequences of the programmes.
■ The effect of broadcasting an 'unintended' recording of the British Prime Minister.
■ The impact on public health of broadcasts in Africa of programmes about HIV/AIDS.

## Mass murder in England's lakelands

Just after 11.20 a.m. on 2 June, 2010, the normal mid-morning programme of music and features on BBC Radio Cumbria in north-west England was interrupted by some startling information from the programme's presenter, Liz Rhodes. Information had just been received from the police that residents in the Whitehaven and Egremont area should stay indoors following an incident that had taken place just after 10.30 a.m. There was then a description of a car that police were trying to locate. Naturally, further information was promised as soon as it was received by the station and indeed this was followed up by several other interjections that hour, including from the travel news reporter. By the time of the mid-day news, it was clear that the station had on its patch the story of national and even international significance but it wasn't until the late afternoon that it was confirmed that a disgruntled taxi driver,

Derrick Bird, had gone on a shooting rampage, killing first his twin brother, then his solicitor, attempting to murder a fellow taxi driver and then apparently targeting at random innocent passers-by as he zigzagged his way through a large chunk of the county, eventually killing 12 people in all and then shooting himself.

Its geography means that Cumbria is poorly served by mobile (cell) phone coverage and this being mid-morning, few would be watching TV and, even if they had, technically and, in programming terms, it is still quite difficult for TV channels to interrupt their programming or even to flash up captions. Another factor at that time of year was that it coincided with school half-term holidays and an area which is regarded as one of the most scenic in the country was particularly busy with tourists. Therefore, radio was the only viable, and certainly the most effective method, of informing the public about the unfolding, terrifying drama and most importantly advising them that they should stay indoors and certainly not attempt to tackle the gunman. A common reaction from local residents was disbelief that anything like this could happen in their area: the UK has very low levels of gun crime. This is probably linked with the fact that, with just over five guns owned per 100 of the population, it has some of the lowest gun ownership ratios in the world and certainly some of the toughest regulations on firearms, which had been tightened up after each of the two previous mass killings in Britain, roughly a decade apart. The Cumbria mass murders were the country's first such case of the 21st century.

The credibility and authority of the BBC and its reputation of not sensationalising or 'hyping up' news was also another important factor in the effectiveness of the local coverage. In short, people trusted the station to give them accurate information. Just a few months before, the station had been vital in providing life-saving information of a different sort and in different circumstances when its transmission area was hit by devastating floods.

The local commercial stations also carried updated news and information and this, of course, was also vital. Given the relatively small newsrooms on such services it was to that extent fortunate that the shooting incident happened during daytime hours on a weekday, rather than, say, on a Sunday or public holiday, when it would be unlikely that there would be on-site news staffing. Nevertheless, there was public praise for radio's role in overall this mercifully rare but devastating incidents.

## Does television 'encourage' mass killings?

Just three weeks after the Cumbria shootings, a former nightclub 'bouncer', Raoul Moat, was released from prison on parole, having been jailed for assaulting a child. His partner had broken up with him and, in a tragically misguided attempt to dissuade him from coming after her, she told him a lie: that her new boyfriend was a police officer. Within hours of his release Moat had shot and seriously wounded his ex-partner and killed her boyfriend. The next day he also shot, full in the face, a police officer, who was sitting in a stationary patrol car. Left for dead, the officer was blinded but survived. For the next few days that part of northern England saw the nation's biggest manhunt in decades, involving at one time about a quarter of the country's police officers trained in firearms, the RAF and special forces. Finally, six days after his last shooting, he was cornered by a river in Rothbury, holding a gun to his throat, for a stand-off with negotiators and armed police that was to last some six hours before he killed himself.[1]

The scene quickly developed something of a carnival atmosphere, with villagers coming out of the pubs, many with their pints of beer in one hand and their Smartphones in another, to witness what was widely, and correctly, expected to be Moat's last hours, phoning friends and adding comments on social network sites. At one stage, an already bizarre, if deadly, situation descended into near farce, as former England and Newcastle footballer, Paul 'Gazza' Gascoigne, turned up in a taxi and, in a state kindly described as 'somewhat the worse for wear', called two local radio stations after being frustrated in his attempt to enter the police cordon. Supplied with a dressing-gown, a chicken, a fishing rod and a pint of beer, Gascoigne claimed that 'Moaty' was a friend of his and if he could be allowed some time with him all would be well.[2]

Rolling TV news crews were able to get within yards from the stand-off. Correspondents such as the BBC's Jon Sopel, excitedly and, in the eyes of some, including Charlie Brooker,[3] gratuitously, almost salivatingly, interviewed those who had been trapped inside the police cordon or had come into close contact with Moat.

Another media critic, Mark Lawson,[4] argued that the history of television news was a changing relationship between the importance of the story and the availability of technology and airtime, with competition also a key factor, suggesting that: 'The BBC and ITV were perhaps worried about losing viewers to Sky News, which was mad for Moat'. However, Lawson argued that the main factor in the broadcasters covering the story in this way was because technology enabled them to do so. But, he asked rhetorically: because they can, does that mean they should?

There can be little doubt that the televising of an execution would draw record viewing figures. The British public has not been satiated by a public hanging since the 19th century. However, 'execution porn' is quite readily available on the internet and you can only have to look at the number of 'hits', (to use an unfortunate term in this context) of such scenes to understand the ghoulish fascination of people for such an event. Given that Moat had effectively declared 'they'll never take me alive' it seemed overwhelmingly likely that, once he was cornered, there would be only one outcome. Fortunately, for the TV coverage, he was not holed up inside a building but was very much out into the open. Unfortunately for TV, although the 'end-game' began in Friday night prime-time, the *dénouement* was not reached until approximately 1.15 a.m. on the following morning. This did not please the many hundreds of people who used Twitter and other social media sites to complain that, as they wanted to go to bed, could Moat please hurry up and shoot himself, or the police do the job for him? There was real frustration amongst the innumerable instances of bad or sick jokes, that the stand-off was dragging on. The public, it seemed, had paid its money and wanted it all over within a couple of hours – just like a Bruce Willis movie. Amongst all the commentary was, of course, much sneering about the rolling news TV coverage. 'I'll bet that the producers at Sky News are masturbating at the thought of capturing a single shot ringing out', wrote one. But that clearly didn't stop the critics of rolling news from devouring every second.

Unfortunately for those watching the rolling news channels' greenish night-vision coverage and who were hoping to witness the moment of death, although the sound of gunshot was heard, they did not see Moat's head exploding as he pulled the trigger.

What followed was, in the views of many, including the Prime Minister, David Cameron – as he made clear in a House of Commons statement early in the following week – even more grotesque, with 'tribute' sites opening up, and comments on the YouTube clips of Moat's death openly stating that he was a hero and was 'harder than any of the police'. Two days after Moat's death, his brother, Angus, gave an exclusive interview to Sky News in which he – rather ironically given the channel on which he chose to give the interview – criticised the 'national' TV coverage of a 'public execution'.[5] The character portrait he gave of his brother is somewhat at variance from that given by the murderer's former partner, but Angus Moat was not pressed on his brother's by then well-known psychotic violence, including that inflicted on a child. The interview added to the outlaw status, coupled with the victimhood and narcissism in which the murderer revelled and to which a disturbing percentage of the public responded with empathy, rather than with outrage and disgust.

But did the coverage of Derrick Bird's killing spree encourage Moat (who was in prison at that time but would have had access to TV and radio coverage) to take a similar form of murderous 'revenge'? Indeed, had Bird's murderous actions been inspired, or at least been 'encouraged' by the coverage given to previous mass murderers? True, as noted above, the UK has mercifully few such outrages, but they are quite frequent in the world overall and, such is the nature of television, they also tend to be covered by broadcasters many thousands of miles away. Is there, in other words, a 'copycat' element in these killings and if so, is it desirable – even possible – for television in particular to cover such stories with greater restraint? Once again, we have a problem in proving causality: not only can we not interview the killers – because they usually kill themselves – but we do not have a control group, so can never 'prove' whether or not the incidents would have taken place, even if broadcasting had shown restraint or even self-censorship in its coverage of previous incidents.

In March 2009, Charlie Brooker's satirical BBC TV *Newswipe* programme[6] castigated the TV networks for their alleged irresponsible reporting of a shooting at a school near Stuttgart in southern Germany a week earlier, in which 16 people were killed. In typical polemical style, Brooker inter-cut the suggestions by a forensic psychiatrist, Dr Park Dietz, of ways to minimise a 'copycat' element, with examples of how TV had covered the shooting:

> **Dr Park Dietz**: We've had twenty years of mass murders, throughout which I have repeatedly told CNN and our other media, if you don't want to propagate more mass murders, *don't* start the story with sirens blaring:
> [cuts to video from unidentified news channel of german police cars with sirens blaring]
> **Dietz**: *Don't* have photographs of the killer:
> [cuts to shot of ITV news presenter, who has picture of the killer on big screen behind her]
> **Dietz**: *Don't* make this 24/7 coverage:
> [cuts to Sky News, showing table, covered in microphones but devoid of people, in advance of news conference]. News presenter: 'The German Chancellor is about to give her reaction, we'll bring you that to you live ...'
> **Dietz**: Do everything you can *not* to make the body count the lead story:
> [cuts to opening headlines from itv news]. News presenter: 'Carnage in the classroom – 16 people are dead ...'
> **Dietz**: *Not* to make the killer some kind of anti-hero:
> [cuts to ITV News]. News presenter: 'Dressed in black combat gear, the gunman opened fire at random ...'
> **Dietz**: *Do* localise this story to the affected community and make it as boring as possible in every other market. Because every time we have intense, saturation coverage of a mass murder, we expect to see one or two more within a week.

In short, Brooker showed examples of how broadcast coverage in the UK of the German shootings had been the exact opposite of that recommended by Dietz and, it was implied, TV news outlets had – in the pursuit of ratings and sensational coverage – been wilfully and recklessly cavalier in their reporting.

He seems to have been vindicated by a spate of threats, some more serious than others, at several schools in Germany in the first few days following these shootings, although none of these resulted in loss of life.[7] These are strong accusations, however, and when Dietz was interviewed on Radio 4's *The Media Show* a few days after Moat had killed himself,[8] he seemed to be more tentative about the 'copycat' link than he had appeared to be in the tightly edited piece on *Newswipe* some 16 months previously.

To be able to be absolutely sure we'd have to be able to show that this occurs more often in the aftermath of intense coverage than on other weeks or months. And I think the pattern suggests that, but I haven't done the quantitative analysis to be able to prove it for a Nobel Prize.

Dietz, though, was adamant that the coverage of the Moat case had been highly dangerous and could lead to further murders:

I think there are plenty of people who will identify with anyone who looks like a cop-hating bad guy with a Mohawk [hair cut] and big muscles and that's not really the role-model we would like for our children or our depressed paranoids to adopt … images are key and if the images move they are more powerful and if the images are colourful … it's more powerful … It leads some people to elect to be like that … there are always lots of people at risk because there are other people who see themselves as like this person and those very people are the ones who think that getting news coverage and having 18,000 people on your Facebook page makes you a winner and they want to be like that.

Speaking on the same programme, the BBC's Head of Newsgathering, Fran Unsworth, said that in the modern media world the sorts of restrictions on broadcasters championed by Dietz were unworkable because of the proliferation of news media and that it also raised issues of free speech. If the broadcasters were censored, or self-censored, where would it stop? Would certain movies be banned in case they caused 'copycat' killings? She also stated that the Corporation (along with other media) had complied with one of the two news blackouts requested by the police. She said that in the Moat case there had been:

almost a public information aspect of it for the people of Rothbury. Here was a man who had shot two people, one of them fatally, and he was still on the loose with a shotgun in a particularly small village in the north of England.

Fran Unsworth also pointed out that, shortly after Moat's shootings, the police had said the 'net was closing in' on the killer, so no one had expected the story to go on for so long.

Fellow programme guest, journalism professor and former newspaper editor Roy Greenslade, was even more dismissive of Dietz's claims, and in particular on any link between previous mass shootings in the UK in the 1980s and 1990s and those in Cumbria in June 2010, or Rothbury a few weeks after that:

There is not a shred of evidence to show that reporting of violent crime – serial murders, mass murders – causes copycat crime. … there is no evidence to show … that there is a causation between the two things.

This is clearly not a question that can be resolved and that there are sincere and strongly held views and beliefs on both sides of the argument. In addition, as Fran Unsworth noted, even if cause could be established, what, in practical terms, could be done? It is true that broadcasters and the press do have their ethics' codes and editorial guidelines, on, for example, the coverage of hostage-taking, both domestic and foreign, in particular in not showing footage of the murder of hostages – especially if such footage is supplied by the hostage-takers. Partly, of course, this is on the grounds of taste and decency, but also because, particularly in the case of a country's nationals murdered/executed abroad, it is regarded as providing encouragement and support for the murderers and for them to take more hostages and carry out more murders – exactly the arguments promoted by Dr Dietz. So, it should be possible within one territory such as the UK to draw up a list of guidelines for the coverage of mass murders. In all likelihood though, no serious action will be taken unless and until a future mass murder explicitly states at some stage that he was influenced by coverage of previous murders.

## The leaders' debates and the UK 2010 General Election: did Sky News change the course of British political history?

The UK is unusual in not allowing paid broadcast political commercials. The public service traditions allows for free airtime to be given to the parties to directly make their pitch to the voters, both between and during elections. The first such broadcast was made on the BBC in October 1924, by Prime Minister Ramsay MacDonald. The UK was very slow in allowing broadcasters the scope for election coverage. It was Granada Television – holder of the commercial TV franchise for north-west England – that first defied the ban on reporting campaigns.

By a nice piece of historical completion, the Granada TV studios in Manchester saw the first ever televised election debate between the main UK party leaders. It has been a long road to achieve the kind of debate which the USA had had for 50 years; as noted in Chapter 1, the first, in 1960, saw the famous clashes between Presidential candidates Richard Nixon and John F. Kennedy.[9] As has often been pointed out, however, by those who oppose such debates in Britain, the UK, unlike the USA, does not elect its head of state and has a parliamentary system in which the head of *government*, the Prime Minister, emerges as a result of support in the House of Commons, and is formally appointed by the monarch. Therefore, it is argued, this different process requires a different approach in examining the suitability of leaders and party policies at election times. Furthermore, it was pointed out that, unlike many other countries, the UK's Prime Minister of the day subjects him or herself to a weekly grilling by the Leader of the Opposition – his/her main rival for the job at a general election – and other MPs in the House of Commons in Prime Minister's Questions (PMQs), which are not only broadcast 'live' but the edited highlights of these frequently rowdy exchanges are routinely used in TV news coverage. Nevertheless, broadcasters continued to push for debate between the main party leaders.

A pattern emerged in this public relations battle over several decades: the broadcasters would suggest a debate or debates, the leader of the party which was behind in the opinion polls – usually, but not always the Opposition leader or leaders – would eagerly accept, but the leader of the party with a good poll lead would decline. The one who was apparently in the lead position was reluctant to do something which might jeopardise that position – especially if it was the incumbent Prime Minister, who would also not wish to see his or her main rival given equal status, giving them extra credibility as a potential Prime Minister.

Early in 2009, over a year before the last constitutional date for a general election, Sky News began a rigorous and unrelenting campaign for a TV debate in the election campaign and put specific proposals to the politicians. The debate would run simultaneously on the main commercial radio news network, now run by Sky, as well as on Sky News (television). The leaders of the then opposition Conservative and Liberal Democrat parties quickly agreed to this debate and Sky announced that if the Prime Minister and Labour party leader, Gordon Brown, refused to participate, he would be represented by an empty chair. For the first time, a broadcaster had called the bluff of the incumbent PM and declared that there would be no veto. This would seem to run counter to legislation on broadcasting politics, especially during elections, but it was clear that Sky was prepared to play 'hardball' and it ran a remorseless campaign on both Sky News (a 'ticker-tape' ran between the 'Breaking News' scrolling text at the bottom of the screen) and on its internet sites, urging the public to back its campaign for such a debate. The BBC and ITN entered negotiations at several stages but seemed willing, as before, to accept that participation by all the party leaders would be required.

Then, just before Christmas 2009, to the surprise of all but a few insiders, Gordon Brown announced that he *would* agree to take part in not one, but *three* debates, to be run on consecutive weeks in the general election campaign on each of the three main UK TV news providers. It is a testament to how quickly and successfully Sky News had established itself as a credible and authoritative TV news channel that it would be regarded as having equal footing with the BBC and ITV (with its national and international news provider ITN), established respectively in 1922 and 1955. When it began in 1989 as a direct broadcast satellite service and from very modest studios and offices some distance from the centre of London, Sky was regarded by the broadcasting establishment as something of a joke. How could its news channel be seen as any kind of competitor with the well established and well resourced BBC and ITN services? Furthermore, unlike the BBC and ITV companies, Sky did not have any public service obligations to cover news and current affairs in a thorough manner, or indeed at all; although, like all UK broadcasters, it was obliged to maintain 'due impartiality' in any news coverage that it did provide. But, just as ITN had confounded its critics and a particularly sneering, snobbish attitude back in the 1950s and 1960s, so Sky News in the 1990s and into the 21st century became an acknowledged and indeed feared competitor by the older networks, and by the public as part of the 'natural' television environment.

The fine details of the rules surrounding the TV debates at one stage seemed to even then destroy the project. A document was agreed detailing the 76 rules[10] on the broadcasters and politicians, and indeed the 'live' audience. Unlike the weekly *Question Time* on BBC TV and *Any Questions* on BBC radio, audience members would not be allowed to applaud or provide any other audio commentary on the leaders and, indeed, the rules were so strict that many observers feared that the debate would be sterile and fail to enlighten the public on the leaders and their policies, and – clearly worst of all for the broadcasters – result in a big switch-off. In any event, the two commercial broadcasters would not directly gain any advertising revenues from the broadcasts as they were to be 90 minutes of uninterrupted debate, so for them it was more a matter of public prestige and authority to be entrusted – along with the BBC – to stage one of the debates. There were to be additional debates in Scotland, Wales and Northern Ireland – which not only had devolved administrations governing many important aspects of life and different make-ups in their party representation, notably by nationalist parties – and the rules on these were far less strict, allowing for interjections and challenges from both audience members and the moderator/chair. Nevertheless, this did not stop several of the nationalist parties launching an (unsuccessful) legal challenge to them being excluded from the main, UK-wide TV debates.

## Two-screen audience involvement

Although some of the projections of 20 million or more viewers proved to be wildly optimistic, the first debate, on ITV on 15 April 2010, gained slightly over 10 million viewers at the peak to its 'live' transmission.[11] All three debates were also carried by BBC Radio 4. The websites of the broadcasters and many of the national newspapers carried a 'live' comment thread, and social networking sites enabled the public outside the Granada Studios to comment on the debate and, in particular, the performance of the three party leaders.

Within two months of the general election, Nic Newman, who had been a key figure in the BBC's online strategy for a decade, and by then a visiting Fellow at the Reuters Institute for the Study of Journalism, produced a paper which analysed the effect of social media on the election.[12] In the paper's fifth chapter he analyses the 'social amplification' of the TV debates and quotes from an interview with Richard Allan, Facebook's director of policy in Europe, who said that operating two screens (TV plus mobile or laptop) had by then become commonplace for many of the (by then) 23 million Facebook users in the UK.

This same two-screen approach was apparent on micro-blogging site Twitter, in the first UK general election to take place since its creation. Newman reports that political website Tweetminster reported that 184,000 tweets were posted by 36,000 people during the first debate. Whilst, as Newman notes, this is a fraction of the total TV audience for the first debate (itself barely half that who would watch a key England match in the World Cup soccer tournament two months later), Newman cites arguments that all this activity represents a greater engagement by the public in an election campaign than ever before.[13] Furthermore, it was the reflections of the impact on social media, not least by the broadcasters, which re-enforced the sense that this election campaign was taking off in hitherto unknown ways. This phenomenon extended to people who had not watched the TV debates at all, or consulted any of the mainstream media and so had formed *all* their views on how they were reported and reflected in social media. Naturally, the reaction was followed with no greater interest than by the party leaders and their 'spin doctors', who then, of course, adjusted their approach in the later debates.

Real-time reaction to the debate was demonstrated in innovative ways by the broadcasters. ITV, hosting that first debate, used a 'worm' which tracked the reactions of a focus group and showed which answers were most liked and disliked.

It was the startling response to Nick Clegg, the leader of the smallest of the three national parties, the Liberal Democrats, which proved by far the most significant factor in the first debate. Under the Westminster parliament's first-past-the-post (FPTP) electoral system the third UK-wide party was always at a disadvantage. As a consequence of this system, since 1945 all UK governments had been composed entirely of either Labour or Conservative members. The leader of the third party was never given the credence granted to the 'big two' and was much less well-known to the public. In the coverage of political stories between elections 'balance' was often provided by time given to the government spokesman, followed by that from the main opposition party, ignoring the Liberal Democrats' position. However, the law required a more even approach in elections, with the ratio in time between Labour, Conservatives and the Liberal Democrats at 3:3:2. As a result, the Liberal Democrat party and its predecessors did usually see an increase in support during election campaigns. But to be given equal 'billing' in the first TV leaders' debates was an even more significant matter.

From almost the first minutes of the first TV debate, it was clear from the comments on and off the broadcaster's screen that Nick Clegg was easily seen to be 'winning'. It also seemed clear that Gordon Brown sensed this, and seemed to be keen to ally himself with his younger rival, leading to what became an instant catch-phrase: 'I agree with Nick.'

Polls taken immediately afterwards confirmed this support and the opinion polls of voting intentions in the following days showed the most extraordinary, dramatic turnaround in polling history: the Liberal Democrats shot from third, to second and – in at least two polls – first place.[14] Even though, due to the voting system, this was highly unlikely to result in a Liberal Democrat majority, it represented a truly seismic change in public support. And, unquestionably, this was a direct result of the TV debate.

From that point, it seemed unlikely that any one party would achieve an overall majority (more seats in the House of Commons than all the other parties combined). But before the election – indeed, just one day before the final TV debate, hosted by the BBC – there was one more dramatic and unexpected development and, again, Sky News was at its centre.

## 'Bigot-gate'

On the day before the final leaders' election debate the then Prime Minister, Gordon Brown, was in Rochdale, not far from the location of that first TV debate, on a 'walkabout' amongst what his aides evidently thought were Labour party supporters. The three news broadcasters had, in accordance with common practice, 'pooled' audio, in this case partly via a microphone from Sky News, clipped to Brown's jacket. During the walkabout he entered into what seemed to be a friendly, if rather forced, conversation with a 65-year-old lifetime Labour supporter Gillian Duffy, including a discussion of her worries about the impact of recent immigration from Eastern Europe. Gordon Brown seemed to deal with her concerns in a firm but good-natured way, smiled broadly, and deftly switched the conversation to personal compliments and an apparent interest in Gillian Duffy's family. He then made what turned out to be perhaps a fatal error in his campaign, by failing to remove the microphone when he got into his official car and was being driven away from the walkabout. His tone of voice and overall mood changed immediately he got into the car, out of site of the cameras, and, he thought, microphones:[15]

> GB: That was a disaster. Should never have put me with that woman. Whose idea was that?
> Unknown male: I don't know, I didn't see.
> GB: Sue's, I think. [angry tone] Just ridiculous.
> Unknown male: Not sure if they'll go with that one.
> GB: They will go with it.
> Unknown male: What did she say?
> GB: Everything. She's just this sort of bigoted woman who said she used to be a Labour voter … Ridiculous.
> [Transmission breaks up]

It was a few minutes after this that a Sky News producer realised that this unintended-for-broadcast conversation had been recorded. Sky made the decision to run it, with the other broadcasters quickly following.

The so-called 'bigot-gate' recording was then, excruciatingly, played to Brown a short time later as he sat in the BBC's Manchester studios for a radio interview, which was also videoed. The pictures of him literally with his head in his hands were perhaps the defining and lasting images of the election campaign.[16]

Ethical questions as to whether such a private conversation should have been broadcast were largely brushed aside, although it seems likely that, had it had been the BBC's turn to organise the pooled audio, it might never have been broadcast. The BBC's Editorial Guidelines[17] state that secret recordings must be cleared in advance, but of course in this case there was no plan or expectation that such a recording would be obtained.

Broadcast regulator Ofcom also bars such secret recordings in normal circumstances. But 7.14 of its broadcasting code[18] says (in part): 'it may be warranted to use material obtained through misrepresentation or deception without consent if it is in the public interest and cannot reasonably be obtained by other means'.

It could certainly be argued that, in a crucial stage of a tightly fought election campaign, in which claims and counter-claims about the Prime Minister's character – even his psychological fitness for office – had been raised, this apparent demonstration of Gordon Brown's dismissiveness of what many regard as a legitimate public policy issue, as well his apparent fondness for blaming a subordinate for when things went wrong, a 'two-faced' attitude to the voters and evidence of a much-rumoured (but always denied) bad temper, was very much in the public interest.

How much all of this eventually played out in changing voting behaviour – the 'Media Effects' question – is of course hotly debated, but there has surely never in UK history been such a dramatic change in opinion poll ratings. Although impossible to prove because, as noted above, in this field of study there can never be a control (group), the opinion polling suggests that the debates, plus 'bigot-gate', initiated a highly significant shift in voting intentions towards the Liberal Democrats, which can be stated with near certainty would not otherwise have taken place.

The three broadcasters combined their resources to commission an exit poll, broadcast on each of their election programmes the second the polls closed on election night. This predicted with almost uncanny accuracy the actual result, which wasn't clear until well into the following day; that the UK was to have a 'hung' Parliament. Under the strange impact of the first-past-the-post system, although the Liberal Democrats had significantly increased their vote compared with the 2005 election, they had a slight reduction in seats. However, they quite probably denied the Conservatives from either having an overall majority, or at least having enough seats to form a reasonably effective minority government. Five days later Britain had its first coalition government since 1945, with the Liberal Democrat leader Nick Clegg becoming Deputy Prime Minister, four others from his party in the Cabinet – the first time the third party (formerly the Liberal Party, then in the 1980s the SDP/Liberal Alliance) had been in a peacetime national government since 1922.

The dramatic coverage of Brown's farewell speech outside Number 10 Downing Street, leaving with his wife and two children for Buckingham Palace to offer his resignation to the Queen, and then the arrival of David Cameron at the Prime Minister's residence, after he'd accepted Her Majesty's invitation to form this new style of government, took place in prime time, with the BBC even ditching its top-rating soap opera *EastEnders* for the occasion. The programme and the later news bulletins provided one of the few 21st-century examples of news output reaching the top ten in the weekly national TV ratings.

But potentially the most significant impact of the election may be the decision – in honour of the coalition agreement between the two parties – to consider changing the voting method for elections to the Westminster Parliament to the alternative vote (AV) system. Some two months after the election, the government confirmed that a referendum on such a change would take place in May 2011, which would be only the second UK-wide referendum ever. Although not the proportional voting system type desired by the Liberal Democrats, most political analysts believe the effect of the AV system would be to entrench a coalition-type government in the UK – if it had applied in May 2010 it would probably also have produced a different *type* of coalition government, with Labour, not the Conservatives, being the major partner. The Conservative Prime Minister, David Cameron, announced that he would oppose such a change, whilst Nick Clegg confirmed he would campaign for it – providing the potential for a very interesting political split in the coalition government. In addition, this is an abrogation of the usual convention of 'collective responsibility' in government, in which the 1975 referendum campaign on the UK's continued membership of the then European Economic Community (latterly European Union) provides the only previous, formal example. Given that there would be few, if any, senior editorial figures who had been involved in the 1975 referendum and would still be in a similar position in 2011, this referendum also provided for challenges to the broadcasters in maintaining balance and impartiality.

In the event, a majority of more than two to one voted in favour of maintaining the FPTP system for elections to the House of Commons. Despite efforts by the broadcasters to grab their attention the electorate seemed largely unexcited about the issue or the campaign. This may have been partly due to the fact that elections to the Scottish Parliament, the Wales and Northern Ireland Assemblies, as well as to many local councils in England, took place on the same day, so politicians were campaigning on several fronts at the same time and the broadcasters' news agenda was also crowded, with these and several other major concurrent national and international stories vying for a leading place on the running orders. However, once having been agreed for that general election, it seems highly likely that TV debates will be a major feature of every subsequent UK general election and that, indeed, the TV debates will – as many believe they had been in 2010 – not just *part* of the election campaign but *the* election campaign. In short: Sky News may, both directly and indirectly, have changed the course of British political history.

## How MTV and community radio turned a crisis into a drama and helped prevent many deaths from AIDS

Whilst the previous examples in this chapter are likely to produce subjective responses in the reader as to whether the broadcasts produced a good, bad or neutral effect, the final example is certain to be less tendentious: the positive effect on education of a vital health issue by quite different broadcasters.

Acquired immune deficiency syndrome (AIDS) has been described as a modern-day global plague. By 2008 more than 25 million people worldwide had died from AIDS-related illnesses and some 33 million are thought to have acquired the infection.[19] The impact of the disease is felt by many more millions, including children who are orphaned and frequently destitute and at the mercy of charities – there are many orphanages that exist purely for such children. It is especially prevalent in Africa, largely due to sexual taboos, poverty and gender inequality. Deaths from AIDS are caused by infection of a virus, human immunodeficiency virus (HIV), which is typically transmitted through blood contamination during sexual acts. Because it first came to light in the western world amongst groups of promiscuous homosexual men in urban areas, it acquired the tag 'gay plague', providing both a stigma and an initial lack of public sympathy for its victims. That stigma, although largely eradicated in western cultures was still prevalent in many African countries – many of which outlaw male homosexuality – well into the 21st century, but in any case, in the African continent HIV/AIDS was also spread through heterosexual contact.

Attempts at educating the public to modify sexual behaviour, in particular encouraging 'safe sex', preoccupied many of the health communities and it was realised that the normal advertising/propaganda methods were largely ineffective and that a more creative solution needed to be found, integrating messages into the narrative of popular and compelling dramas.

Researchers at Johns Hopkins University in Baltimore were asked to assess the impact of *Shuga* and of *Tribes*, the dramas made in Trinidad and Tobago,[20] which were at the heart of what MTV calls its Ignite campaign, involving social networking, counselling and testing linked to organised screenings for people without TVs in the home.

The TV dramas proved especially effective in parts of Africa. *Tribes* did reasonably well: it was seen by 8 per cent of the youth of the country. But *Shuga* took Kenya by storm. The Johns Hopkins survey found that 60 per cent of Kenyan youth had seen it and they knew the main messages from the show and could identify the lessons to be learned.[21] This example would seem to provide firm evidence of the media effects theory, although, as ever, we cannot be sure that even a single person did modify their behaviour because of watching either of these dramas.

Romie Singh[22], a media researcher and author of educational dramas had a particular interest in assessing the impact community radio was having on its audience and studied audience responses to specific HIV/AIDS broadcasts, which have been produced and distributed among community radio stations in South Africa. She presented her findings at the 2008 Broadcast Education Association (BEA) convention in Las Vegas.[23] Her paper pointed out that between five and six million people are HIV positive in South Africa. That represents over 25 per cent of the population, of which young women are the most vulnerable. The main thrust of HIV and AIDS messaging had been: abstain – delay your sexual debut; stay faithful – do not have multiple concurrent sexual partners; practise safe sex; use a condom; get tested regularly for HIV. Research has identified the biggest drivers of the HIV/AIDS pandemic as poverty which often drives MCP – multiple concurrent partnerships.

Romie Singh worked at ABC Ulwazi, which was founded in 1995, just after the first democratic elections in South Africa. It is based in Johannesburg and is a non-government (not-for-profit) organisation, offering radio production, training and consultancy for the community radio sector. It produces 'edutainment' radio material for community radio stations throughout South Africa and where required, beyond its borders, to Namibia, Swaziland, Lesotho and other SADEC countries. In addition the company carries out intense liaison work with the participating stations and takes charge of distribution, monitoring and evaluation of the programmes it distributes. ABC Ulwazi also provides support by way of radio training courses for community radio broadcasters who receive specific training in radio skills, as well as in the content and in how to contextualise the content in order to make the material relevant for their particular community in their own language. This goes some way to ensuring that local presenters are informed in the subject of the programme: democracy, human rights, women and children's rights, community enterprises, governance, and, of top priority, HIV and AIDS.

In 2006 the Johns Hopkins University carried out a National HIV and AIDS Communication Survey in South Africa to examine the overall impact of 19 AIDS communication programmes on listeners and viewers. They found that the 'cumulative exposure' of all 19 HIV communication programmes broadcast over 12 months on national television, public and community radio stations in South Africa led to:

1. higher levels of 'condom self-efficacy' and condom use;
2. higher numbers of partners discussing an HIV test with their sexual partner and actually having a test within the last 12 months;
3. higher knowledge about the availability of anti-retroviral treatment;
4. higher willingness to engage with people infected and affected by HIV/AIDS.

Just as dramas had the most impact on TV stations, so it proved in community radio. Romie Singh reported that ABC Ulwazi confirmed in its 2007 'Body, Mind and Soul Impact Study', that the radio drama format has the greatest edutainment value in terms of learning and changing behaviour within the community. Several factors were key in their effectiveness:

- identification with main character
- listener loyalty
- increased listenership: more phone calls; more participation at Listeners' Association level
- increased community activity around HIV/AIDS
- increased buy-in by Community Radio

The effective use of both radio and television – and the eagerness of broadcasters, health professionals and charities to work together to provide life-saving education, in a form which engages its target audience, provides an encouraging example of the positive use of broadcasting in the 21st century.

## Notes and references

1. Mendock, R. and Leach, B. (11 July, 2010) 'Raoul Moat: "I've no dad, no one cares about me"', *Telegraph.co.uk*, available online at: http://www.telegraph.co.uk/news/uknews/crime/7883742/Raoul-Moat-Ive-no-dad-no-one-cares-about-me.html.

2. Taylor, A. (10 July, 2010) 'Gazza brings Moat chicken', *The Sun*, available online at: http://www.thesun.co.uk/sol/homepage/news/3048989/Gazza-brings-Moat-chicken.html.

3. Brooker, C. (17 July, 2010) 'Charlie Brooker's screen burn: the news', *Guardian.co.uk*, available online at: http://www.guardian.co.uk/tv-and-radio/2010/jul/17/charlie-brooker-screen-burn.

4. Lawson, M. (15 July, 2010) 'TV matters: Raoul Moat and live television news coverage', *Guardian.co.uk*, available online at: http://www.guardian.co.uk/tv-and-radio/2010/jul/15/raoul-moat-live-television-news.

5. Evans, M. (11 July, 2010) 'Raoul Moat's final hours were like "public execution", says brother', *Telegraph.co.uk*, available online at: http://www.telegraph.co.uk/news/uknews/crime/7884129/Raoul-Moats-final-hours-were-like-public-execution-says-brother.html.

6. BBC Four (25 March, 2009). *Charlie Brooker's Newswipe*. BBC Four.

7. Davies, L. (13 March, 2009. 'German school shooting sparks copycat threats', *Guardian.co.uk*, available online at: http://www.guardian.co.uk/world/2009/mar/13/albertville-school-shooting-copycats.

8. BBC Radio 4 (14 July, 2010) *The Media Show*.

9. It should also be noted, however, that such was the alarm caused to the elites over the apparent power of television in that election – Kennedy won by a tiny margin, which was credited to public reaction to his performance on TV – that no such debates were held for another 16 years.

10. Couzens, J. (3 March, 2010) 'Stage Set For Historic TV Election Debates', *Sky News Online*, available online at: http://news.sky.com/skynews/Home/Politics/Leaders-Debates-TV-Format-For-Historic-Debates-Agreed-By-Political-Parties-And-Broadcasters/Article/201003115566087.

11. Parker, R. (16 April, 2010) 'Election debate peaks with 10.3m', *Broadcastnow*, available online at: http://www.broadcastnow.co.uk/ratings/terrestrial/election-debate-peaks-with-103m/5012811.article.

12. Newman, N. (July 2010) 'UK election2010, mainstream media and the role of the internet: how social and digital media affected the business of politics and journalism', Reuters Institute for the Study of Journalism, available online at: http://reutersinstitute.politics.ox.ac.uk/fileadmin/documents/Publications/Working_Papers/Social_Media_and_the_Election.pdf.
13. *Ibid.*
14. Leach, B. (18 April, 2010) 'General Election 2010: Lib Dems take lead in a new poll', *Telegraph.co.uk*, available online at: http://www.telegraph.co.uk/news/election-2010/7605260/General-Election-2010-Lib-Dems-take-lead-in-new-poll.html.
15. Channel 4 News (28 April, 2010) 'When Gillian met Gordon, the full transcript', available online at: http://www.channel4.com/news/articles/vote_2010/when+gillian+met+gordon+the+full+transcript/3629187.
16. BBC Mobile (28 April, 2010) 'Election 2010', available online at: http://news.bbc.co.uk/1/hi/uk_politics/election_2010/8649200.stm.
17. BBC (n.d.) 'Secret recordings from outside sources', *BBC Editorial Guidelines*, available online at: http://www.bbc.co.uk/guidelines/editorialguidelines/edguide/privacy/secretoutside.shtml
18. Ofcom (December, 2009) 'Deceptions, set-ups and "wind up" calls', *The Ofcom Broadcasting Code*, available online at: http://stakeholders.ofcom.org.uk/binaries/broadcast/code09/bcode.pdf.
19. AVERT (13 July, 2010) 'AIDS and HIV around the world', available online at: http://www.avert.org/aroundworld.htm.
20. Plusnews (21 July, 2010) 'GLOBAL: MTV drama brings cool to HIV prevention', available online at: http://www.plusnews.org/Report.aspx?ReportId=89907.
21. Boseley, S. (20 July, 2010) 'Aids-related soap is big hit in Africa', *Guardian.co.uk*, available online at: http://www.guardian.co.uk/world/2010/jul/20/shuga-aids-soap-africa-mtv.
22. The 'pen name' of Romie Mürkens.
23. BEA (2008) *The New Communication Frontier*, Conference program available online at: http://www.beaweb.org/Content/NavigationMenu/Events1/BEA2008Program.pdf.

# Conclusion

This book has discussed a very wide range of examples and issues. There is clearly a danger that the breadth of the material will confuse rather than enlighten and so it falls on this final section to pull together what I think are the overall 'answers' to the issues and questions posed in the Introduction and the most important strands in the arguments derived from the various case studies and empirical evidence in the main chapters and then come to some concluding remarks and, necessarily, subjective comment.

Given that the focus of the book is the changing and evolving relationship between citizens and broadcasters, the most obvious aspect is the fragmentation of audiences in the 21st century. It is a sobering and even profound thought, however, that in the thousands of years of human history perhaps only two generations will have the cultural and psychological experience of listening to and/or viewing the same material at the same time as half of the rest of their fellow citizens in that country, ranging from the royal family to the humblest of subjects. We shall never again have the pleasure of going into workplace, store or other social space and be able to refer to jokes and sketches on the previous night's TV, safe in the knowledge that most of the people would have seen the same programmes. True, as mentioned in the Introduction, certain TV 'event shows' such as *The X Factor* on Britain's main commercial network can still have a major impact on public conversation (as well as having many detractors) but, as I demonstrated in Chapter 3, even the figures for the top-rated entertainment and drama shows in the 21st century are barely that achieved on a regular basis for daily news bulletins in the pre-fragmentation/time-shifting era of the mid-1970s, especially when taking account the approximately 20 per cent increase in the UK's population since then.

It is hard not to be concerned about the evidence of the decline in viewing to 'serious' programmes in the UK and USA, especially the quite dramatic fall-off in the regular, mass viewing of 'hard' news programmes, with their coverage of political, economic and international affairs. This has run parallel in the decline in readership of 'serious' newspapers (indeed, almost all newspapers). Before the arrival of mass-circulation newspapers at the turn of the 20th century, the daily engagement with such matters was largely the preserve of an educated elite. By the mid-20th century, however, both newspaper readership and radio listening, then TV viewing, of such material was the common, 'normal' experience. The multiplicity of channels and fragmentation of audiences has generally resulted in a migration to the 'lighter' end of the broadcasting output and the danger of a return to the pre-mass-literacy/engagement era.

This is partly the result of a fundamental change in the delicate ecology of broadcasting: if there is insufficient competition, broadcasters become lazy and arrogant; too much and the fragmentation of audiences and of revenue streams means a drive to the bottom in terms of quality (so far as that can be defined to most people's agreement), of material that challenges the mind, and the output also becomes derivative, safe and formulaic. Private companies can, and often do, provide dynamism and innovation, but only when they don't have to worry about every last bit of revenue. Public service broadcasters such as the BBC, with a secure (if reduced) revenue stream, can and have experimented with all kinds of genre, and provided a 'permission to fail.' We may never again have a situation when, for example, the Corporation gives money and studio time to a group of recent graduates and just tells them to make some 'funny programmes' – as happened to what became the *Monty Python* team at the end of the 1960s – or provide similar support and only the most limited oversight to radical film-makers such as Ken Loach. He has complained bitterly about the layers of commissioning editors and compliance directives that, he argued, was stifling his creativity and storytelling, but it is vital that public service broadcasters give patronage to the young and for the experimental and innovative. In other words, a 'mixed economy' in terms of finance and a wide market-place of ideas is most likely to produce the best results for the viewer and listener and refresh and re-invigorate the whole sector.

The first BBC broadcasts coincided with only the second UK general election held under universal suffrage (women and most working-class men only being given the vote in 1918), so the development of broadcasting and that of democracy even in supposed 'advanced' countries such as Britain have been intertwined. But a mass democracy and robust, informed debate by an informed citizenry does not always suit vested interests. Like nature, the airwaves abhor a vacuum and if the space left – or is never occupied by – public service broadcasters, with the requirement for news and debate that does not privilege or exclude any particular viewpoint or faction, it will soon be filled by those who are well-financed and pursue a populist agenda which, history also shows, can easily turn into demagoguery. A meaningful democracy has to be more than the ability to cast a vote every four or five years; it requires an engaged and informed citizenry that can not only understand the issues but can affect the decision-making process.

There may not be a formal, organised international conspiracy in which powerful people agree to find ways to distract and divert the population's attention with a seductive but bland torrent of diversionary entertainments, but it is surely in the interests of the rich and powerful that it should be so. Furthermore, in a technological world, the understanding of science and of the causes and effects of such phenomena as climate change is crucial, and broadcasting has a vital role to play here.

But the communal experience of broadcasting goes much deeper than that; as I hope to have amply demonstrated in this book, in the UK, in much of western Europe and many other countries there is a kind of 'folk' memory at work; the shared pleasures and excitements of growing up at a particular time, and immense nostalgia for the broadcasting of the period. No other form of mass communications has achieved that level of affection and identification. This produces a unique relationship and a feeling that broadcasting is not just a service like any other but is part of, and belongs to, the public and is an integral part of society again, in a way that no other for the mass communication.

The accusation that broadcasting – in common with other mass media – has 'dumbed down' is easy to make when reviewing this evidence: easy, but wrong. Programmes that are intellectually demanding, have high production values and do not rely simply on the allure of celebrity and fantasy, continue to perform well in the audience ratings. Broadcasters such as Britain's David Attenborough are hugely respected and his programmes continue to command substantial audiences who have, after all, in the 21st century, so many alternative technological distractions in the home and, indeed, when on the move. In a broader sense, a curious mind can find unexpected and hitherto undiscovered interests and knowledge. We all consist of both majorities and minorities in our tastes and interests, so we can all find pleasure from niche and mass appeal programmes; from aural and visual 'comfort blankets', but if we only absorb the tried and familiar (the great fear of Reith and others at the start of broadcasting) we will miss out on so much potential. Reith referred to 'balance' in the programme output, equivalent to the necessity of a balanced food diet. Another simile is browsing through library shelves and discovering a work or a subject hitherto unknown to you, compared with, say, going straight to the section on thrillers by a well-known author whose novels you have read many times. In fact, in the UK the rise in mass education at the further and higher education levels, like democracy, ran in tandem with the development of broadcasting. There is a virtuous connection between all three.

I've been very moved in researching the changes to children's television, in particular, at just how fragile and precious broadcasting is for this age-group. All of us, no matter how rich or poor, whatever age we are born into and wherever we find ourselves in the world, have only one childhood. I believe there must be special protection and increased energy, commitment and resources for children's broadcasting and that must include older children to the age of 16.

The case strongly argued by David Simon, creator of *The Wire*, of the benefits of subscriber-based cable television, rather than free-to-air advertising-funded broadcasting, is hard to counter but although the subscription-based broadcasters may well produce high-quality, original and challenging content, they will only do so to the extent that it will appeal to those with the discretionary income to fund the subscriptions. The point about public service television, especially that paid by the whole community of viewers, is that it can and should provide such programmes, whatever the socio-demographics of the audience and, indeed, should particularly serve those such as the poor and the elderly, who generally have less disposable income and are therefore often marginalised by the mainstream, commercial media.

Which brings me to the next main point and theme of the book: the power and prominence of myths (not least about broadcasting and its past) and the conflicts between different interpretations of 'reality', with its twin subject of bias and impartiality, linked to an argument that broadcasting covers science poorly because the nature of scientific discovery and endeavour does not easily fit with the demands and expectations of broadcasting and journalists. These areas comprise two substantial chapters in the book but in fact they also invaded other areas, such as the chapters on the erosion of time and spatial dimensions, and the continuing appeal, along with sustained myths and folk-lore, of 'pirate' radio. Although it was somewhat beyond the scope of this book, or the knowledge and competence of the author, the argument from psychiatrist Dorothy Rowe that there can never be one fixed 'reality' because of our different experiences and interpretations of the world does beg the question as to whether even the most scrupulous and open-minded broad-caster and journalist, working for the most independent and ethical organisa-tion, can ever produce programmes that would satisfy everyone – even those who are broadly in the same cultural and political environment. That does not of course mean that they shouldn't try. The arguments and evidence that BBC staff have, at different times (and perhaps on occasions at the same time), been both too uncritical of the *status quo* and also been too dismissive of people and opinions who have a different view from the Corporation's personnel seem to be strong. This is not to doubt the sincerity and commitment of, for example, its journalists in maintaining due impartiality and objectivity, but is rather the result, as Andrew Marr and others have argued, of their rather narrow and similar backgrounds. This in turn feeds in to a particular work culture or 'group-think', which is also true in a different way of those in commercial organisations.

The third theme became clear to me – as is often the way with research and is one of its most rewarding aspects – late on in the writing of the book; that is, how much the power and impact of broadcasting is related to its trust and credibility. The final chapter provided evidence of the 'media effects' theory; that broadcasting does have a direct impact on the attitudes and conduct of its audience. Whilst it is always difficult to find direct cause and effect, particu-larly at the extremes of human behaviour such as the alleged influence on the psyche of potential mass murderers, I found the 'evidence' for this convincing. As is often argued, advertisers would not spend billions of pounds if they did not think their ads would influence our behaviour; and politicians and the military, whether in authoritarian regimes or liberal democracies, would not be so concerned about broadcasting if they did not believe it could sway opin-ion, up to the point of sparking or inflaming revolt in their countries. And if, as seems undeniable, the TV leaders' debates in the UK 2010 general election campaign did have a direct bearing on public support for at least one of the party leaders, could not very different 'messages' and images influence the (unstable) mind of a potential killer? There then follows the very different question as to what can or should be done by broadcasters to minimise such harm to public safety. The final example of the positive use of radio and television to educate and inform – whilst continuing to entertain – in order to combat HIV/AIDS, demonstrated the power and potential of broadcasting to do good.

A fourth major theme that emerged in the book and which is clearly linked to the first was the removal of time and space constraints on broadcasting output; in turn this is connected to technological developments, notably the internet, the move from analogue to digital systems and the convergence of media. The implications for broadcasting are immense but have also been oversold and some technologies, such as digital audio broadcasting, have lacked the kind of appeal necessary for mass adoption.

On the broader question of the public's use of technology there is a clear demarcation between radio and television. The willingness of the public in wealthier countries to spend significant sums of disposable income on new, flat-screen, high definition and even 3-D sets, is in marked contrast to the readiness to spend on radio receivers. Indeed, the idea of many in the younger age group buying anything called 'a radio' as such is laughable. So, radio will need to engage young people at a new, innovative level, or face a slow but certain death as a truly mass medium.

The interactive nature of the new technologies and the relative cheapness of the software and hardware is an important sub-theme in this area -- a point that was made forcibly by many contributors in several other chapters, even if interactivity in television is, and is likely to remain, a minority interest, at any rate at a deeper level than voting in a reality TV show. That is not to say that this is not a significant development but, as the BBC's Peter Horrocks pointed out, broadcasters would be wise to concentrate on the 100 per cent of people who are viewing the programme, rather than the 1 per cent or so who are reacting to it. The new technologies, however, have enabled the public to contribute audio and video to the broadcasters, in the form of the so-called user generated content, or citizens' journalism, as well as other types of material in the form of multimedia websites, podcasts, vodcasts, etc. For radio – the original interactive medium – the use of social networking and micro-blogging sites such as Twitter enabled the already deep and unique connection between broadcaster and audience, discussed in Chapter 4, to be further strengthened. Now, presenters do not have to 'sign off' at the end of their on-air shift but can continue the conversation and the connection with their audiences pretty well 24 hours a day if they wish.

This in turn connects back to the reality question, because it requires a new, negotiated *persona* both on and off the air, with the one possibly compromised by the other and with organisations such as the BBC concerned that their on-air performers do not break their editorial guidelines or otherwise cause embarrassment. Of course, for the listener and viewer too, there is a sort of 'variable geometry' in our persona within these interactions. Many citizens in a multicultural country such as the UK have to negotiate a number of identities, and broadcasting – as discussed in Chapter 10 – can help both resolve and clarify these. At the same time and conversely, it is often argued, not least by the founder of Facebook, that social media blurs the different identities or characters we project in, for example, the work and family situations. And this is where public service broadcasting really is important, because the market will inevitably seek to increase its domination of the individual's time and resources. Only PSB or community-based media can afford to encourage the public to spend *less* time with the media and to stimulate the individual to go out and get involved in all kinds of social, cultural and even scientific activities. A purely market-driven broadcasting system will invariably want the public to continue to 'just sit there' or, better still, sit there and buy something! It wants them to interact and to have a 'content-rich experience', but only to the extent that it can increase its revenue from the subscriber.

The fifth and final major theme is the continued importance of 'the local' in broadcasting. Reading through individual chapters I was struck by how often the discussion centred on the apparent contradictions of living in a far more integrated world than ever before in terms of culture, economy and politics, and yet how much of our lives continues to centre on our sense of place. Whilst it is true that there are very important 'communities of interest' that bind people even in different geographical areas (not least in the academic life), there continues to be a desire and need for local relevance, and that broadcasters ignore this desire at their peril. This is most pertinent in the future pattern of local radio, especially commercial music stations. In this 'back to the future' scenario, local radio stations are rediscovering importance of local, relevant content, rather than relying on a highly restricted number of music tracks, calculated to offend the least number of people. I was also impressed by Andrew David's arguments and descriptions of how community radio takes a completely different view from both the BBC and commercial services on how to gauge the value and effectiveness of their broadcasts and of the social gain provided by such stations.

It is easy, though, for those of us living in the rich industrialised world, with the latest gadgets and gizmos, our broadband and our wide choice of channels and services, to forget that, as of the end of 2010, around a third of the world's population exists on less than two US dollars a day; two-thirds do not have access to the internet and around a quarter do not have reliable electricity supplies. So, radio – cheap to buy and to use, mobile and able to draw in signals from outside the region, nation or even continent of the listener – provides the main source of information and entertainment for hundreds of millions, and remains the most democratic and ubiquitous medium on earth. In addition, when catastrophe strikes, such as the earthquake and tsunami in Japan in March 2011, many citizens in even wealthy countries rely on battery-powered radio for vital news and information.

The importance of international broadcasters was highlighted yet again in November 2010 with the release of the Burmese opposition leader Aung San

Suu Kyi, who had been held under house arrest for 15 years. In subsequent interviews she stressed how important had been the BBC World Service's news output in keeping her informed of what was really going on in her own country, as well as providing companionship and a feeling of being connected to the outside world. The human rights group, Amnesty International, took the opportunity to push its 'buy a radio for Burma', stressing the impact of independent, uncensored news in a country whose military leaders censor and try to snuff out all such material and those who provide it. Amnesty's campaign pointed out that one radio can be listened to by 100 people. During the 'Arab Spring' of 2011, protestors in Syria carried placards saying 'Thank you, BBC' to recognise the importance of the World Service's coverage of their government's crackdown against the uprisings there. The BBC's motto 'nation shall speak peace unto nation' therefore equates to the spread of democracy and the role of international broadcasters from Britain and other countries in wielding so-called 'soft power', which may be even more important in the 21st century that it was in the 20th.

This book was completed on almost exactly the 90th anniversary of the first regularly scheduled one-to-many broadcasting. Another 90 years from that point will take as to the end of the 21st century. Although the title of the book suggests an overview of how broadcasting will develop in the whole of that 100 years it would be arrogant in the extreme to imagine that I can do other than report on the situation at present and perhaps speculate on the next decade or so, even if some of the technologies do have a 'long tail'. The direction of travel seems clear; increasing convergence between old and new technologies in content and in devices and the blurring of the hitherto rigid distinction between broadcaster and audience. The seamless integration of the personal computer, phones, other mobile devices, game stations and the TV set and the breaking down of 'live' and on-demand content was swiftly becoming a reality at the book's completion. What cannot be predicted is how politics, economics and culture will define the content and its accessibility.

In essence, this book is a plea for the protection, continuation and development of broadcasting in the public interest and other public benefit. For the richer part of the world at least, the converging technologies provides a fascinating and exciting opportunity for a level of individual and group development and stimulus that John Reith and the other early pioneers of broadcasting would have envied. Even more importantly, in an ever more interconnected world, but one in which there seems ever greater chasms between different faiths and ideologies, and where technological advances can so easily be used for destructive purposes, the existence of a mass, public and freely available space, in which rational and respectful but lively and robust informed debate can take place, may not just be desirable: it might even save our lives.

# Chronology

(Unless otherwise stated, events refer to the UK.)

1887    Hertz proves Maxwell's theory of existence of radio waves.

1895    Marconi sends and receives a radio signal.

1899    Marconi sends a wireless signal across the English Channel.

1901    Marconi sends a wireless signal across the Atlantic.

1906    Fessenden sends voice and music over the wireless.

1919    RCA is formed by General Electric.

1920    Regularly scheduled programmes begin on KDKA, Pittsburgh, Pennsylvania.
       Marconi opens Britain's first public radio station; broadcast by Dame Nellie Melba heard as far as Newfoundland.

1921    US President Warren G. Harding speaks to the nation over radio.

1922    British Broadcasting Company starts broadcasting in major UK cities; coverage of results of the general election.
       First transatlantic broadcast.

1924    First broadcast to schools.

1925    Baird demonstrates first television pictures.
       Fashion talk, sponsored by Selfridges and organised by Captain Leonard Plugge, broadcast to Britain from Paris.

1926    British Broadcasting Company is granted a Royal Charter and becomes British Broadcasting Corporation – a public service monopoly.

1927    US Congress passes the Radio Act, creating the Federal Radio Commission and concept of 'public interest, convenience and necessity' broadcasting.
       First football commentary.
       First radios in automobiles (USA)

1928    Baird sends television signal across Atlantic.
       First colour TV demonstration.

1930    First transmission of 30-line television with synchronised sound.

1931    In USA, 15 experimental TV stations are on air; first BBC television programme.

1932    Broadcasting House, in London's West End, becomes official HQ of BBC.
        Start of BBC's Empire Service, from transmitters in Daventry.

1933    Radio Luxembourg begins regular schedule of programmes in English.

1934    Armstrong demonstrates FM radio.

1936    First regularly scheduled 'high definition' television service from BBC. King Edward VIII broadcasts his abdication speech 'live' from Windsor castle.

1937    First BBC TV outside broadcast – Coronation of King George V1.

1938    Arabic service is first BBC broadcast in foreign language.
        *The War of the Worlds* broadcast causes panic in USA.

1939    Prime Minster Neville Chamberlain announces declaration of war on BBC radio.
        BBC television closed down on Britain's declaration of war.

1940    Start of Forces Programme.

1941    First commercial TV station begins broadcasting in the USA.

1942    First broadcast of *Britain to America* from BBC North American service, re-broadcast by NBC in USA.

1945    Start of Light Programme.

1946    BBC TV resumes.
        Cable TV demonstrated in USA.
        Radio Luxembourg resumes English-language commercial service.
        BBC starts 'high-brow' radio Third Programme'.

1947    Harry S. Truman makes first televised presidential address in USA.

1948    First BBC *Newsreel*.

1950    First television coverage of general election results.

1953    Coronation of Queen Elizabeth II is televised.

1954    Television Act establishes 'independent' television in the UK.
        First Eurovision exchange of television programmes; eight countries take part.

1955    First UK VHF/FM broadcasts.
        First UK 'independent' Television (ITV) goes on air.
        First rock 'n' roll music on radio airwaves in USA.

1956   Ampex introduces video-tape recorder.
       The cordless remote control is introduced by Zenith in the USA.
       First *Eurovision Song Contest*.
       First television ministerial broadcast (made by Anthony Eden).

1957   Nat 'King' Cole becomes first black performer to have own US
       network show.
       First TV broadcast of The Queen's Christmas Day message.

1958   Challenges by ITN and Granada to ban on coverage of election
       campaigns and to '14-day rule' that barred coverage of events to come
       before Parliament in next two weeks, lead to abandonment of both
       restrictions.

1960   First programmes from BBC Television Centre (TC).
       Nixon–Kennedy debates broadcast on US radio and TV networks.

1962   First satellite transatlantic TV pictures.
       BBC begins experimental stereo radio broadcasts.

1963   Transatlantic satellite brings coverage of aftermath of assassination of
       President Kennedy in Dallas, Texas, to UK.

1964   Radio Caroline goes on-air off the coast of Essex.
       Opening of BBC2.

1965   Most US network broadcasts now in colour.

1966   First videotape recorders in US homes.
       Highest-ever UK TV audiences reached, for coverage of soccer World
       Cup Final, England v. West Germany.

1967   In USA, the Public Broadcasting Act is passed and Corporation for
       Public Broadcasting established.
       First regular colour transmissions on BBC2.
       ITV begins UK's first daily half-hour news programme, *News At Ten*.
       Marine (etc.) (Broadcasting) Offences Act forces most of the 'pirate'
       stations to close.
       Start of BBC Radio 1 – other BBC networks re-named Radios '2', '3'
       and '4'.
       First experimental BBC local radio broadcasts on VHF/FM.

1969   Public broadcasting system (PBS) begins in the USA.
       Colour begins on BBC1 and ITV

1971   Start of Open University (university degrees) broadcasts.
       Radio-only licence abolished.

1973   First licensed UK 'independent' radio stations go on air – BBC radio
       monopoly finally broken.

1974    Start of CEEFAX (text news/information) on BBC TV channels.

1975    First experimental radio broadcasting of House of Commons proceedings.

1976    Home Box Office (HBO) uses satellites to distribute material to local cable systems.

1977    Sony introduces Betamax video-cassette deck

1979    Radio broadcasting of House of Commons allows nation to hear 'live' the vote of no confidence in the government and announcement by Prime Minister of a general election

1980    Cable News Network (CNN) – the first 24-hour news service – goes on air.

1981    Start of MTV.

1982    Launch of Channel 4.
        Launch of direct broadcasting by satellite, later re-named Sky.

1983    Breakfast-time television begins on both BBC and ITV.
        Highest-ever TV audiences in USA, for final episode of *M\*A\*S\*H*.

1986    BBC begins full daytime television service.

1987    Launch of MTV Europe.

1988    ITV broadcasting 24/7 in all regions.

1989    First 'incremental' commercial radio stations go on air.
        Full Sky DBS service launched.
        First experimental TV broadcasting of House of Commons proceedings.

1990    Broadcasting Act substantially de-regulates UK commercial broadcasting and creates separate regulators for commercial radio (Radio Authority) and television (Independent Television Commission)
        Sky TV takes over British Satellite Broadcasting to form BskyB.
        BBC Radio 5 (to become 'Radio 5 Live') launched.

1991    BBC World Service Television launched.
        Start of BBC Nicam stereo sound services.
        World Service TV launches Asian Service – to become first BBC 24/7 channel.

1992    First national commercial radio station, Classic FM, goes on air.
        Radio Luxembourg closes.

1996    Broadcasting Act further de-regulates UK broadcasting; Telecommunications Act does same in USA

1997    Launch of Channel 5 – last analogue terrestrial channel.
        BBC News 24 launched on cable networks, simulcast on BBC1 overnight.

1998    Sky digital TV services begin.
        'On Digital' DTT begins.
        BBC Choice launched – digital 'catch up' (repeat) channel; the Corporation's first new domestic TV service since 1964.

1999    National commercial digital radio service begins.
        End of *News At Ten* (but see entry under 2007).

2000    Channel 4 broadcasts first UK *Big Brother* show, starting the phenomenon of Reality TV.
        First local digital radio services.

2001    'Tipping point' for interactive television as BBC offers a 'mosaic' of five simultaneous matches for its coverage of the Wimbledon Lawn Tennis Championships

2002    Communications Act further de-regulates UK broadcasting; five regulatory bodies to be replaced by 'super-regulator' Ofcom, covering all broadcasting and communications services except BBC.
        Freeview – with backing of BBC – takes over DTT service and leads to mass take-up of digital television.
        BBC 7 goes on air and completes the BBC's portfolio of digital radio networks.

2005    ITV news channel goes off air.

2006    First HD transmissions, on Sky and BBC.

2007    First analogue TV switch-off; Whitehaven in Cumbria leads the 'digital revolution'.
        ITV announces that *News at Ten* is to return in January 2008 on four nights a week, again presented by Trevor McDonald.

2009    National switch-off of analogue terrestrial television in USA; north-west England becomes first major UK region to have full TV 'digital switch-over'.
        Announcement that all national radio stations will cease to broadcast on analogue after 2015 – if certain conditions are met.
        Channel 4 announces next season of *Big Brother* will be the last.
        Oprah Winfrey announces her next season of talk shows in USA will be her last.
        Trials of 3-D television on BBC TV.

2010    Record radio audiences in UK since current methodology began in 1999.
        New all-time high TV audience in USA (Superbowl XLIV).

First TV leaders' debates in UK General election.

World Cup coverage sees 'tipping point' of HD Television in UK.

Start of regular 3-D TV services in UK.

Coalition Government announces BBC must fund World Service from 2014 out of licence fee, this and other new obligations estimated to cut BBC's funding by approximately 25 per cent over five years.

Announcement of 'YouView' service, to link computers with TV, backed by major UK public service broadcasters, to begin in 2011.

# Selected Bibliography and Further Reading

This is necessarily a *very* selective list. Many more texts in books and journals have informed this book; direct references to specific points alluded to in the text, mostly for sources available online, are given in the 'Notes and References' at the end of each chapter but these will provide greater depth and development of specific areas. Paperback editions are given where possible. Those that are relevant to specific chapters are indicated in **bold** for each entry; where no chapter is given – generally those that deal with media and communications overall, especially theory – this is because of their all-encompassing nature, and useful reading can be found in these to provide additional understanding for each chapter.

Abercrombie, N. and Longhurst, B. (2007) *Dictionary of Media Studies,* London: Penguin.

Aster, H. and Olechowska, E. (eds) (1998) *Challenges for International Broadcasting – The Audience First?,* Oakville, Ontario: Buffalo Press **9, 10.**

Barfe, L. (2008) *Turned Out Nice Again – the Story of British Light Entertainment,* London: Atlantic Books **1, 4**

Baum, M. (2003) *Soft News Goes to War – Public Opinion and American Foreign Policy in the New Media Age,* Princeton: Princeton University Press **5, 9.**

Bignell, J. (2005) *Big Brother: Reality TV in the Twenty-First Century,* Basingstoke: Palgrave Macmillan **5.**

Branston, G. and Stafford, R. (2010) *The Media Student's Book,* London: Routledge.

Briggs, A. and Burke, P. (2002) *A Social History of the Media – From Gutenberg to the Internet,* Cambridge: Polity.

Brown, M. (2007) *A Licence to be Different – The Story of Channel 4,* London: BFI **1, 5, 6.**

Chalaby, J. (ed.) (2005) *Transnational Television Worldwide – Towards a New Media Order,* London: I.B. Tauris **10.**

Chambers, D., Steiner, L. and Fleming, C. (2004) *Women and Journalism,* London: Routledge **6, 7, 12.**

Cherry, S. (2005) *ITV: The People's Channel,* London: Reynolds & Hearn **1, 3.**

Corner, J. and Pels, D. (eds) (2003) *Media and the Restyling of Politics: Consumerism, Celebrity and Cynicism,* London: Sage    **3, 5, 12.**

Crisell, A. (1997) *An Introductory History of British Broadcasting,* London: Routledge    **1, 3, 4.**

Curran, J. (2002) *Media and Power,* London: Routledge    **6, 7, 12.**

Curran, J. and Seaton, J. (2009) *Power Without Responsibility: Press and Broadcasting in Britain,* London: Routledge.

Currie, T. (2004) *A Concise History of British Television 1930–2000,* Tiverton: Kelly Publications    **1, 3, 6, 7.**

Douglas, S. J. (2004) *Listening In – Radio and the American Imagination,* University of Minnesota Press    **1, 4, 8.**

Frost, C. (2007) *Journalism Ethics and Regulation,* London: Pearson Longman    **3, 6, 7, 12.**

Glasgow Media Group, (ed.) Philo, G. (1995) *Glasgow Media Group Reader Vol. 2 – Industry, Economy, War and Politics,* London: Routledge    **1, 4, 5, 6, 7, 8, 12.**

Harcup, T. (2009) *Journalism: Principles and Practice,* London: Sage    **3, 6, 7, 9, 11, 12.**

Harris, P. (2007) *When Pirates Ruled the Waves,* Glasgow: Kennedy and Boyd    **1, 4, 8.**

Helm, D., *et. al.* (2005) *Can the Market Deliver? Funding Public Service Television in the Digital Age,* Eastleigh: John Libbey    **2, 11, 12.**

Hendy, D. (2000) *Radio in the Global Age,* London: Polity Press    **4, 8, 9, 12.**

Hendy, D. (2008) *Life On Air: A History of Radio Four,* Oxford: Oxford University Press    **1, 6, 7.**

Herman, S. and Chomsky, N. (2006) *Manufacturing Consent: The Political Economy of the Mass Media,* London: Vintage    **1, 7, 12.**

Hill, A. (2005) *Reality TV – Audiences and Popular Factual Television,* London: Routledge    **5, 8.**

Hilmes, M. and Jacobs, J. (2003) *The Television History Book,* London: BFI    **1, 5, 9, 10, 12.**

Johns, A. (2011) *Death of a Pirate – British Radio and the Making of the Information Age,* New York: W.W. Norton and Company    **1, 4, 5, 7, 11.**

Kavanagh, K. and Cowley, P. (2010) *The British General Election of 2010,* Basingstoke: Palgrave Macmillan    **12.**

Keith, M. C. (2001) *Sounds in the Dark – All-Night Radio in American Life,* Iowa: Iowa State University Press    **1, 4, 6.**

Lister, D. (1997) *In the Best Possible Taste – The Crazy Life of Kenny Everett,* London: Bloomsbury    **4, 8.**

Loviglio, J. (2005) *Radio's Intimate Public – Network Broadcasting and Mass-Mediated Democracy,* Minneapolis: University of Minnesota Press    **1, 4, 6, 8.**

McChesney, R. and Nichols, J. (2010) *The Death and Life of American Journalism – The Media Revolution That Will Begin the World Again*, Philadelphia: Nation Books **3, 5, 6, 7, 11, 12**.

McNair, B. (2003) *An Introduction to Political Communication*, London: Routledge **6, 7, 12**.

McQuail, D. (ed.) (2002) *McQuail's Reader in Mass Communication Theory*, London: Sage.

McQuail, D. (2010) *McQuail's Mass Communications Theory*, London: Sage.

Mitchell, M. (2000) (ed.) *Women and Radio – Airing Differences*, London: Routledge **4, 6, 7, 12**.

Morley, D. and Robins, K. (1995) *Spaces of Identity – Global Media, Electronic Landcapes and Cultural Boundaries*, London: Routledge **3, 9, 10**.

O'Neill, B., Ala-Fossi, M., Jauert, P., Lax, S., Nyre, L., Shaw, H. (eds) (2011) *Digital radio in Europe – Technologies, Industries and Cultures*, Bristol: Intellect **1, 2, 4, 11**.

Page, B. (2003) *The Murdoch Archipelago*, London: Simon & Schuster **3, 9, 10, 11**.

Papathanassopoulos, S. (2002) *European Television in the Digital Age*, Cambridge: Polity **2, 8, 9, 10**.

Ross, S.M. (2008) *Beyond the Box – Television and the Internet*, Oxford: Blackwell **2, 5, 10, 11**.

Ruddock, A. (2007) *Investigating Audiences*, London: Sage **1, 2, 3, 8, 9**.

Scannell, P. (1996) *Radio, Television and Modern Life*, Oxford: Blackwell **1, 2, 4, 8**.

Scannell, P. (2007) *Media and Communication*, London: Sage.

Seymour-Ure, C. (1999) *The British Press and Broadcasting since 1945*, Oxford: Blackwell **1,3**.

Sissons, P. (2010) *When One Door Closes*, London: Biteback **1, 3, 6, 7, 12**

Sposato, S. and Smith, W. (2005) *Radio – A Post Nine-Eleven Strategy for Reaching the World's Poor*, Lanham: University Press of America **4, 9, 10**.

Starkey, G. (2004) *Radio in Context*, Basingstoke: Palgrave Macmillan **4, 6, 7, 12**.

Starkey, G. (2007) *Balance and Bias in Journalism – Representation, Regulation and Democracy*, Basingstoke: Palgrave Macmillan **3, 6, 7, 12**.

Starks, M. (2007) *Switching to Digital Television – UK Public Policy and the Market*, Bristol: Intellect **2, 3, 12**.

Street, S. (2002) *A Concise History of British Radio 1922–2002*, Tiverton: Kelly Publications **1, 4**.

Street, S. (2006) *Crossing the Ether: British Public Service Radio and Commercial Competition 1922–1945*, Eastleigh: John Libbey Publishing **1, 3, 4**.

# Index